CAPTAIN AMERICA

★

★

LIVING LEGEND

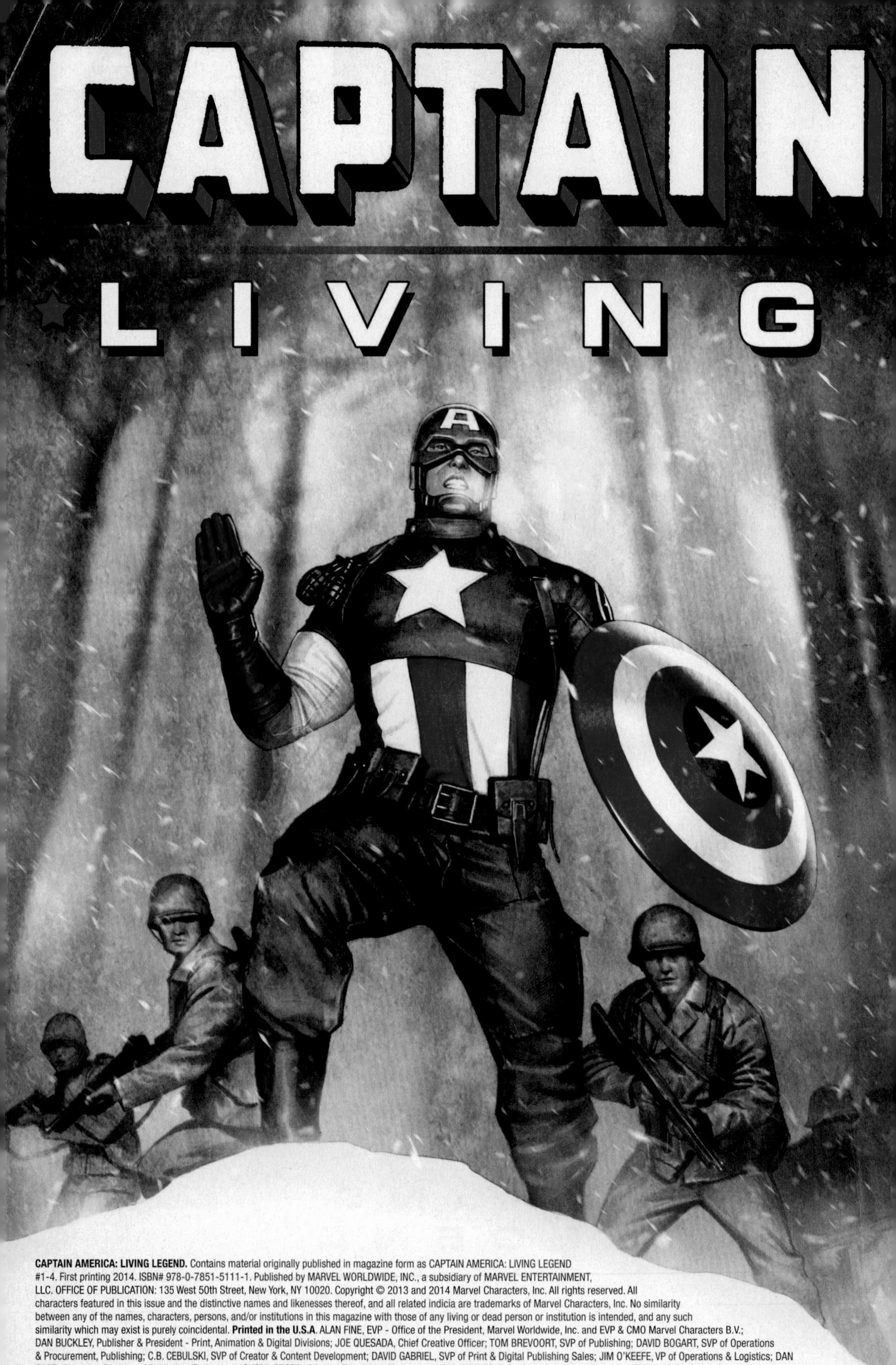

CAPTAIN
★LIVING

CAPTAIN AMERICA: LIVING LEGEND. Contains material originally published in magazine form as CAPTAIN AMERICA: LIVING LEGEND #1-4. First printing 2014. ISBN# 978-0-7851-5111-1. Published by MARVEL WORLDWIDE, INC., a subsidiary of MARVEL ENTERTAINMENT, LLC. OFFICE OF PUBLICATION: 135 West 50th Street, New York, NY 10020. Copyright © 2013 and 2014 Marvel Characters, Inc. All rights reserved. All characters featured in this issue and the distinctive names and likenesses thereof, and all related indicia are trademarks of Marvel Characters, Inc. No similarity between any of the names, characters, persons, and/or institutions in this magazine with those of any living or dead person or institution is intended, and any such similarity which may exist is purely coincidental. **Printed in the U.S.A.** ALAN FINE, EVP - Office of the President, Marvel Worldwide, Inc. and EVP & CMO Marvel Characters B.V.; DAN BUCKLEY, Publisher & President - Print, Animation & Digital Divisions; JOE QUESADA, Chief Creative Officer; TOM BREVOORT, SVP of Publishing; DAVID BOGART, SVP of Operations & Procurement, Publishing; C.B. CEBULSKI, SVP of Creator & Content Development; DAVID GABRIEL, SVP of Print & Digital Publishing Sales; JIM O'KEEFE, VP of Operations & Logistics; DAN CARR, Executive Director of Publishing Technology; SUSAN CRESPI, Editorial Operations Manager; ALEX MORALES, Publishing Operations Manager; STAN LEE, Chairman Emeritus. For information regarding advertising in Marvel Comics or on Marvel.com, please contact Niza Disla, Director of Marvel Partnerships, at ndisla@marvel.com. For Marvel subscription inquiries, please call 800-217-9158. **Manufactured between 12/13/2013 and 1/20/2014 by R.R. DONNELLEY, INC., SALEM, VA, USA.**

10 9 8 7 6 5 4 3 2 1

AMERICA

LEGEND ★

S T O R Y
ANDY DIGGLE
& ADI GRANOV

S C R I P T
ANDY DIGGLE WITH
EDDIE ROBSON (#3-4)

★

I L L U S T R A T I O N S
ADI GRANOV (#1) & **AGUSTIN ALESSIO** (#2-4)

★

L E T T E R E R
VC'S JOE CARAMAGNA

★

A S S I S T A N T   E D I T O R S
JAKE THOMAS & **JOHN DENNING**

★

E D I T O R S
TOM BREVOORT WITH **LAUREN SANKOVITCH**

★

C O V E R   A R T
ADI GRANOV

COLLECTION EDITOR: **MARK D. BEAZLEY** ASSISTANT EDITORS: **NELSON RIBEIRO** & **ALEX STARBUCK**
EDITOR, SPECIAL PROJECTS: **JENNIFER GRÜNWALD** SENIOR EDITOR, SPECIAL PROJECTS: **JEFF YOUNGQUIST**
BOOK DESIGN: **RODOLFO MURAGUCHI**

★

SVP OF PRINT & DIGITAL PUBLISHING SALES: **DAVID GABRIEL**
EDITOR IN CHIEF: **AXEL ALONSO** CHIEF CREATIVE OFFICER: **JOE QUESADA**
PUBLISHER: **DAN BUCKLEY** EXECUTIVE PRODUCER: **ALAN FINE**

★

C A P T A I N   A M E R I C A   C R E A T E D   B Y
JOE SIMON & **JACK KIRBY**

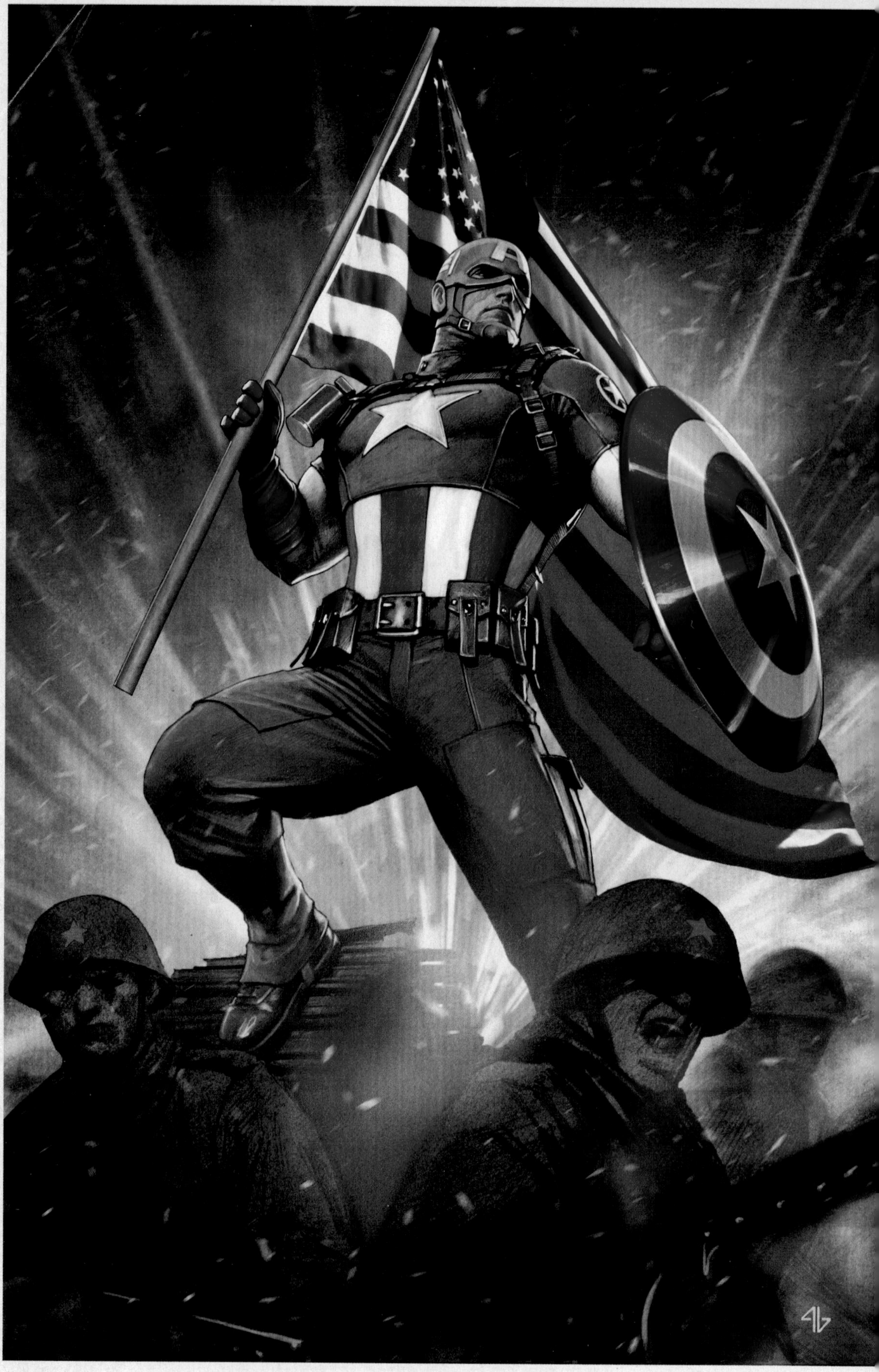

★ CHAPTER ONE ★

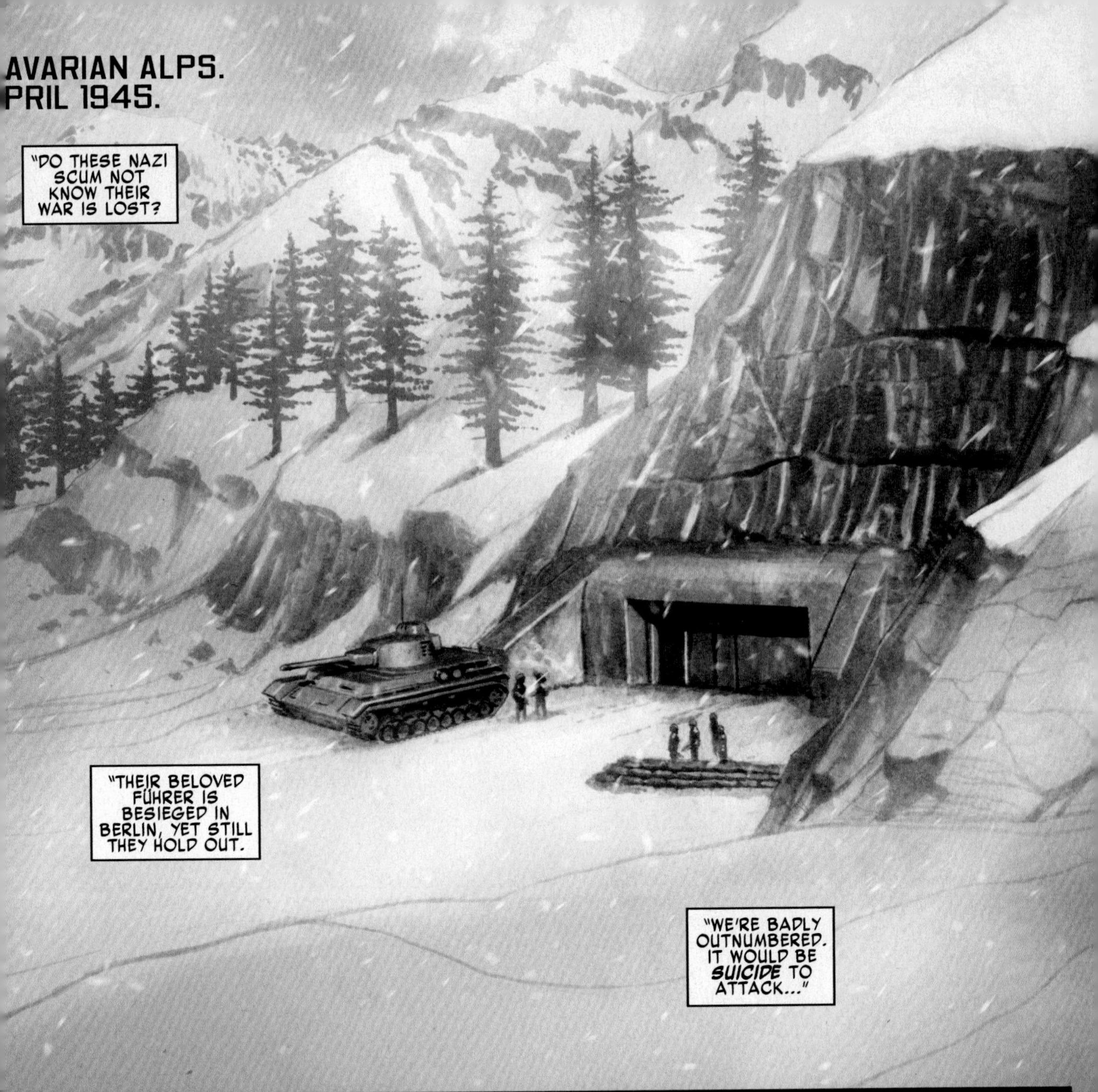
AVARIAN ALPS.
PRIL 1945.
"DO THESE NAZI SCUM NOT KNOW THEIR WAR IS LOST?
"THEIR BELOVED FÜHRER IS BESIEGED IN BERLIN, YET STILL THEY HOLD OUT.
"WE'RE BADLY OUTNUMBERED. IT WOULD BE SUICIDE TO ATTACK..."

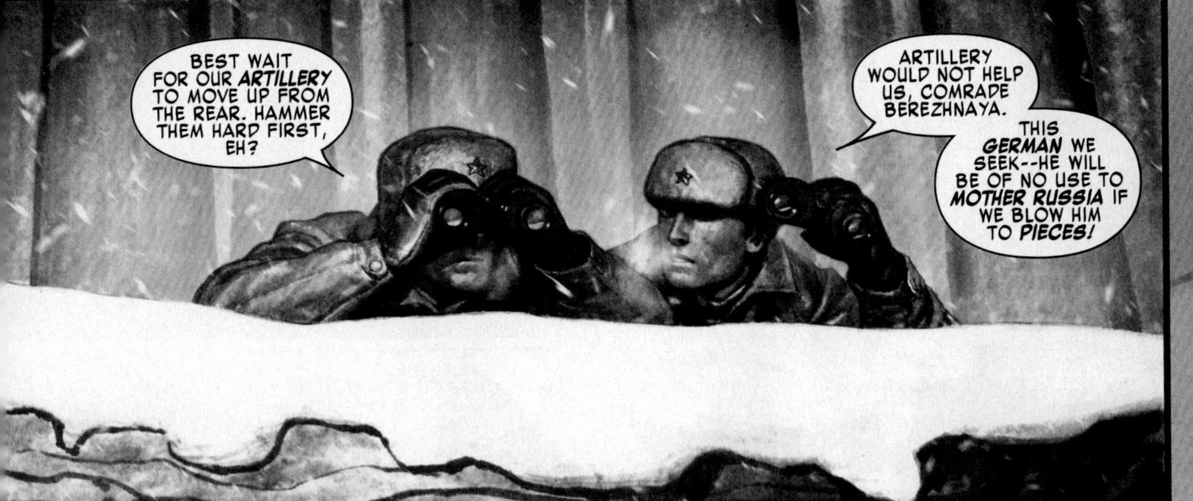
BEST WAIT FOR OUR ARTILLERY TO MOVE UP FROM THE REAR. HAMMER THEM HARD FIRST, EH?
ARTILLERY WOULD NOT HELP US, COMRADE BEREZHNAYA.
THIS GERMAN WE SEEK--HE WILL BE OF NO USE TO MOTHER RUSSIA IF WE BLOW HIM TO PIECES!

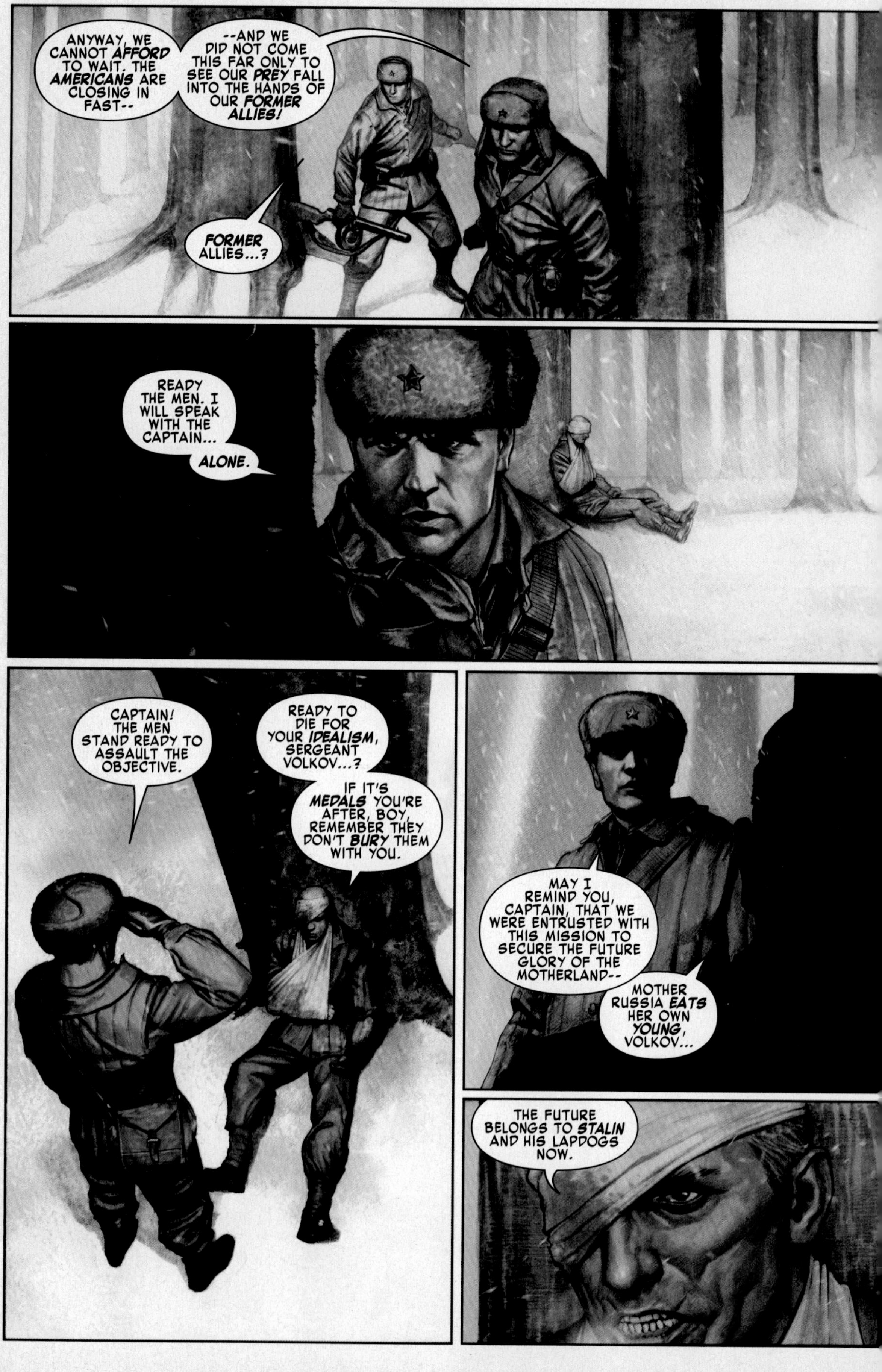

ANYWAY, WE CANNOT AFFORD TO WAIT. THE AMERICANS ARE CLOSING IN FAST--
--AND WE DID NOT COME THIS FAR ONLY TO SEE OUR PREY FALL INTO THE HANDS OF OUR FORMER ALLIES!
FORMER ALLIES...?
READY THE MEN. I WILL SPEAK WITH THE CAPTAIN...
ALONE.
CAPTAIN! THE MEN STAND READY TO ASSAULT THE OBJECTIVE.
READY TO DIE FOR YOUR IDEALISM, SERGEANT VOLKOV...?
IF IT'S MEDALS YOU'RE AFTER, BOY, REMEMBER THEY DON'T BURY THEM WITH YOU.
MAY I REMIND YOU, CAPTAIN, THAT WE WERE ENTRUSTED WITH THIS MISSION TO SECURE THE FUTURE GLORY OF THE MOTHERLAND--
MOTHER RUSSIA EATS HER OWN YOUNG, VOLKOV...
THE FUTURE BELONGS TO STALIN AND HIS LAPDOGS NOW.

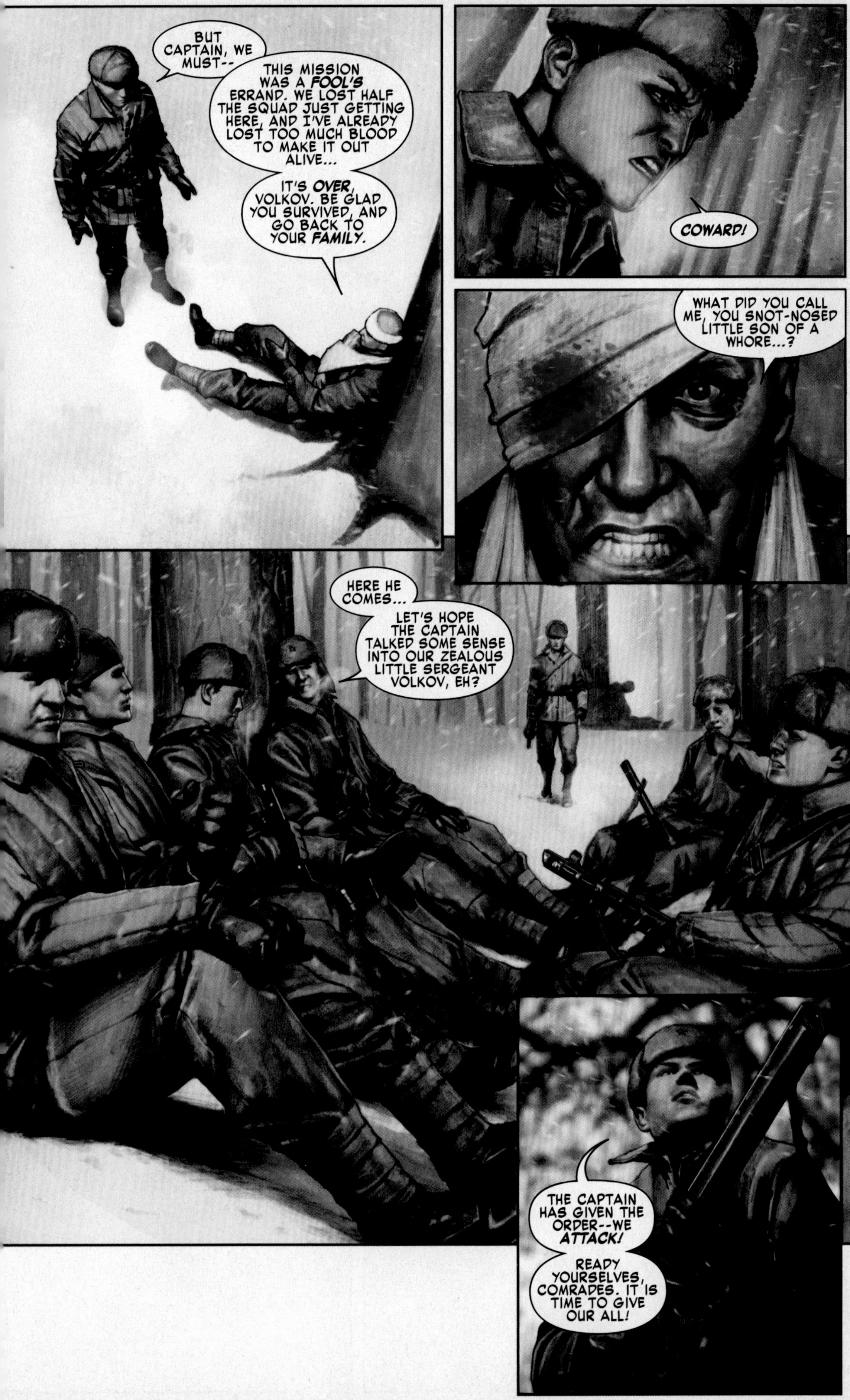
BUT CAPTAIN, WE MUST--
THIS MISSION WAS A FOOL'S ERRAND. WE LOST HALF THE SQUAD JUST GETTING HERE, AND I'VE ALREADY LOST TOO MUCH BLOOD TO MAKE IT OUT ALIVE...
IT'S OVER, VOLKOV. BE GLAD YOU SURVIVED, AND GO BACK TO YOUR FAMILY.
COWARD!
WHAT DID YOU CALL ME, YOU SNOT-NOSED LITTLE SON OF A WHORE...?
HERE HE COMES...
LET'S HOPE THE CAPTAIN TALKED SOME SENSE INTO OUR ZEALOUS LITTLE SERGEANT VOLKOV, EH?
THE CAPTAIN HAS GIVEN THE ORDER--WE ATTACK!
READY YOURSELVES, COMRADES. IT IS TIME TO GIVE OUR ALL!

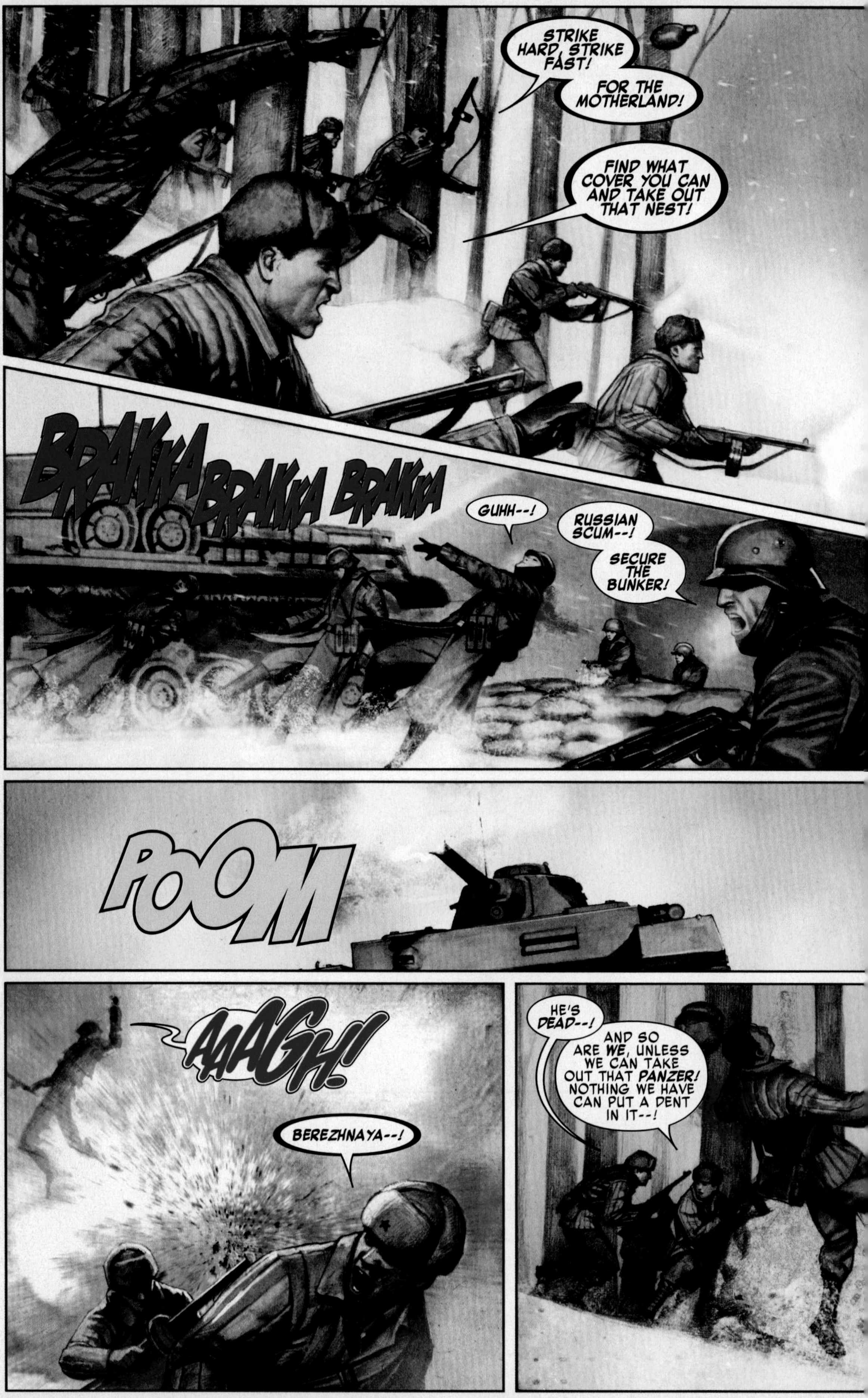
STRIKE HARD, STRIKE FAST!
FOR THE MOTHERLAND!
FIND WHAT COVER YOU CAN AND TAKE OUT THAT NEST!
BRAKKA BRAKKA BRAKKA
GUHH--!
RUSSIAN SCUM--!
SECURE THE BUNKER!
POOM
AAAGH!
BEREZHNAYA--!
HE'S DEAD--!
AND SO ARE WE, UNLESS WE CAN TAKE OUT THAT PANZER! NOTHING WE HAVE CAN PUT A DENT IN IT--!

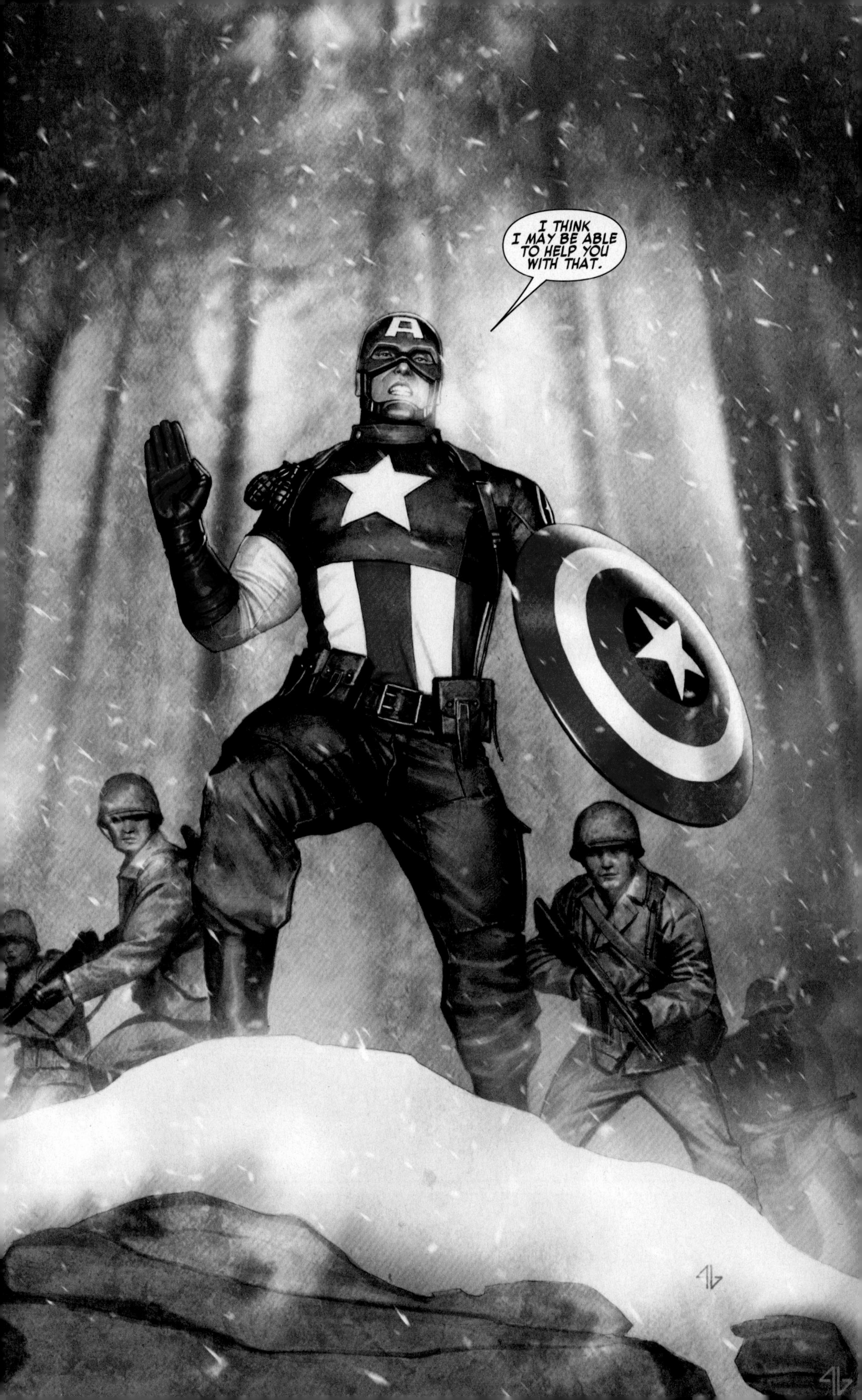
I THINK I MAY BE ABLE TO HELP YOU WITH THAT.

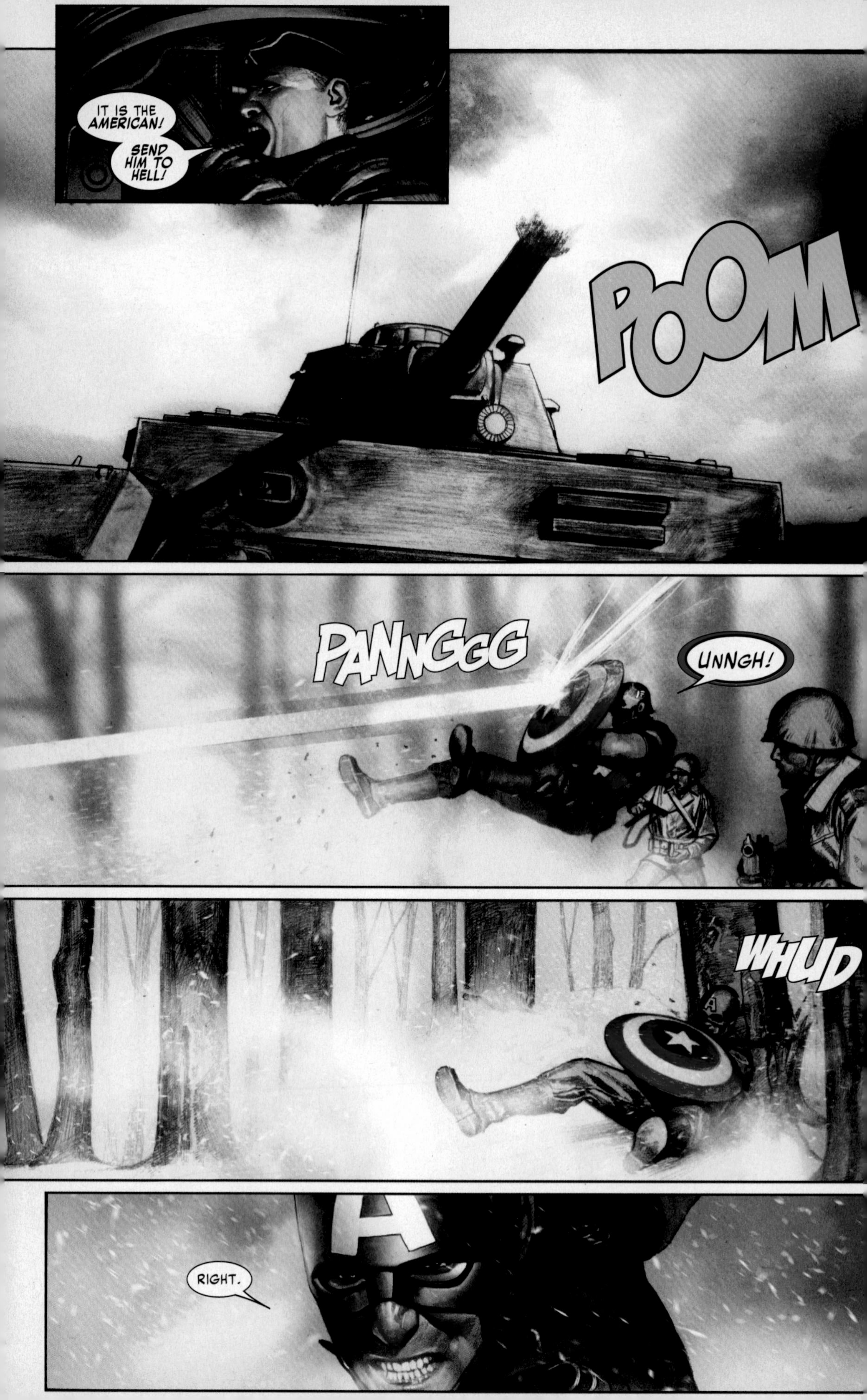
IT IS THE AMERICAN!
SEND HIM TO HELL!
POOM
PANNGGG
UNNGH!
WHUD
RIGHT.

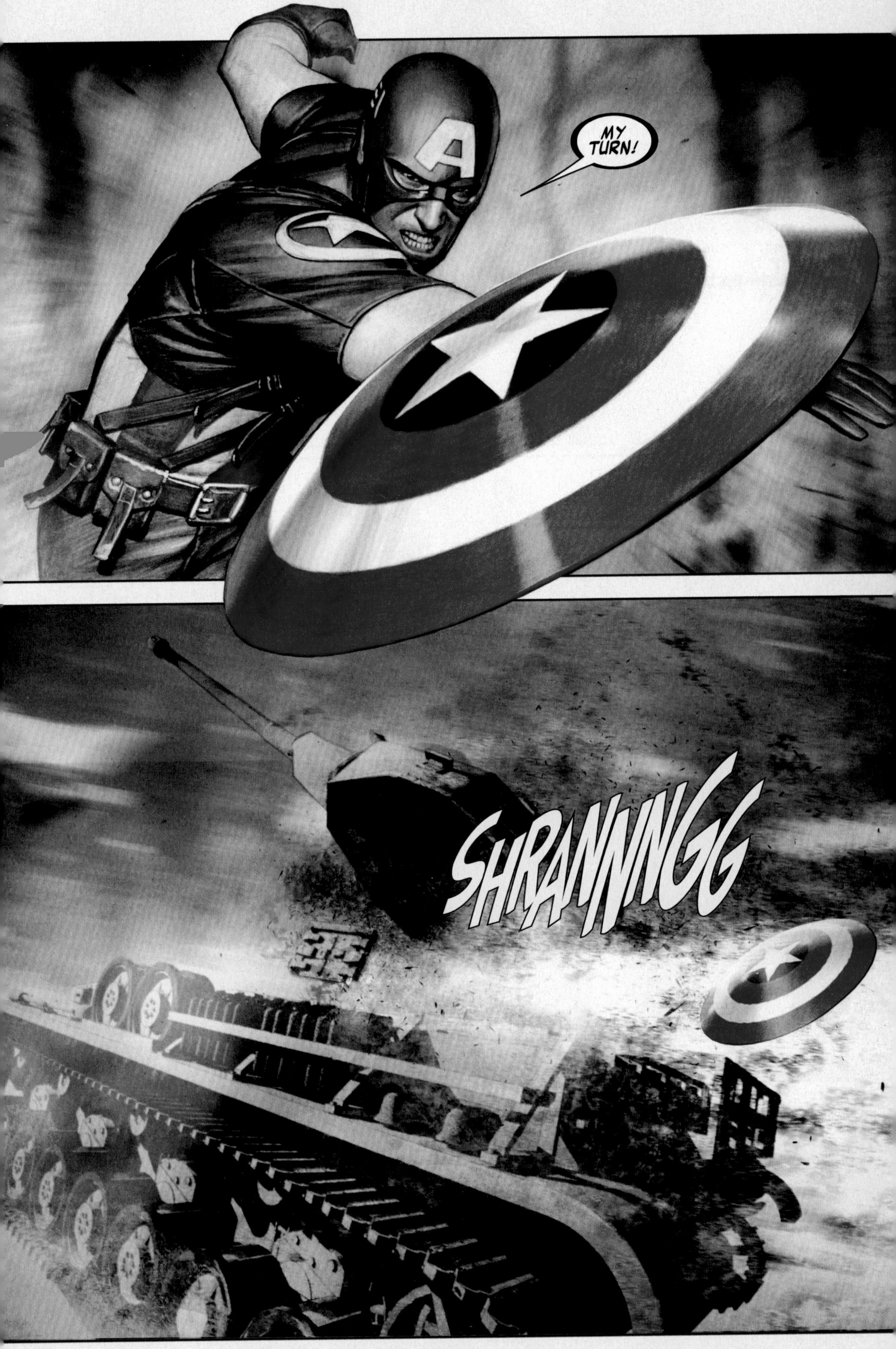
MY TURN!
SHRANNNGG

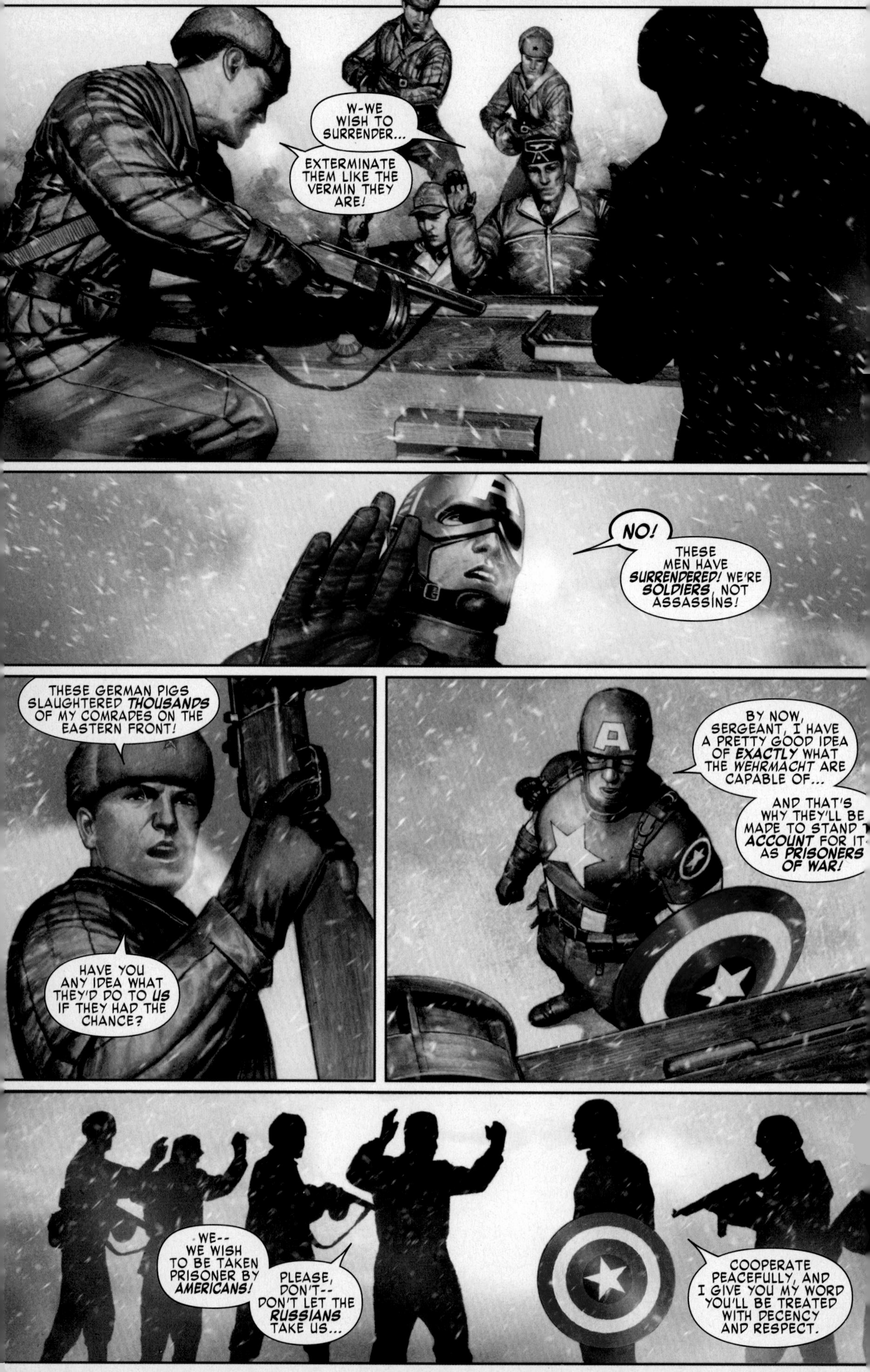
W-WE WISH TO SURRENDER...
EXTERMINATE THEM LIKE THE VERMIN THEY ARE!
NO!
THESE MEN HAVE SURRENDERED! WE'RE SOLDIERS, NOT ASSASSINS!
THESE GERMAN PIGS SLAUGHTERED THOUSANDS OF MY COMRADES ON THE EASTERN FRONT!
HAVE YOU ANY IDEA WHAT THEY'D DO TO US IF THEY HAD THE CHANCE?
BY NOW, SERGEANT, I HAVE A PRETTY GOOD IDEA OF EXACTLY WHAT THE WEHRMACHT ARE CAPABLE OF...
AND THAT'S WHY THEY'LL BE MADE TO STAND T ACCOUNT FOR IT AS PRISONERS OF WAR!
WE-- WE WISH TO BE TAKEN PRISONER BY AMERICANS!
PLEASE, DON'T-- DON'T LET THE RUSSIANS TAKE US...
COOPERATE PEACEFULLY, AND I GIVE YOU MY WORD YOU'LL BE TREATED WITH DECENCY AND RESPECT.

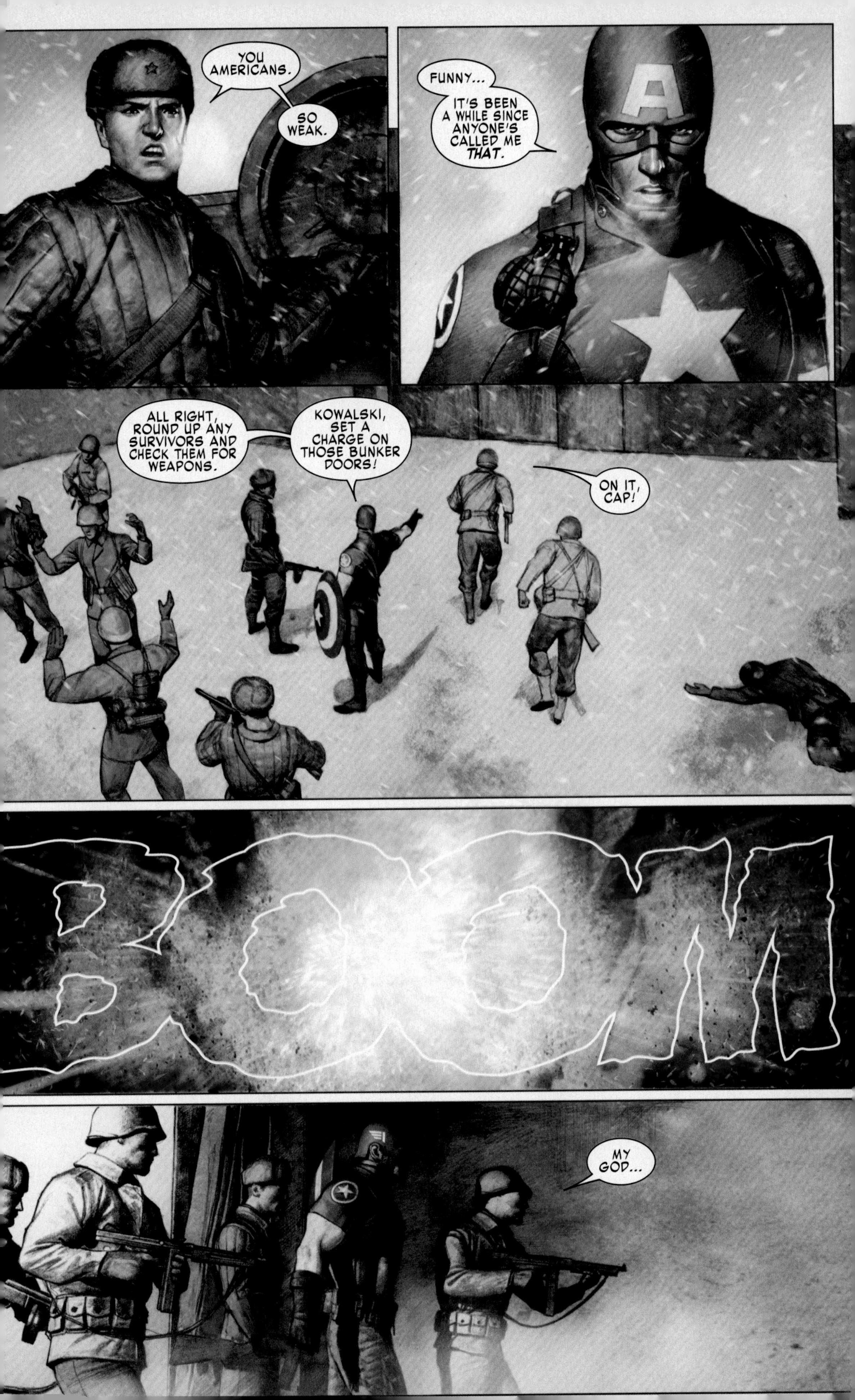
YOU AMERICANS.
SO WEAK.
FUNNY...
IT'S BEEN A WHILE SINCE ANYONE'S CALLED ME *THAT*.
ALL RIGHT, ROUND UP ANY SURVIVORS AND CHECK THEM FOR WEAPONS.
KOWALSKI, SET A CHARGE ON THOSE BUNKER DOORS!
ON IT, CAP!
BOOM
MY GOD...

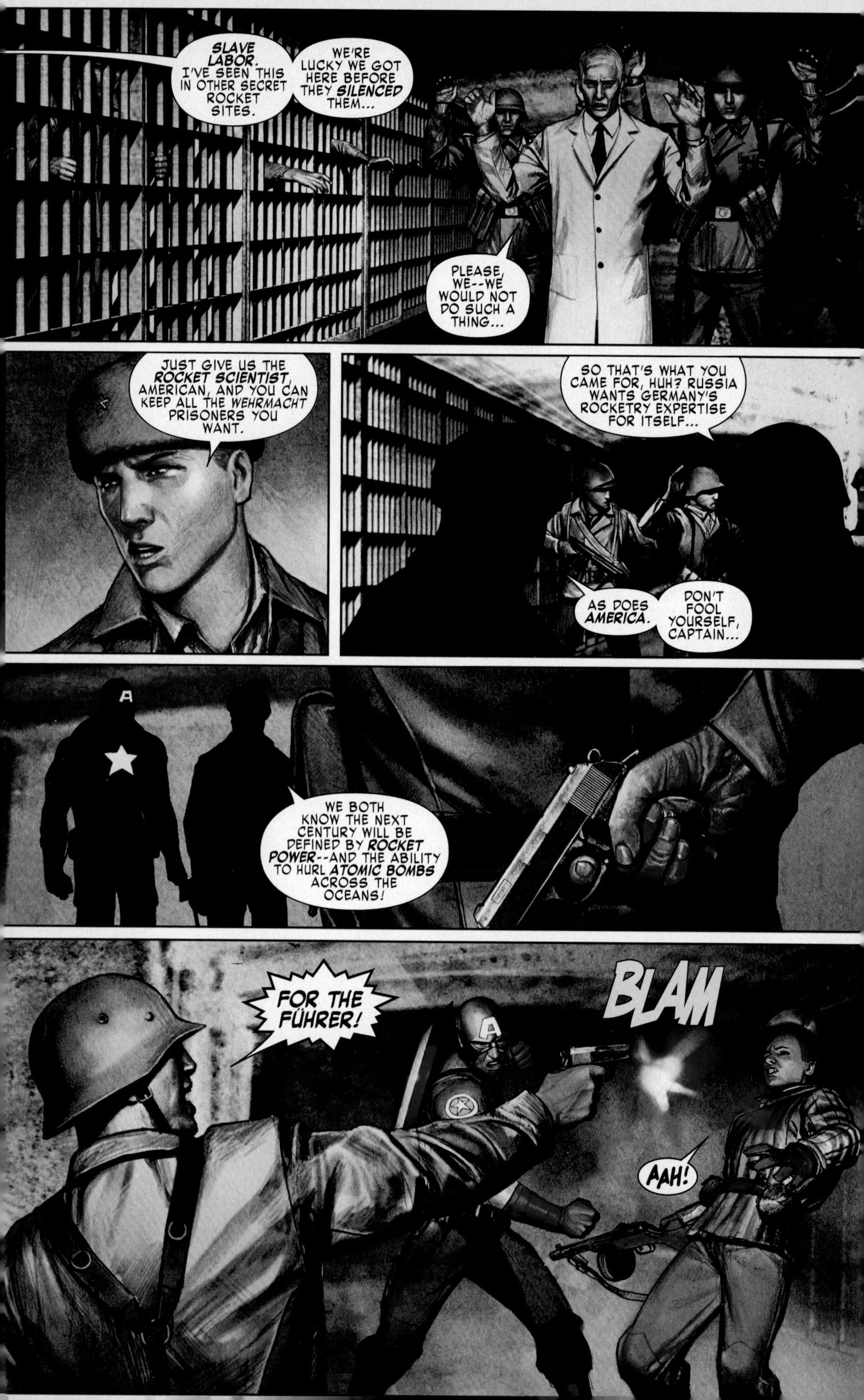
SLAVE LABOR. I'VE SEEN THIS IN OTHER SECRET ROCKET SITES.
WE'RE LUCKY WE GOT HERE BEFORE THEY SILENCED THEM...
PLEASE, WE--WE WOULD NOT DO SUCH A THING...
JUST GIVE US THE ROCKET SCIENTIST, AMERICAN, AND YOU CAN KEEP ALL THE WEHRMACHT PRISONERS YOU WANT.
SO THAT'S WHAT YOU CAME FOR, HUH? RUSSIA WANTS GERMANY'S ROCKETRY EXPERTISE FOR ITSELF...
AS DOES AMERICA.
DON'T FOOL YOURSELF, CAPTAIN...
WE BOTH KNOW THE NEXT CENTURY WILL BE DEFINED BY ROCKET POWER--AND THE ABILITY TO HURL ATOMIC BOMBS ACROSS THE OCEANS!
FOR THE FÜHRER!
BLAM
AAH!

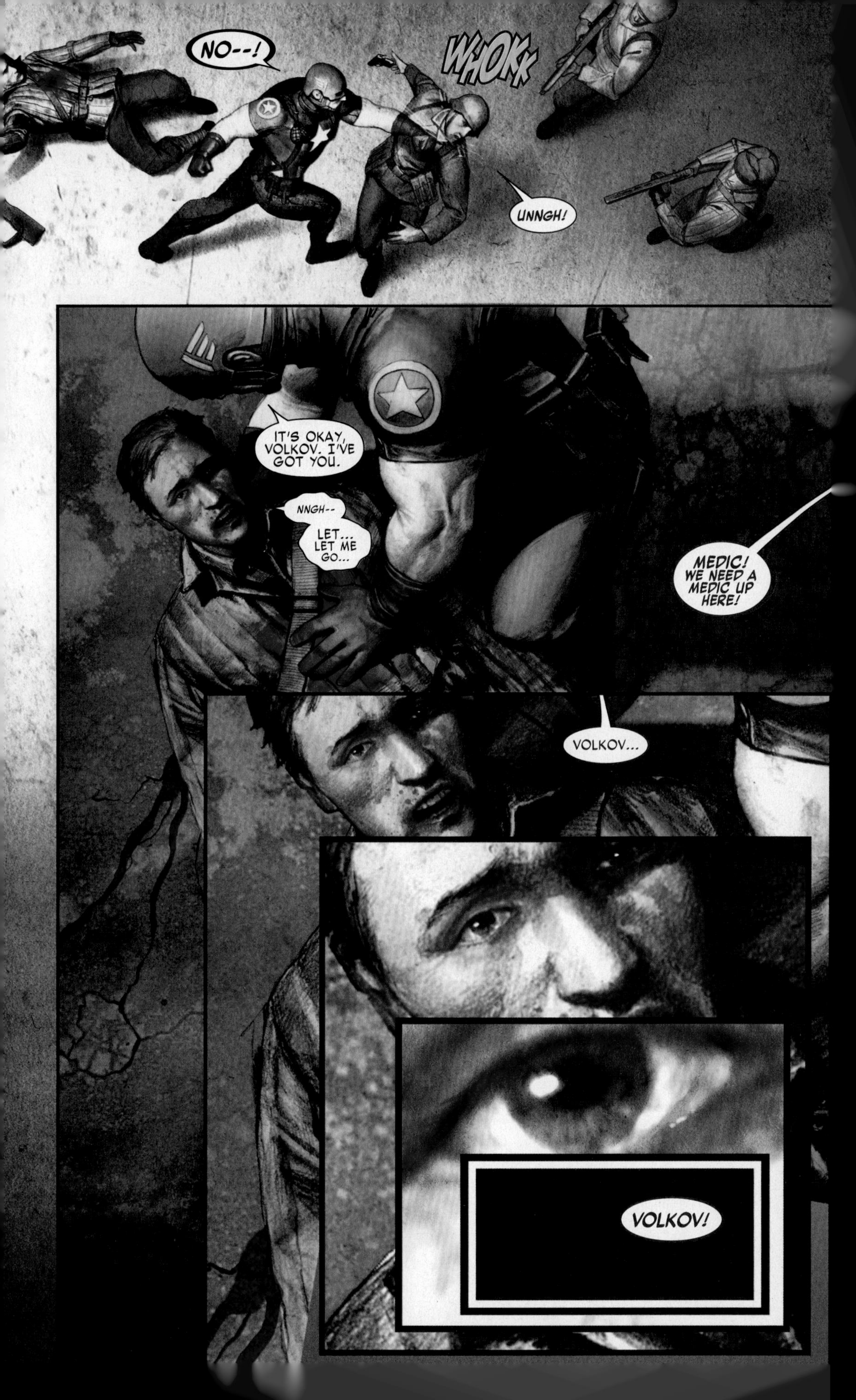
NO--!
WHOKK
UNNGH!
IT'S OKAY, VOLKOV. I'VE GOT YOU.
NNGH--
LET... LET ME GO...
MEDIC! WE NEED A MEDIC UP HERE!
VOLKOV...
VOLKOV!

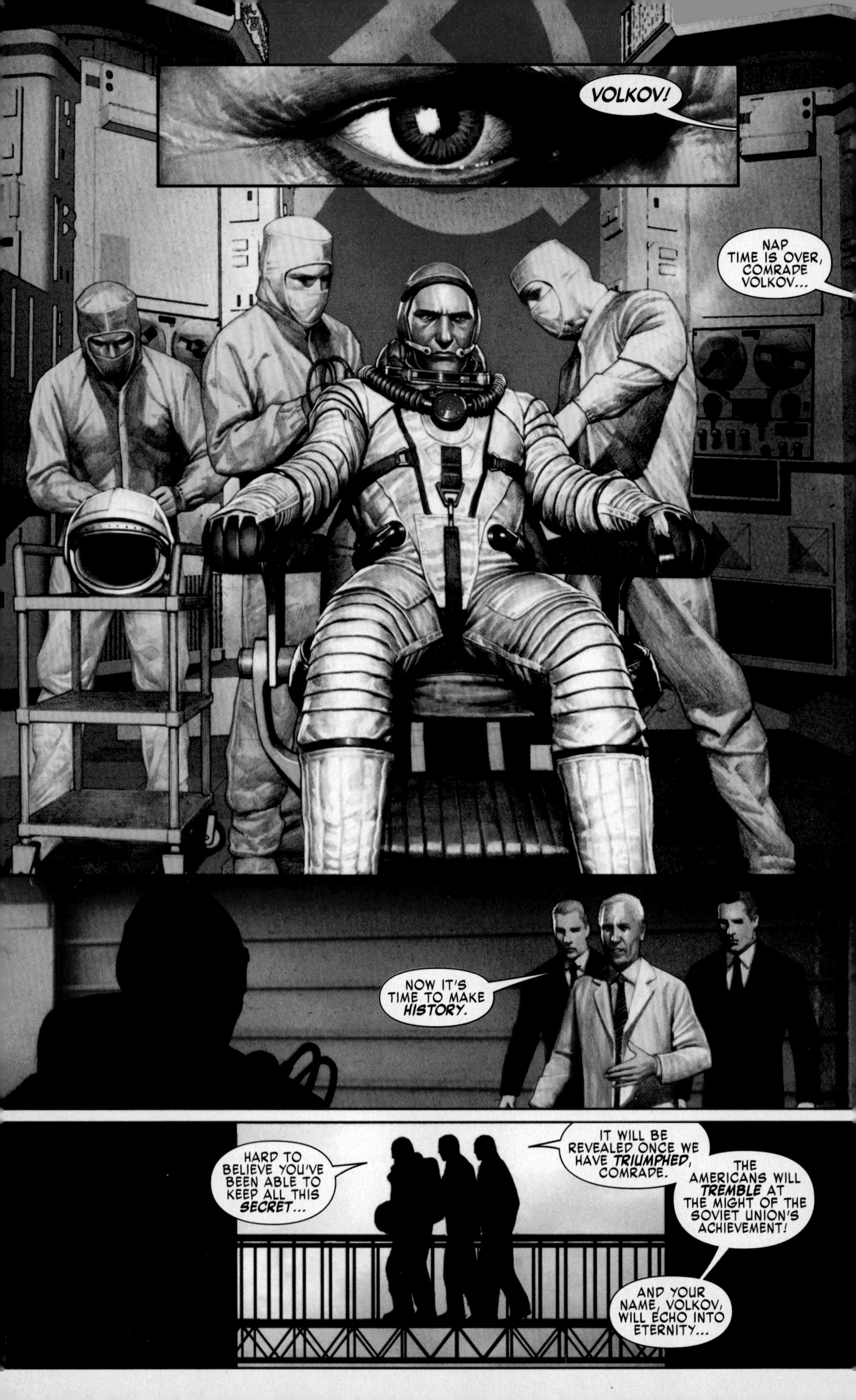
VOLKOV!
NAP TIME IS OVER, COMRADE VOLKOV...
NOW IT'S TIME TO MAKE HISTORY.
HARD TO BELIEVE YOU'VE BEEN ABLE TO KEEP ALL THIS SECRET...
IT WILL BE REVEALED ONCE WE HAVE TRIUMPHED, COMRADE.
THE AMERICANS WILL TREMBLE AT THE MIGHT OF THE SOVIET UNION'S ACHIEVEMENT!
AND YOUR NAME, VOLKOV, WILL ECHO INTO ETERNITY...

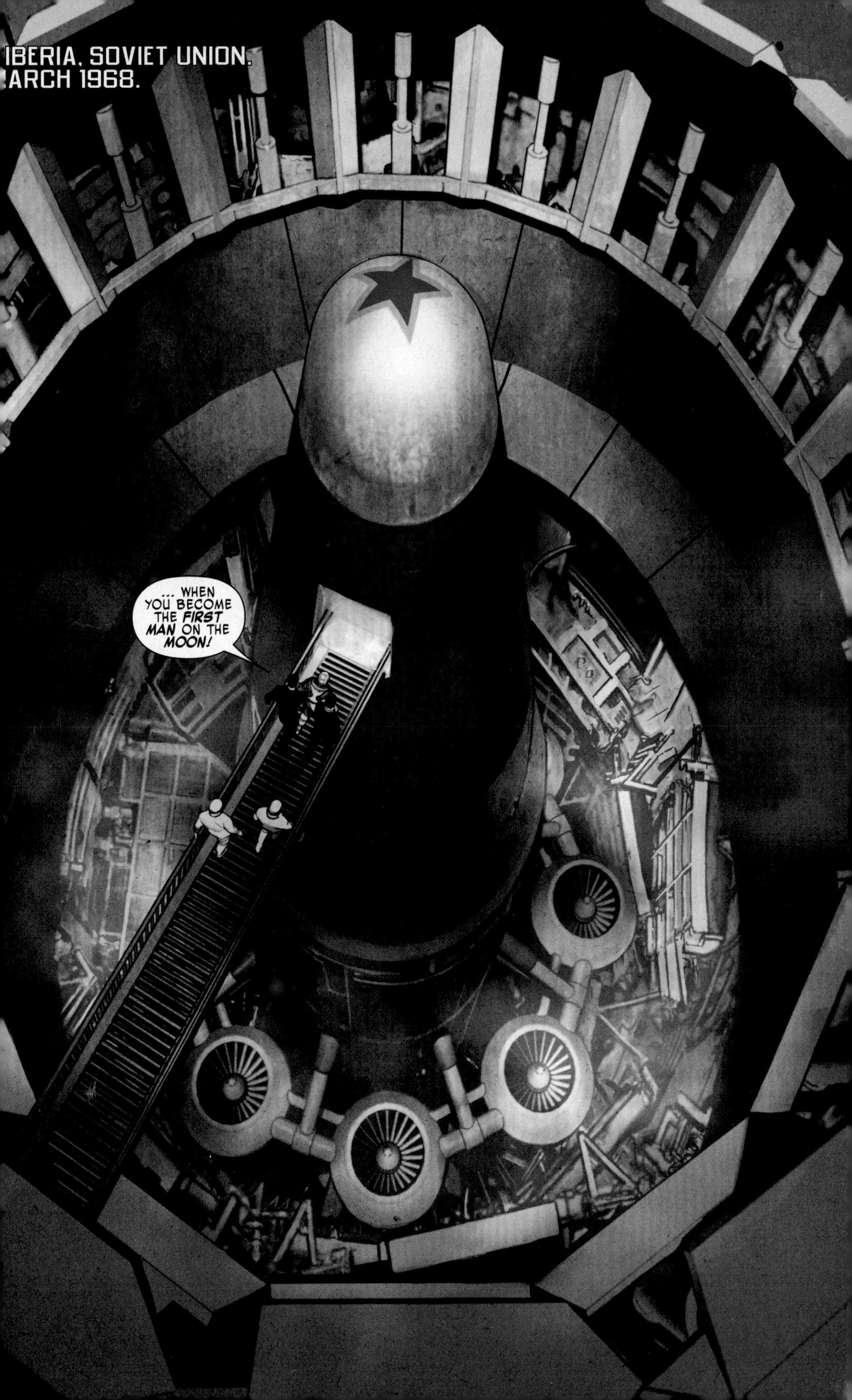
IBERIA, SOVIET UNION.
ARCH 1968.
... WHEN YOU BECOME THE *FIRST MAN* ON THE *MOON!*

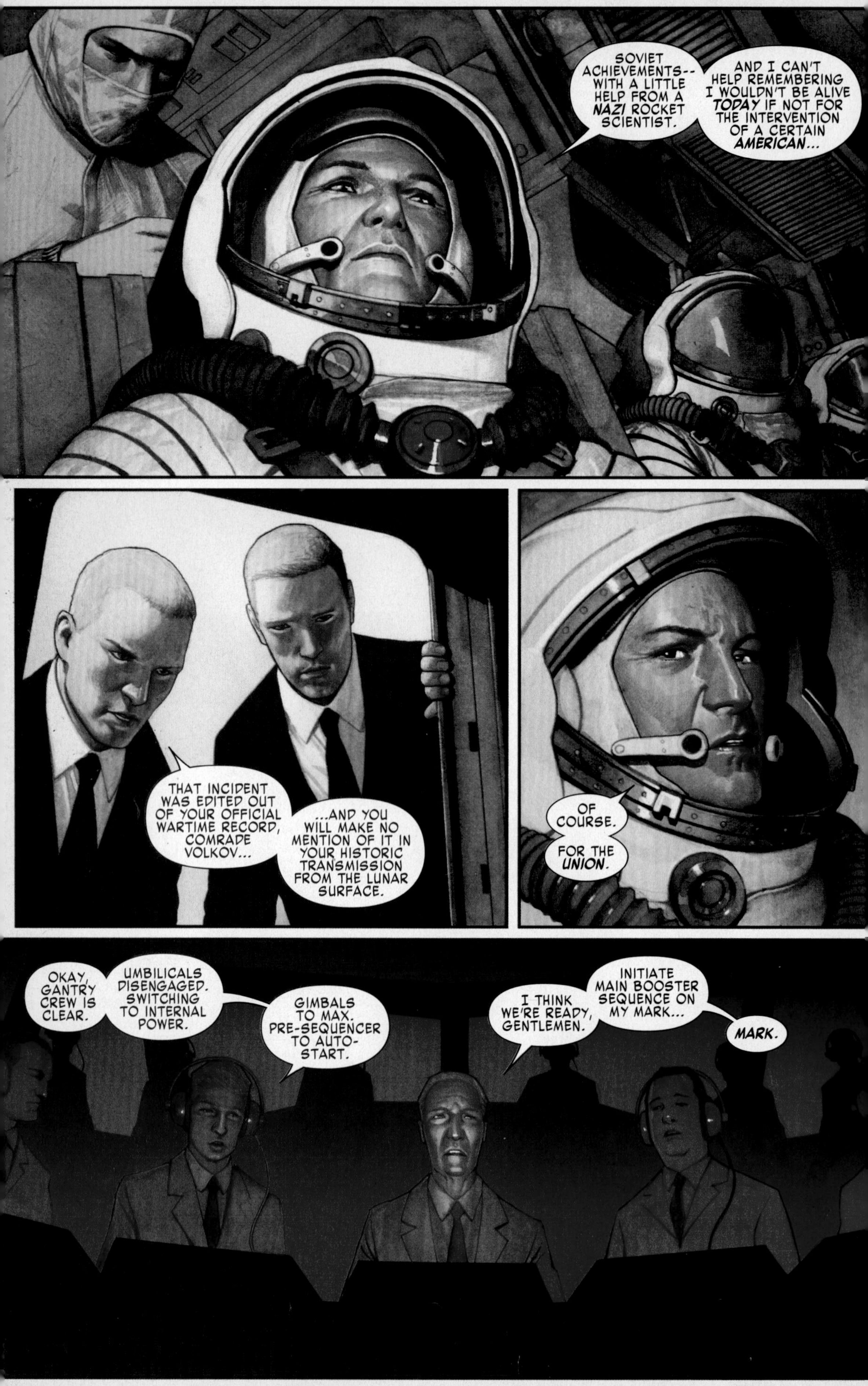
SOVIET ACHIEVEMENTS-- WITH A LITTLE HELP FROM A NAZI ROCKET SCIENTIST.
AND I CAN'T HELP REMEMBERING I WOULDN'T BE ALIVE TODAY IF NOT FOR THE INTERVENTION OF A CERTAIN AMERICAN...
THAT INCIDENT WAS EDITED OUT OF YOUR OFFICIAL WARTIME RECORD, COMRADE VOLKOV...
...AND YOU WILL MAKE NO MENTION OF IT IN YOUR HISTORIC TRANSMISSION FROM THE LUNAR SURFACE.
OF COURSE.
FOR THE UNION.
OKAY, GANTRY CREW IS CLEAR.
UMBILICALS DISENGAGED. SWITCHING TO INTERNAL POWER.
GIMBALS TO MAX. PRE-SEQUENCER TO AUTO-START.
I THINK WE'RE READY, GENTLEMEN.
INITIATE MAIN BOOSTER SEQUENCE ON MY MARK...
MARK.

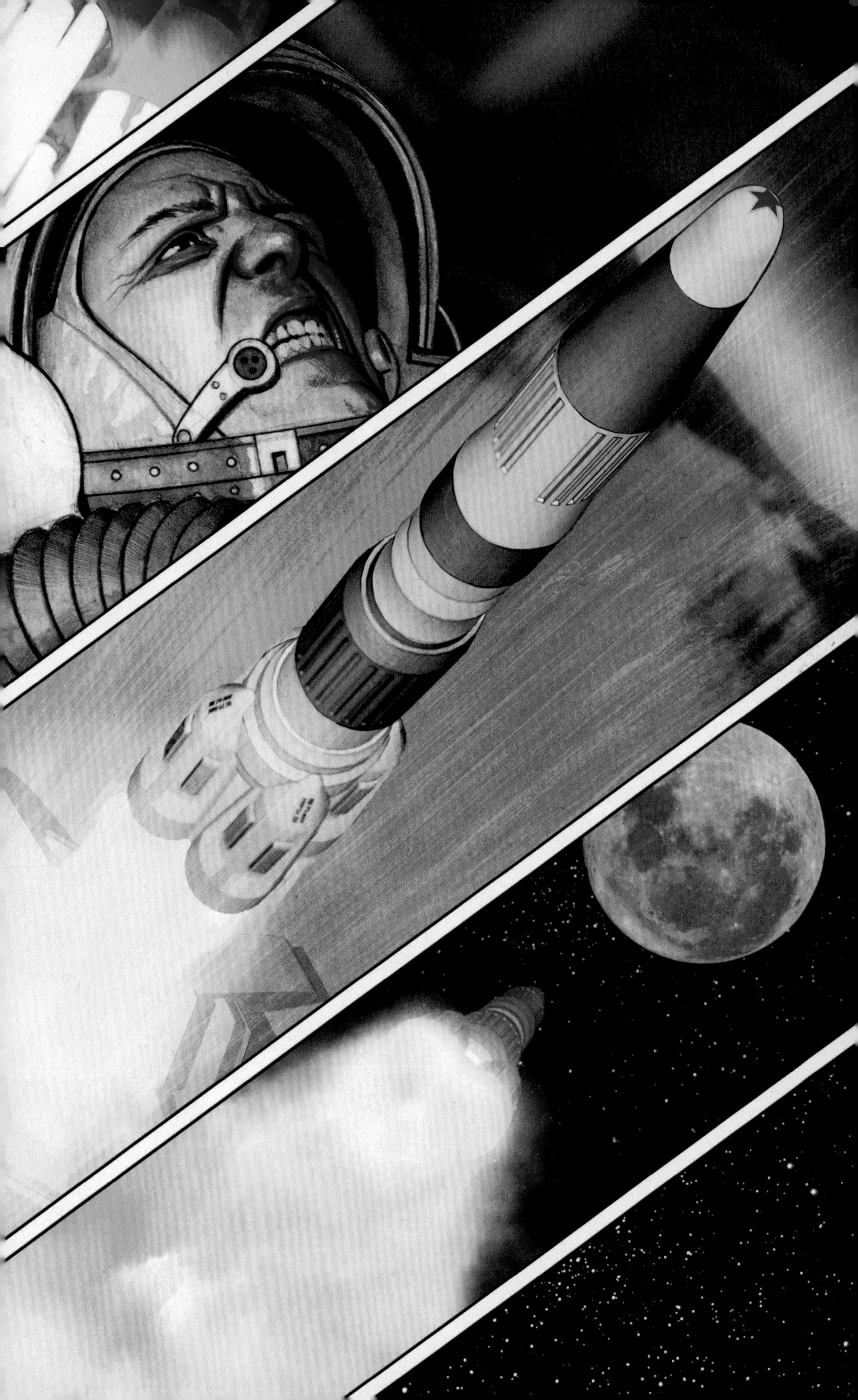

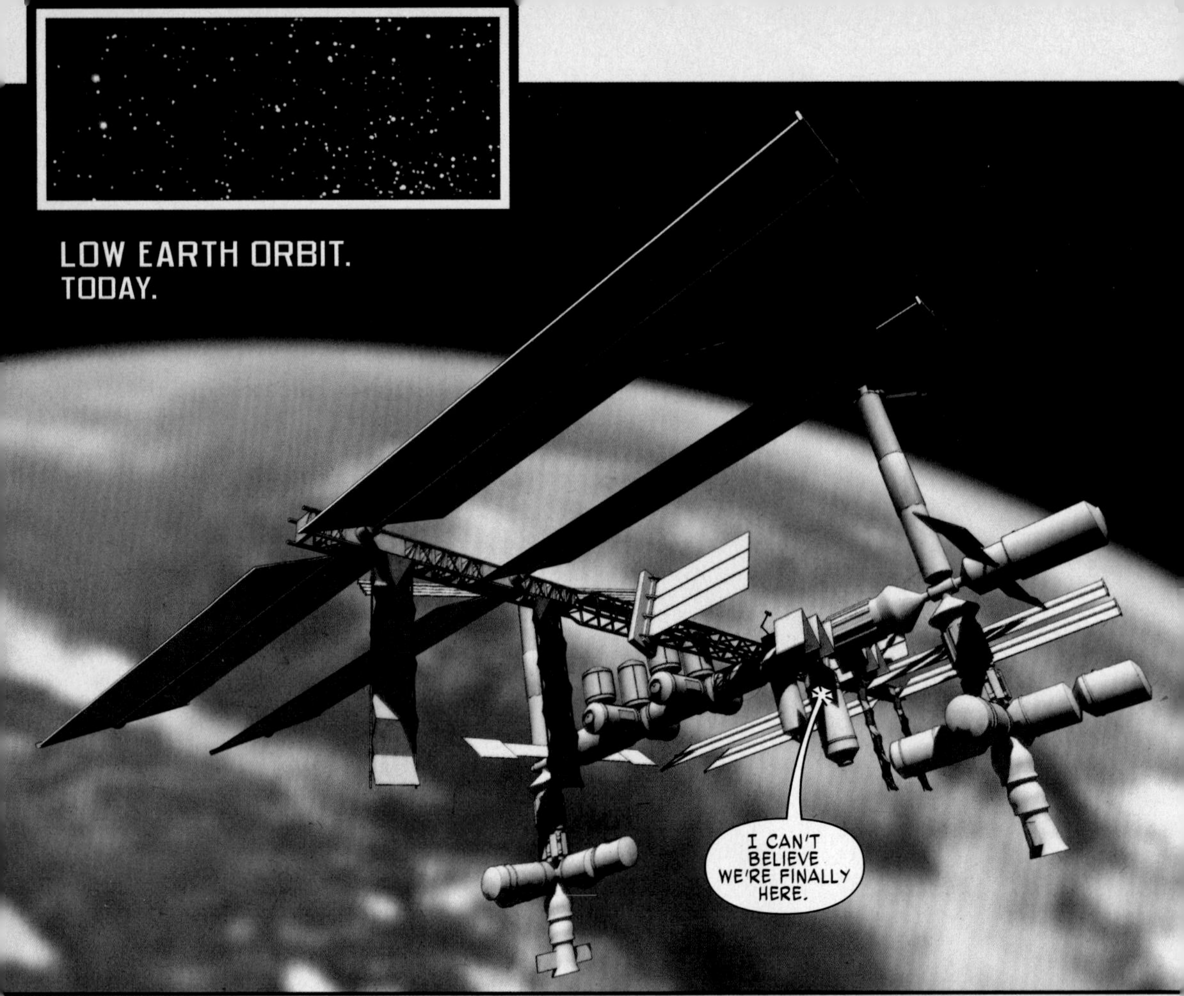
LOW EARTH ORBIT.
TODAY.
I CAN'T BELIEVE WE'RE FINALLY HERE.

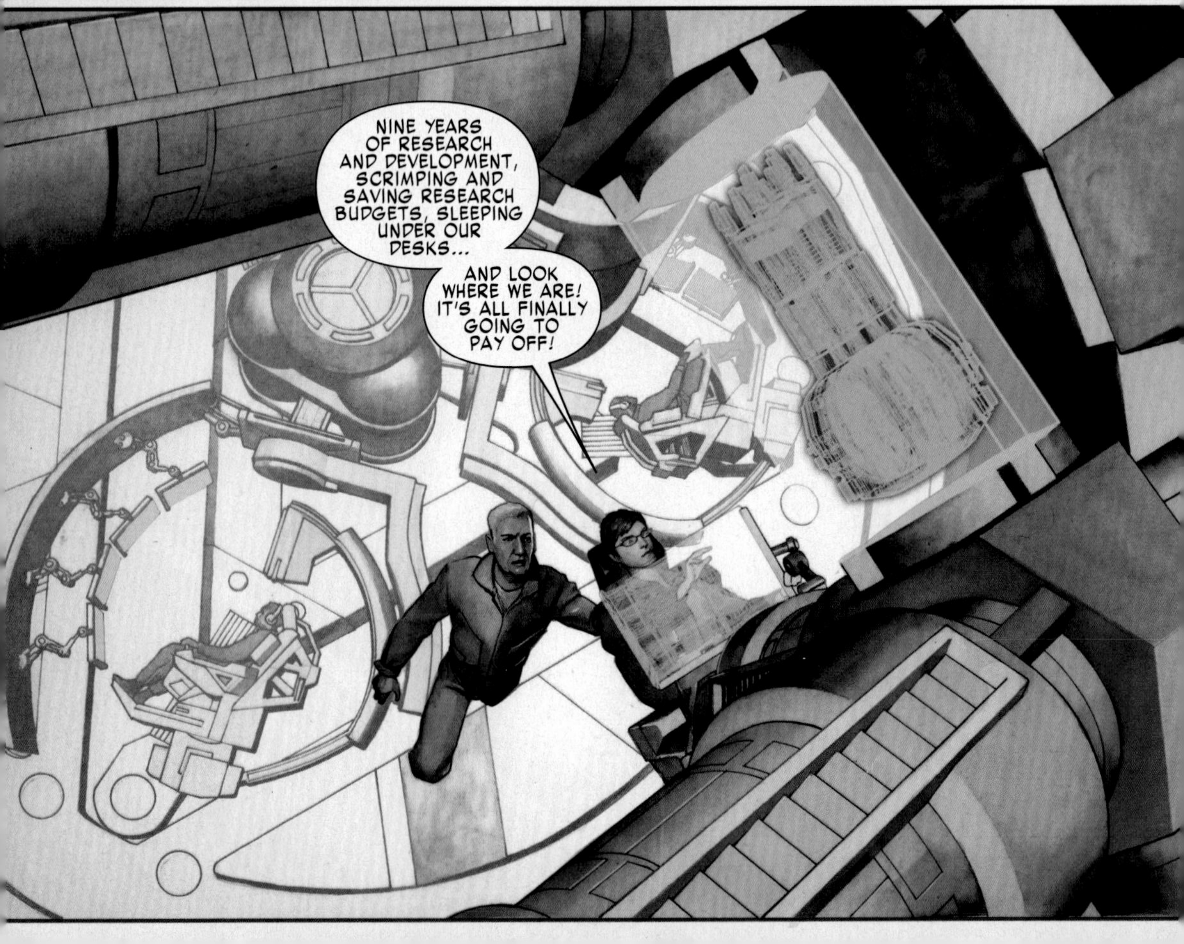
NINE YEARS OF RESEARCH AND DEVELOPMENT, SCRIMPING AND SAVING RESEARCH BUDGETS, SLEEPING UNDER OUR DESKS...
AND LOOK WHERE WE ARE! IT'S ALL FINALLY GOING TO PAY OFF!

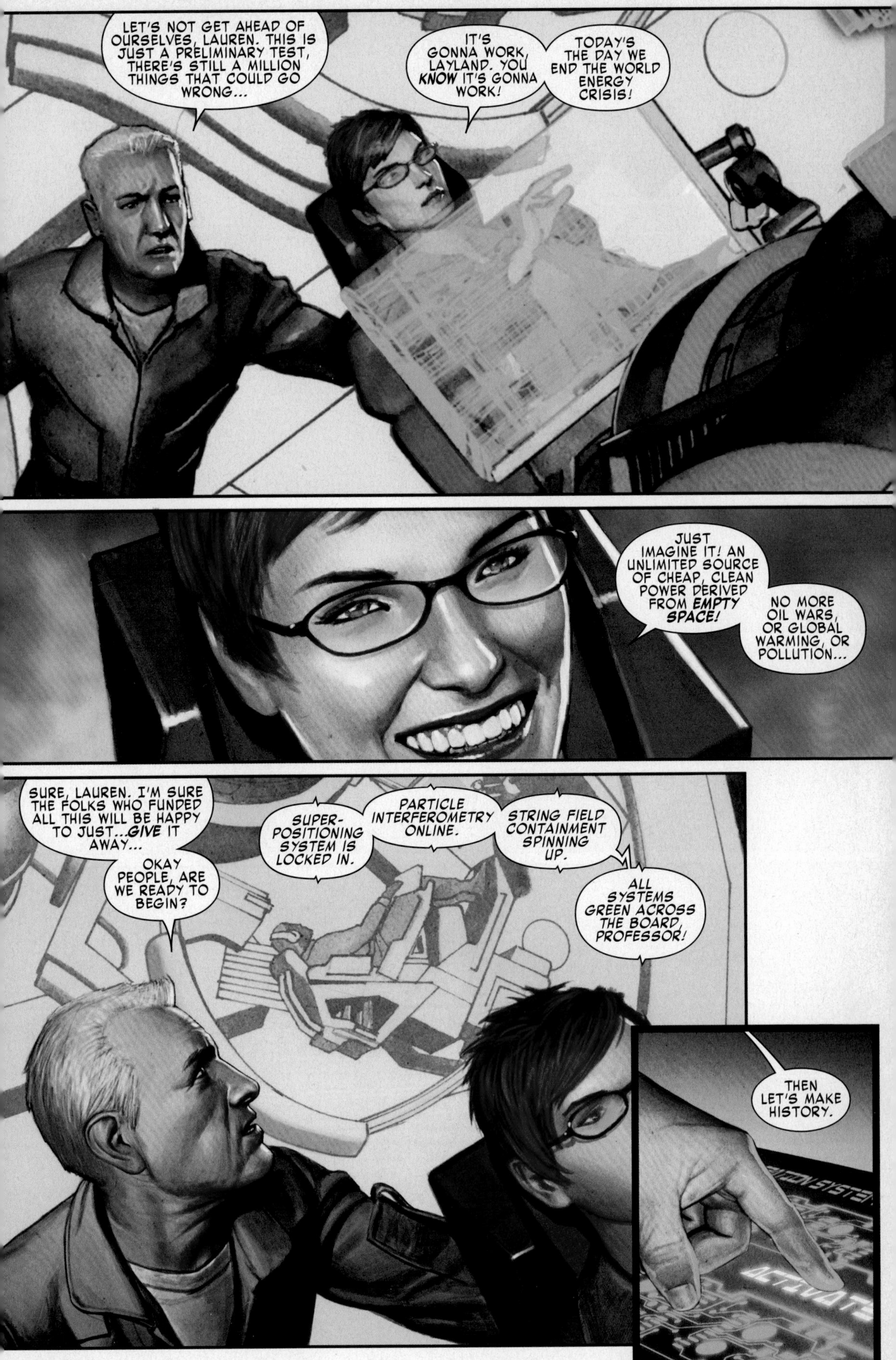
LET'S NOT GET AHEAD OF OURSELVES, LAUREN. THIS IS JUST A PRELIMINARY TEST, THERE'S STILL A MILLION THINGS THAT COULD GO WRONG...
IT'S GONNA WORK, LAYLAND. YOU *KNOW* IT'S GONNA WORK!
TODAY'S THE DAY WE END THE WORLD ENERGY CRISIS!
JUST IMAGINE IT! AN UNLIMITED SOURCE OF CHEAP, CLEAN POWER DERIVED FROM *EMPTY SPACE!*
NO MORE OIL WARS, OR GLOBAL WARMING, OR POLLUTION...
SURE, LAUREN. I'M SURE THE FOLKS WHO FUNDED ALL THIS WILL BE HAPPY TO JUST...*GIVE* IT AWAY...
OKAY PEOPLE, ARE WE READY TO BEGIN?
SUPER-POSITIONING SYSTEM IS LOCKED IN.
PARTICLE INTERFEROMETRY ONLINE.
STRING FIELD CONTAINMENT SPINNING UP.
ALL SYSTEMS GREEN ACROSS THE BOARD, PROFESSOR!
THEN LET'S MAKE HISTORY.
ACTIVATE

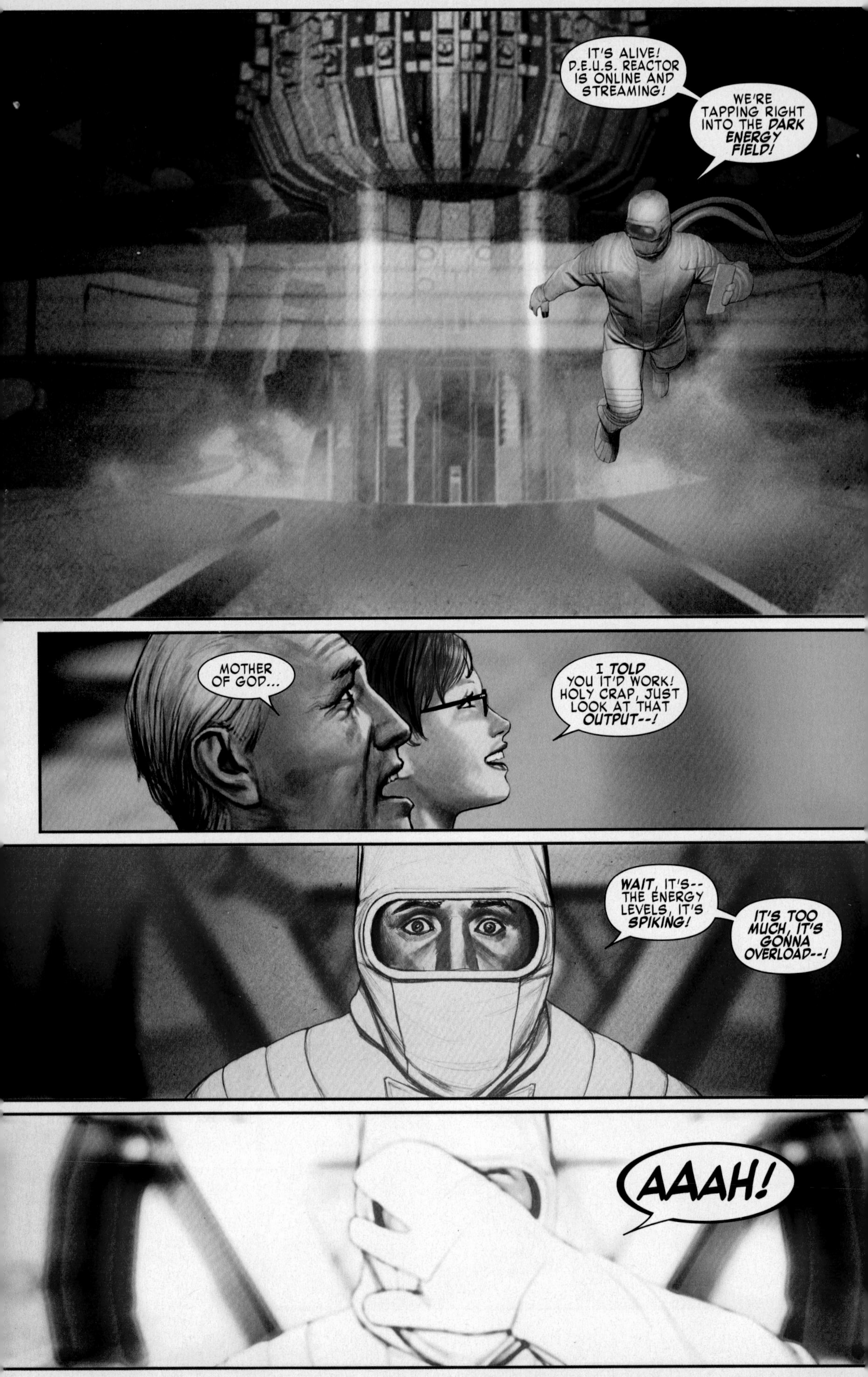
IT'S ALIVE! D.E.U.S. REACTOR IS ONLINE AND STREAMING!
WE'RE TAPPING RIGHT INTO THE DARK ENERGY FIELD!
MOTHER OF GOD...
I TOLD YOU IT'D WORK! HOLY CRAP, JUST LOOK AT THAT OUTPUT--!
WAIT, IT'S-- THE ENERGY LEVELS, IT'S SPIKING!
IT'S TOO MUCH, IT'S GONNA OVERLOAD--!
AAAH!

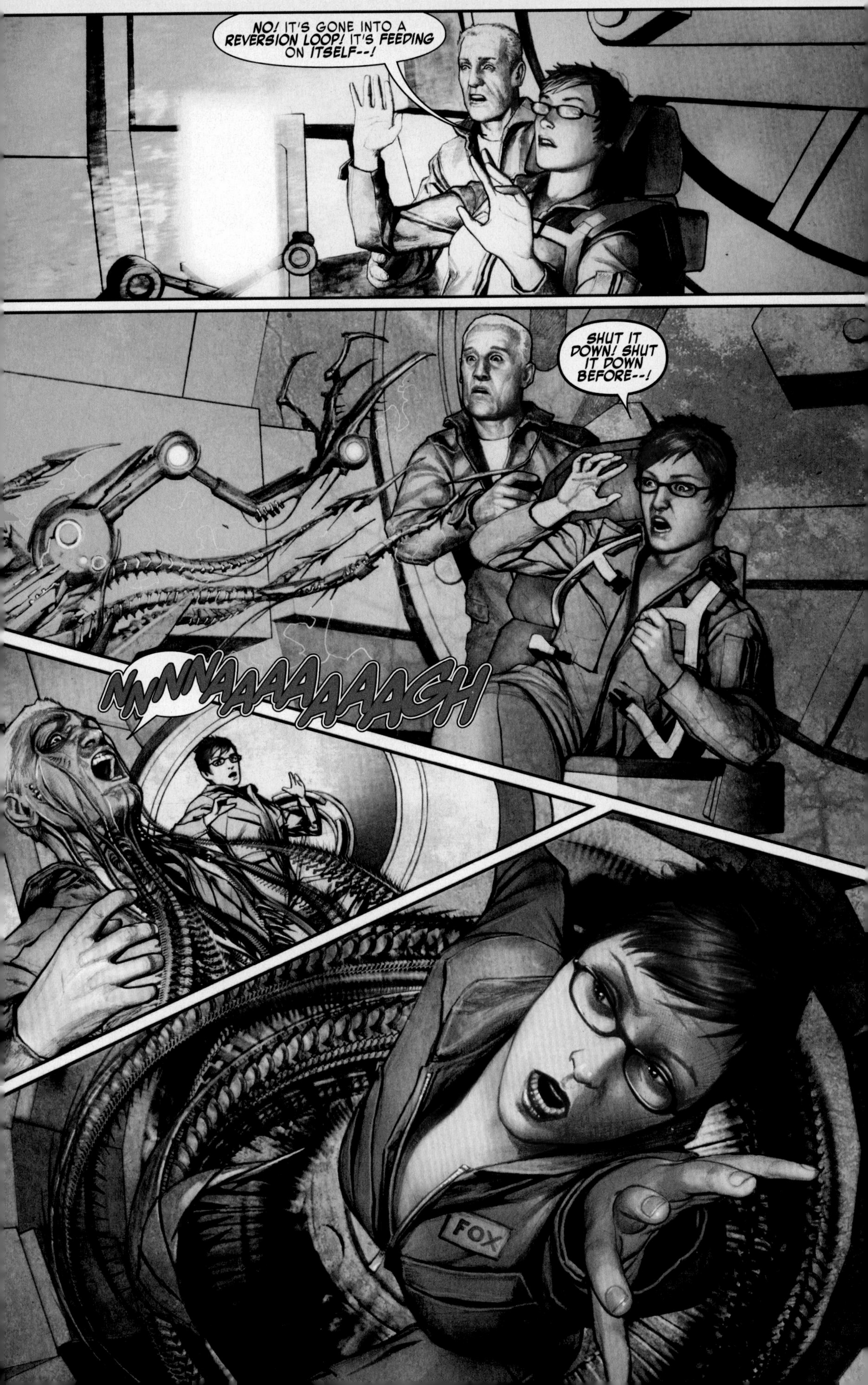
NO! IT'S GONE INTO A REVERSION LOOP! IT'S FEEDING ON ITSELF--!
SHUT IT DOWN! SHUT IT DOWN BEFORE--!
NNNNAAAAAAAAGH
FOX

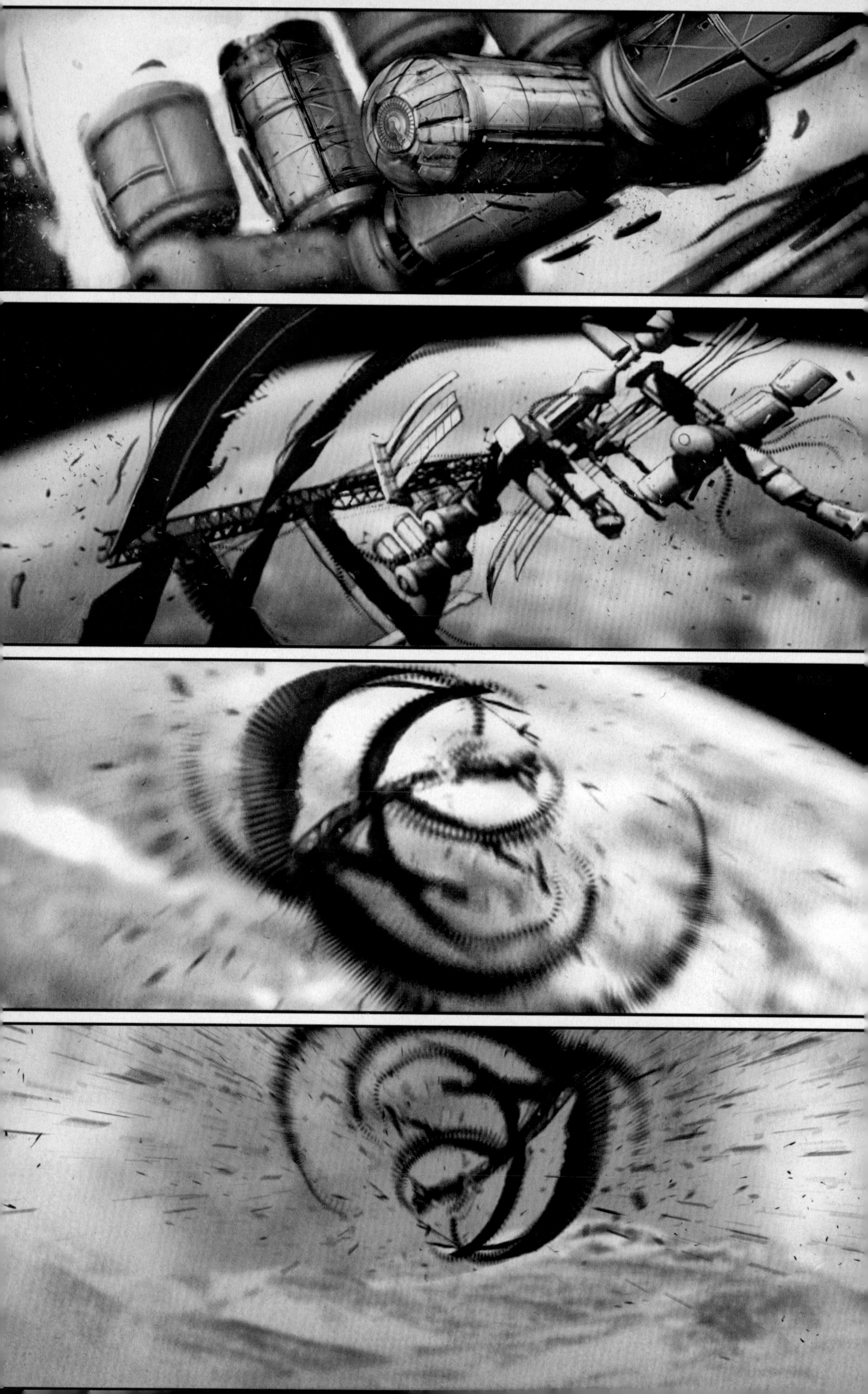

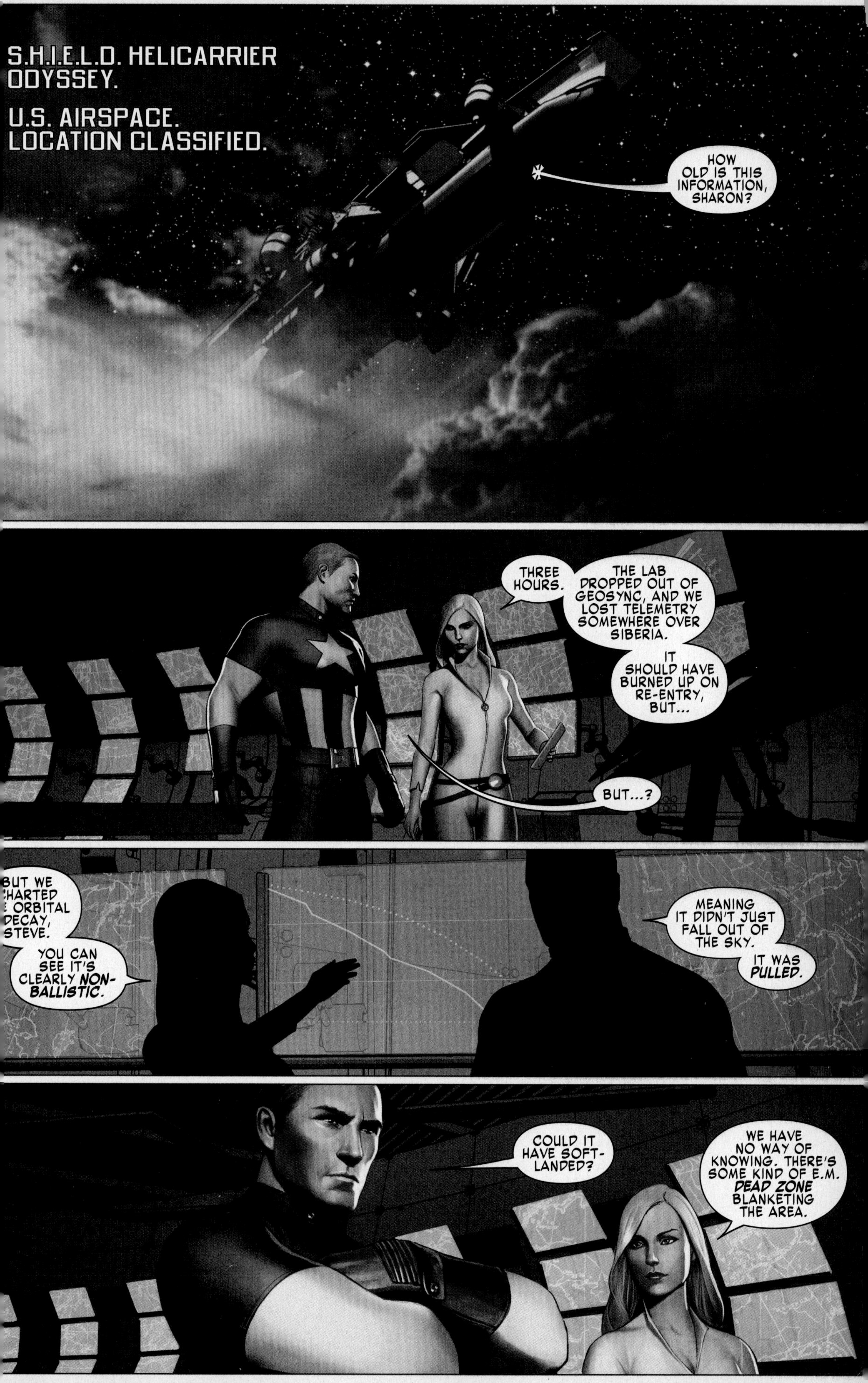
S.H.I.E.L.D. HELICARRIER ODYSSEY.
U.S. AIRSPACE. LOCATION CLASSIFIED.
HOW OLD IS THIS INFORMATION, SHARON?
THREE HOURS.
THE LAB DROPPED OUT OF GEOSYNC, AND WE LOST TELEMETRY SOMEWHERE OVER SIBERIA.
IT SHOULD HAVE BURNED UP ON RE-ENTRY, BUT...
BUT...?
BUT WE CHARTED THE ORBITAL DECAY, STEVE.
YOU CAN SEE IT'S CLEARLY NON-BALLISTIC.
MEANING IT DIDN'T JUST FALL OUT OF THE SKY.
IT WAS PULLED.
COULD IT HAVE SOFT-LANDED?
WE HAVE NO WAY OF KNOWING. THERE'S SOME KIND OF E.M. DEAD ZONE BLANKETING THE AREA.

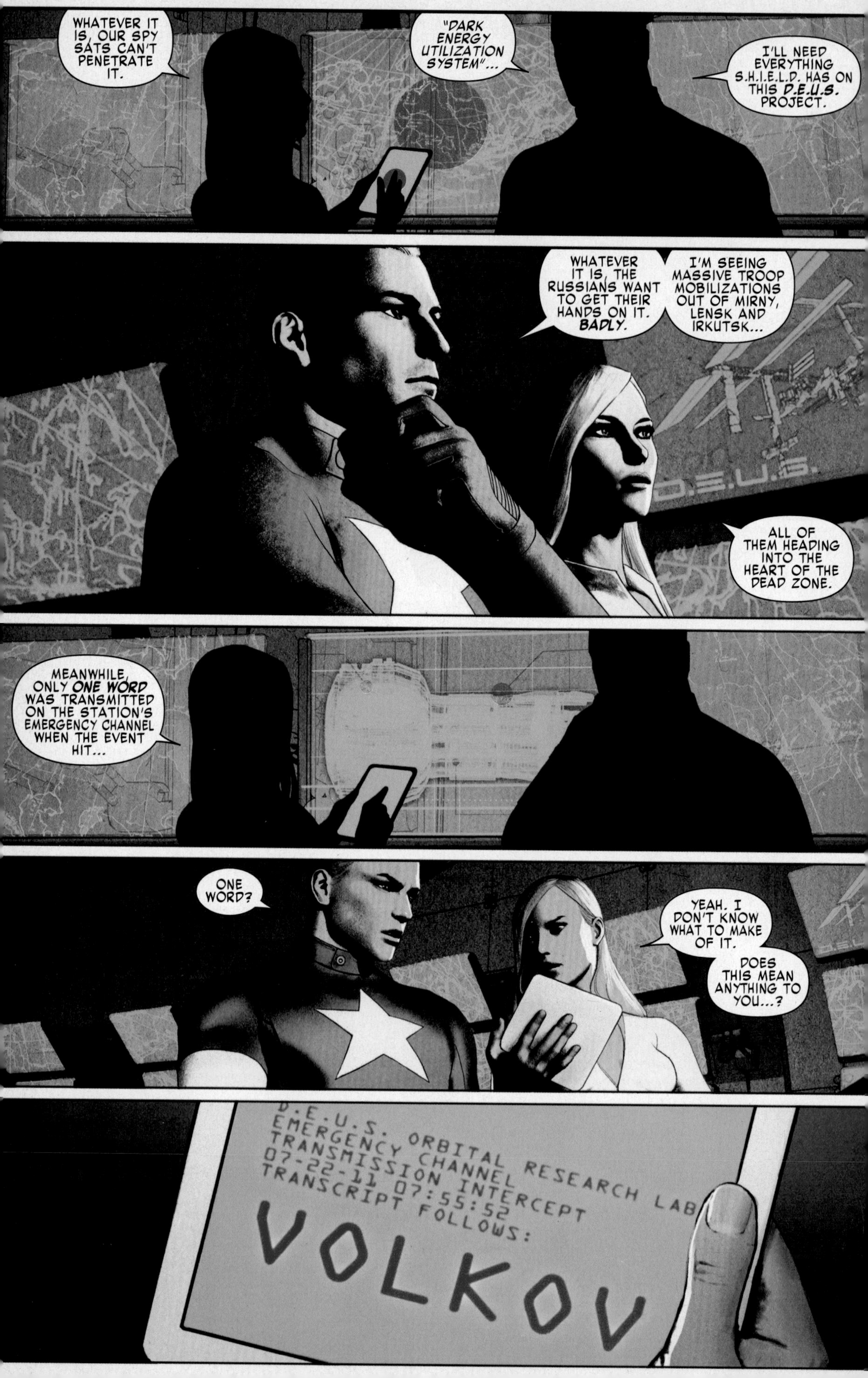
WHATEVER IT IS, OUR SPY SATS CAN'T PENETRATE IT.
"DARK ENERGY UTILIZATION SYSTEM"...
I'LL NEED EVERYTHING S.H.I.E.L.D. HAS ON THIS D.E.U.S. PROJECT.
WHATEVER IT IS, THE RUSSIANS WANT TO GET THEIR HANDS ON IT. BADLY.
I'M SEEING MASSIVE TROOP MOBILIZATIONS OUT OF MIRNY, LENSK AND IRKUTSK...
D.E.U.S.
ALL OF THEM HEADING INTO THE HEART OF THE DEAD ZONE.
MEANWHILE, ONLY ONE WORD WAS TRANSMITTED ON THE STATION'S EMERGENCY CHANNEL WHEN THE EVENT HIT...
ONE WORD?
YEAH. I DON'T KNOW WHAT TO MAKE OF IT.
DOES THIS MEAN ANYTHING TO YOU...?
D.E.U.S. ORBITAL RESEARCH LAB
EMERGENCY CHANNEL
TRANSMISSION INTERCEPT
07-22-11 07:55:52
TRANSCRIPT FOLLOWS:
VOLKOV

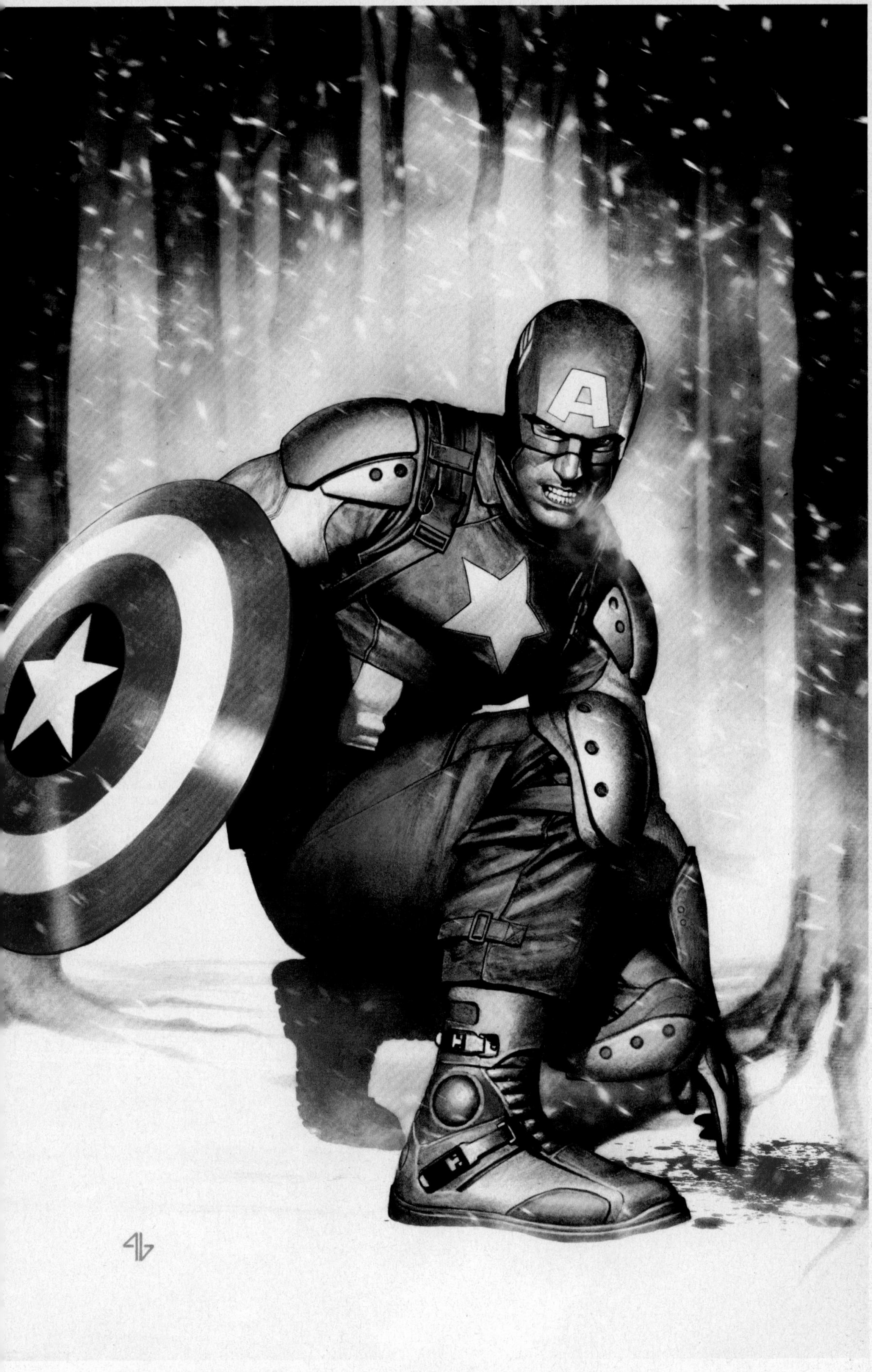

★ CHAPTER TWO ★

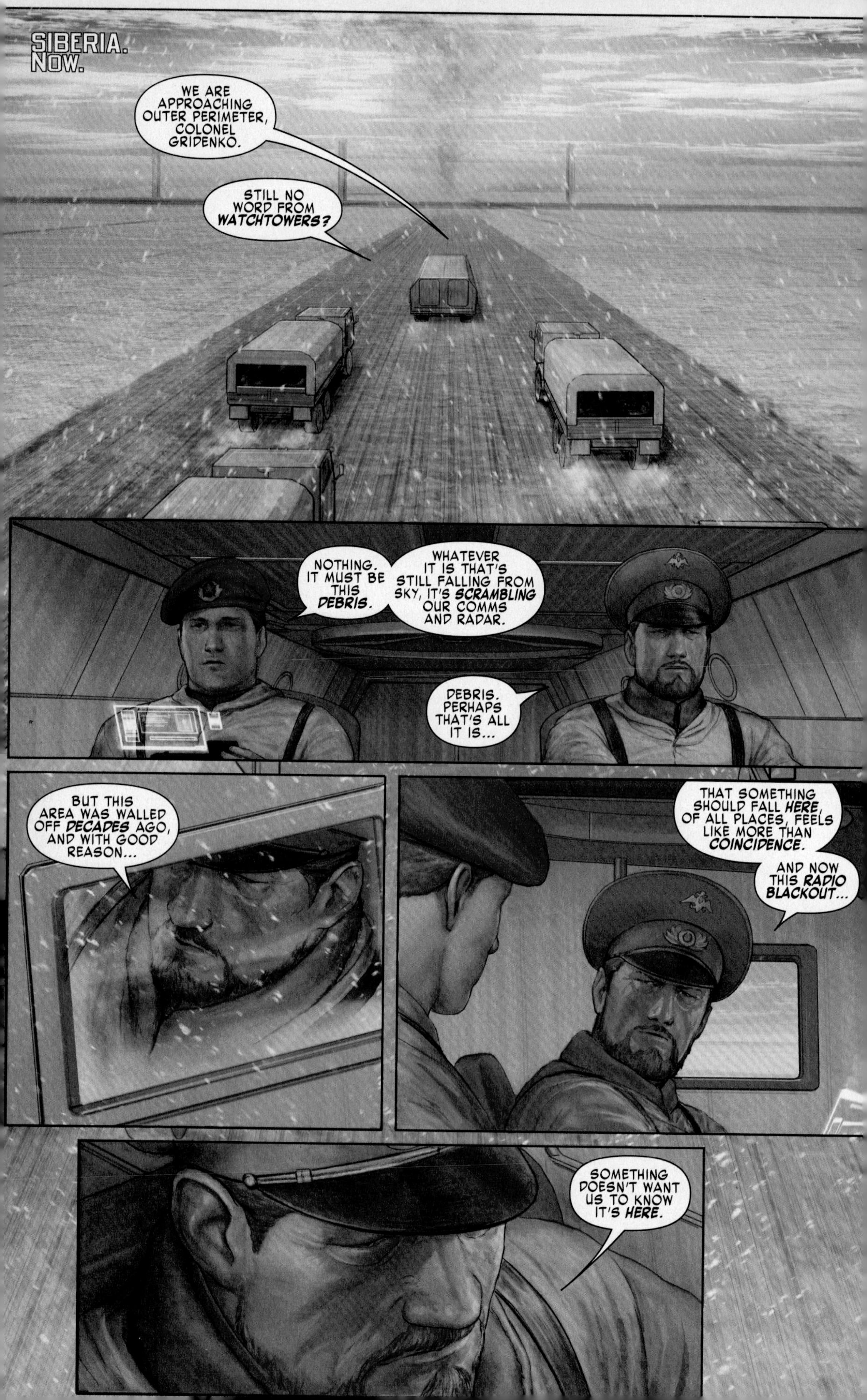

SIBERIA. NOW.
WE ARE APPROACHING OUTER PERIMETER, COLONEL GRIDENKO.
STILL NO WORD FROM WATCHTOWERS?
NOTHING. IT MUST BE THIS DEBRIS.
WHATEVER IT IS THAT'S STILL FALLING FROM SKY, IT'S SCRAMBLING OUR COMMS AND RADAR.
DEBRIS. PERHAPS THAT'S ALL IT IS...
BUT THIS AREA WAS WALLED OFF DECADES AGO, AND WITH GOOD REASON...
THAT SOMETHING SHOULD FALL HERE, OF ALL PLACES, FEELS LIKE MORE THAN COINCIDENCE.
AND NOW THIS RADIO BLACKOUT...
SOMETHING DOESN'T WANT US TO KNOW IT'S HERE.

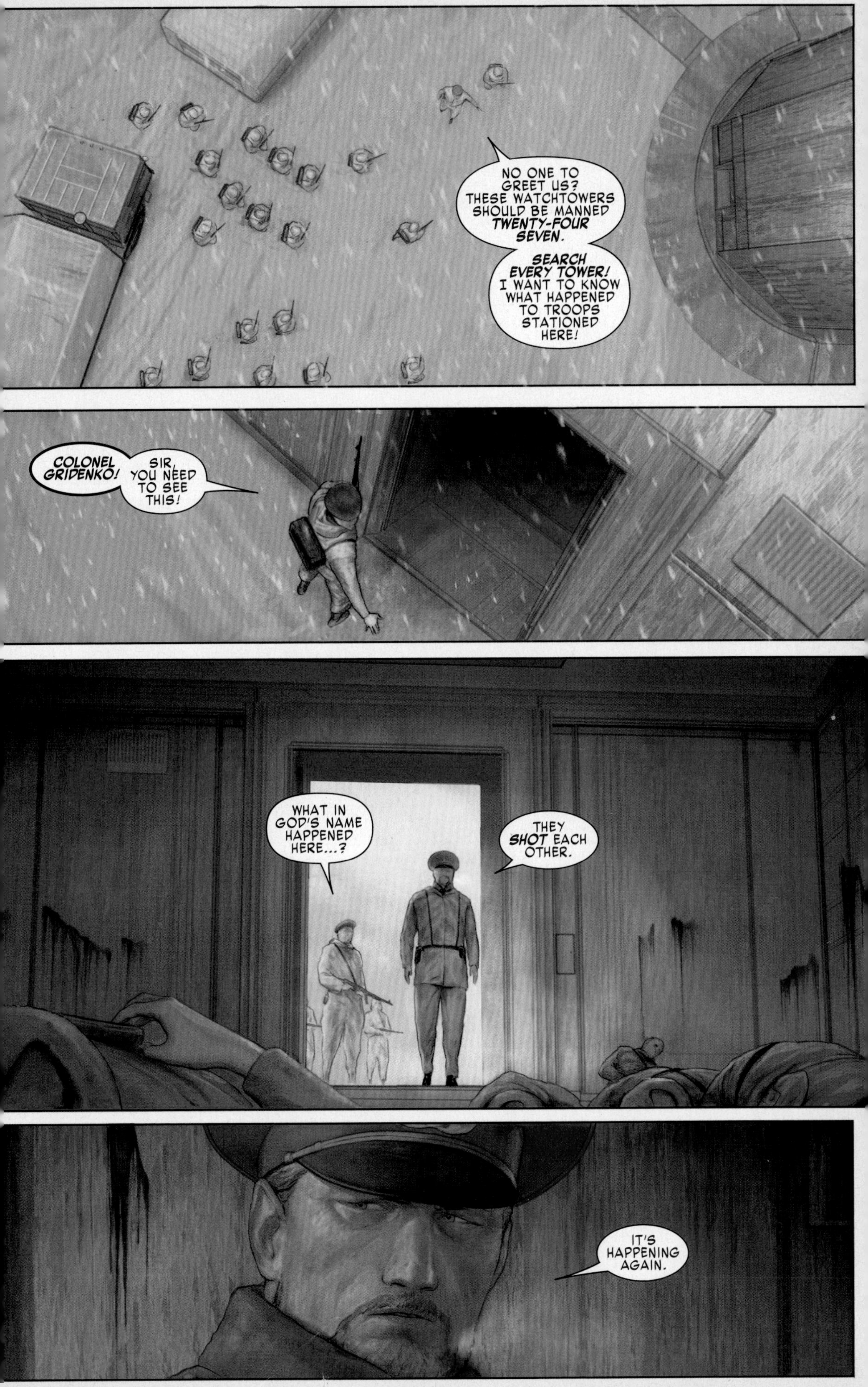
NO ONE TO GREET US? THESE WATCHTOWERS SHOULD BE MANNED TWENTY-FOUR SEVEN.
SEARCH EVERY TOWER! I WANT TO KNOW WHAT HAPPENED TO TROOPS STATIONED HERE!
COLONEL GRIDENKO!
SIR, YOU NEED TO SEE THIS!
WHAT IN GOD'S NAME HAPPENED HERE...?
THEY SHOT EACH OTHER.
IT'S HAPPENING AGAIN.

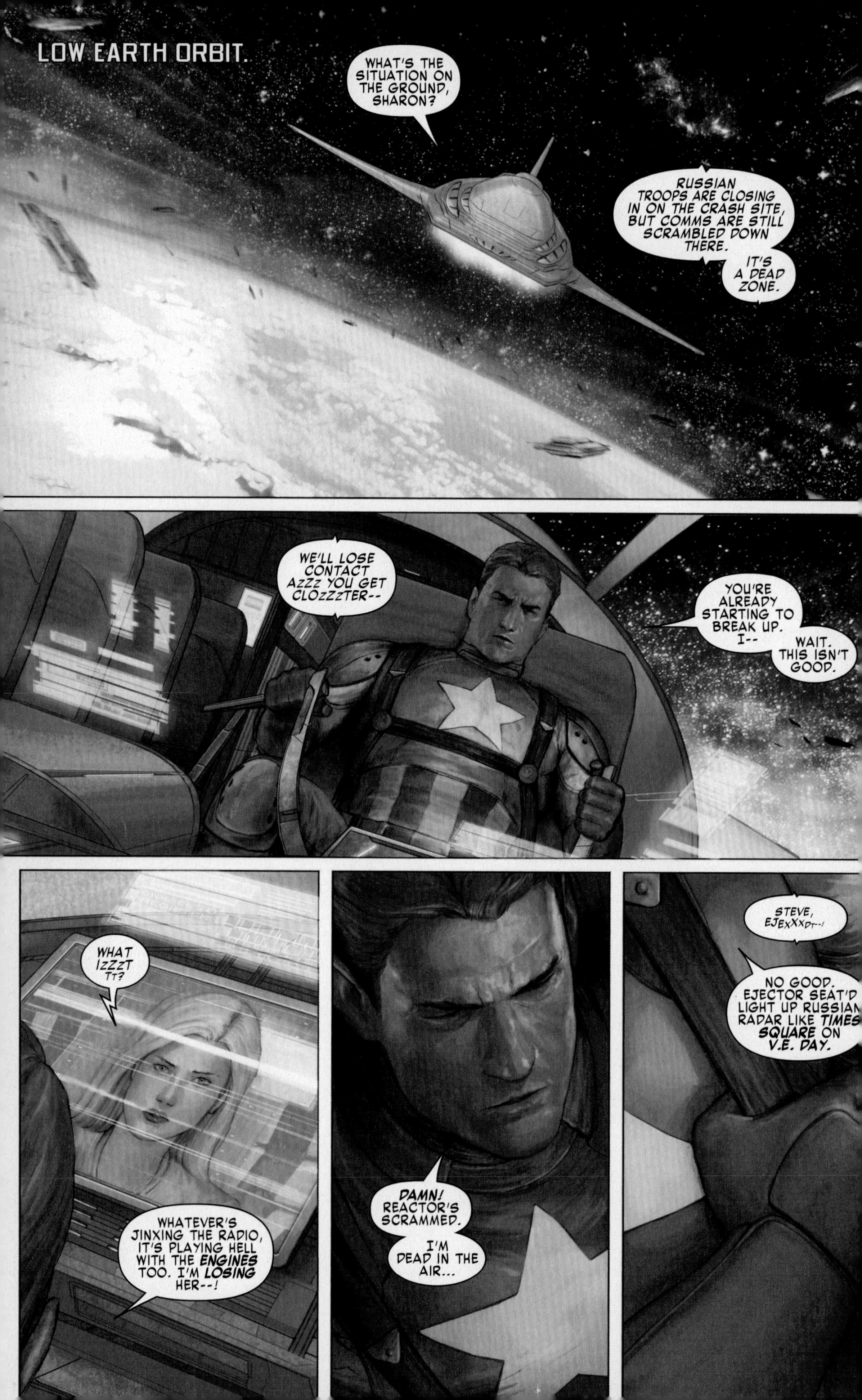

LOW EARTH ORBIT.
WHAT'S THE SITUATION ON THE GROUND, SHARON?
RUSSIAN TROOPS ARE CLOSING IN ON THE CRASH SITE, BUT COMMS ARE STILL SCRAMBLED DOWN THERE.
IT'S A DEAD ZONE.
WE'LL LOSE CONTACT AZZZ YOU GET CLOZZZZTER--
YOU'RE ALREADY STARTING TO BREAK UP. I--
WAIT. THIS ISN'T GOOD.
WHAT IZZZT TT?
WHATEVER'S JINXING THE RADIO, IT'S PLAYING HELL WITH THE ENGINES TOO. I'M LOSING HER--!
DAMN! REACTOR'S SCRAMMED.
I'M DEAD IN THE AIR...
STEVE, EJEXXXDT--!
NO GOOD. EJECTOR SEAT'D LIGHT UP RUSSIAN RADAR LIKE TIMES SQUARE ON V.E. DAY.

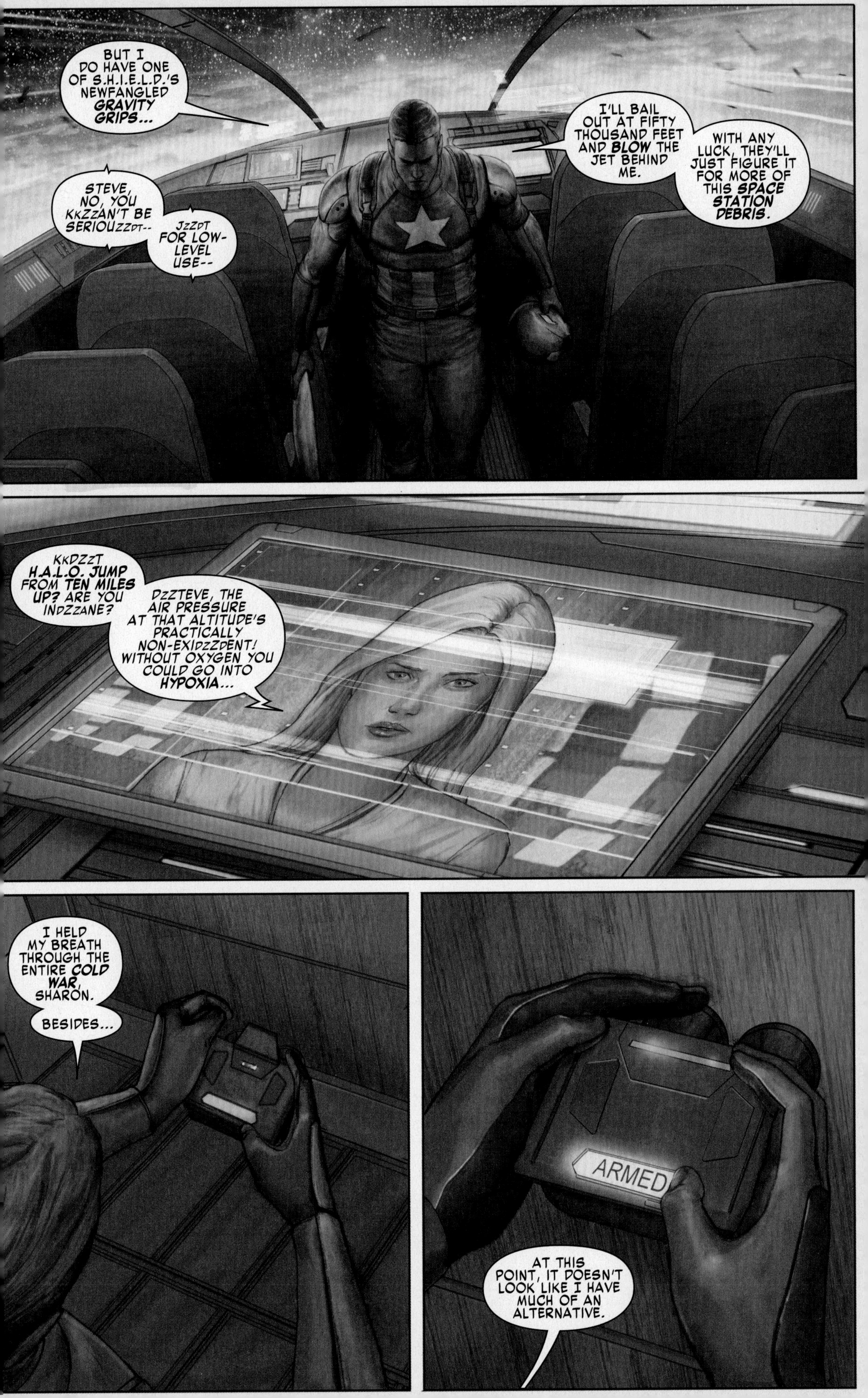
BUT I DO HAVE ONE OF S.H.I.E.L.D.'s NEWFANGLED GRAVITY GRIPS...
STEVE, NO, YOU KKZZAN'T BE SERIOUZZDT--
JZZDT FOR LOW-LEVEL USE--
I'LL BAIL OUT AT FIFTY THOUSAND FEET AND BLOW THE JET BEHIND ME.
WITH ANY LUCK, THEY'LL JUST FIGURE IT FOR MORE OF THIS SPACE STATION DEBRIS.
KKDZZT H.A.L.O. JUMP FROM TEN MILES UP? ARE YOU INDZZANE?
DZZTEVE, THE AIR PRESSURE AT THAT ALTITUDE'S PRACTICALLY NON-EXIDZZDENT! WITHOUT OXYGEN YOU COULD GO INTO HYPOXIA...
I HELD MY BREATH THROUGH THE ENTIRE COLD WAR, SHARON.
BESIDES...
ARMED
AT THIS POINT, IT DOESN'T LOOK LIKE I HAVE MUCH OF AN ALTERNATIVE.

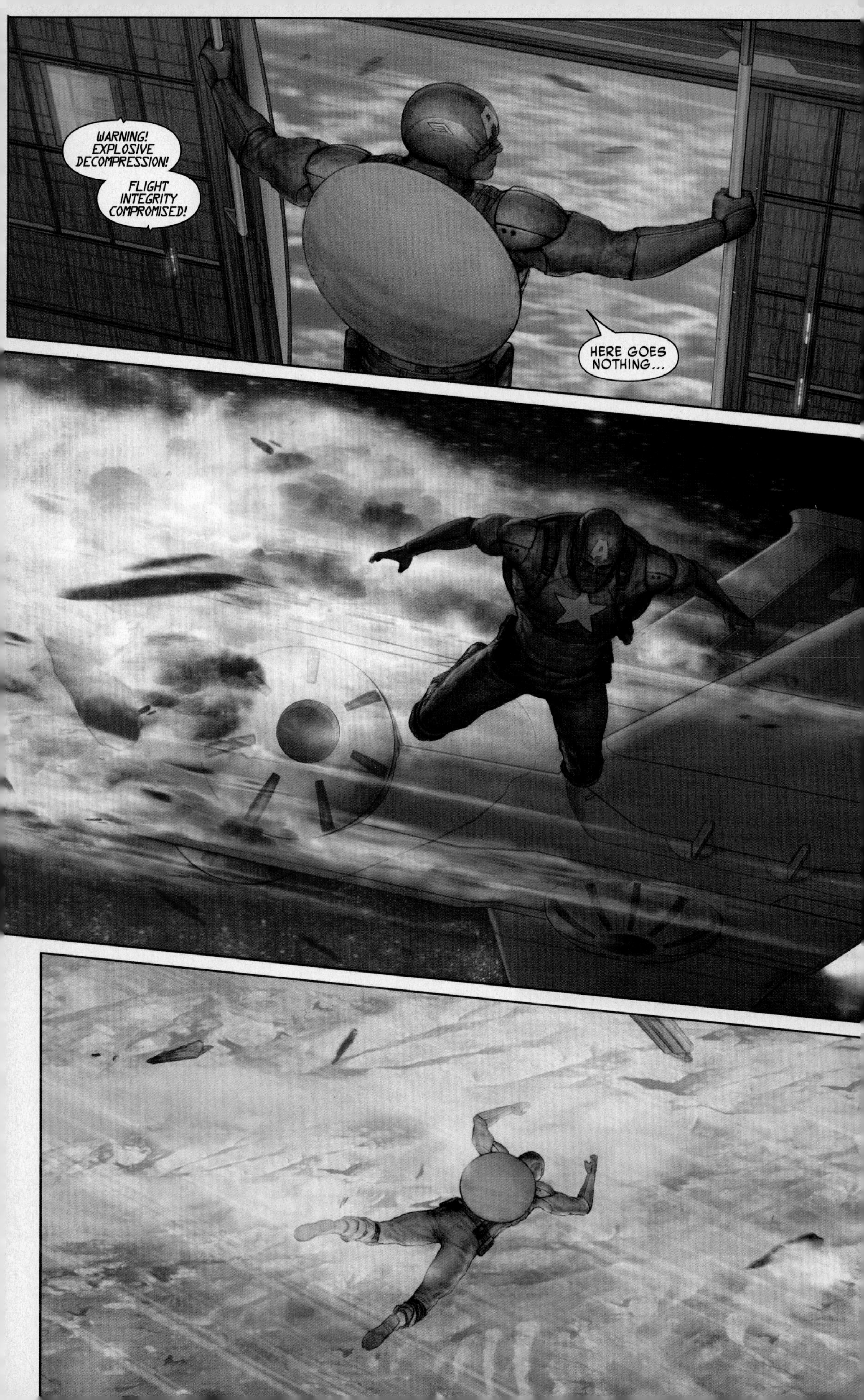
WARNING! EXPLOSIVE DECOMPRESSION!
FLIGHT INTEGRITY COMPROMISED!
HERE GOES NOTHING...

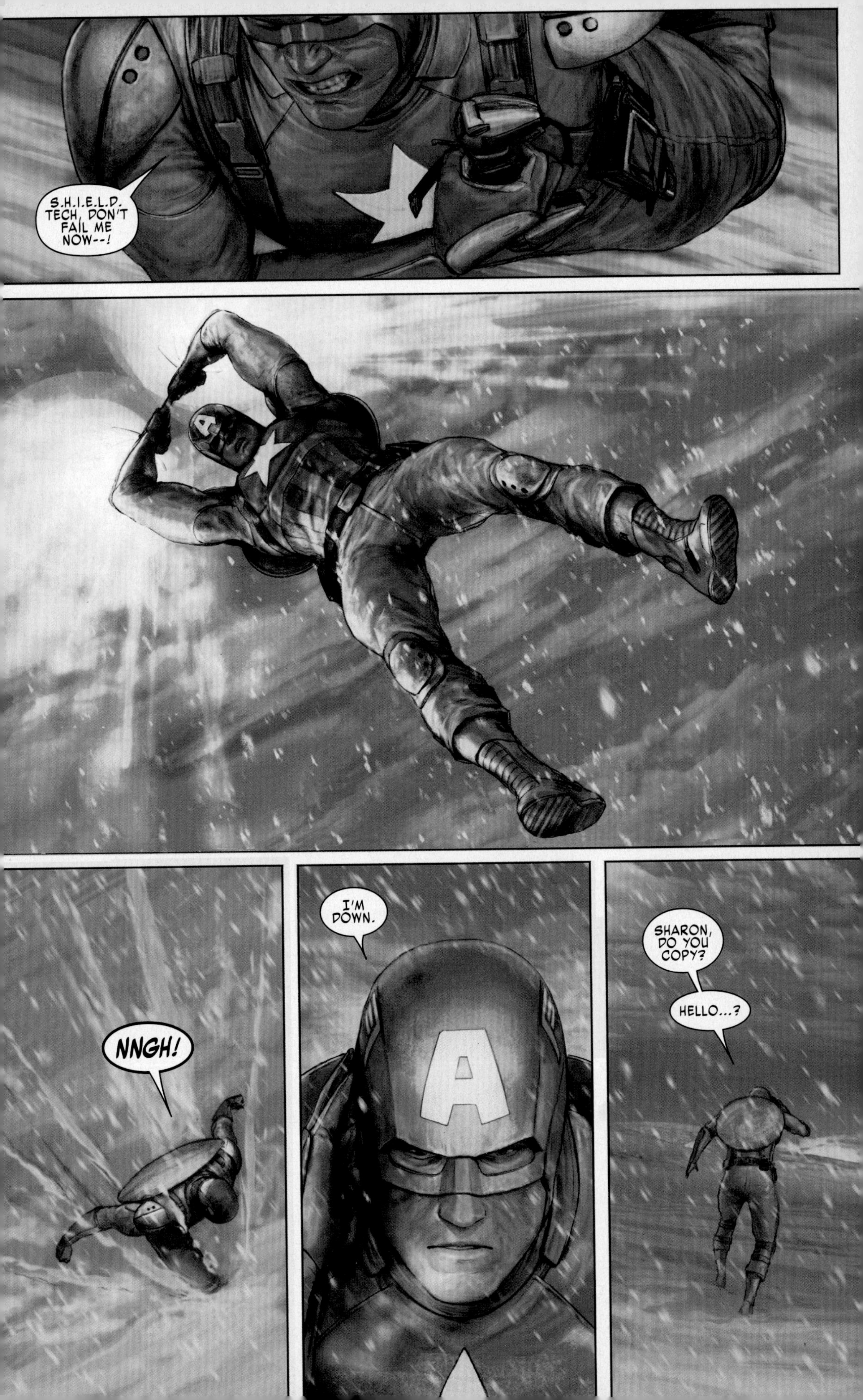

S.H.I.E.L.D. TECH, DON'T FAIL ME NOW--!
NNGH!
I'M DOWN.
SHARON, DO YOU COPY?
HELLO...?

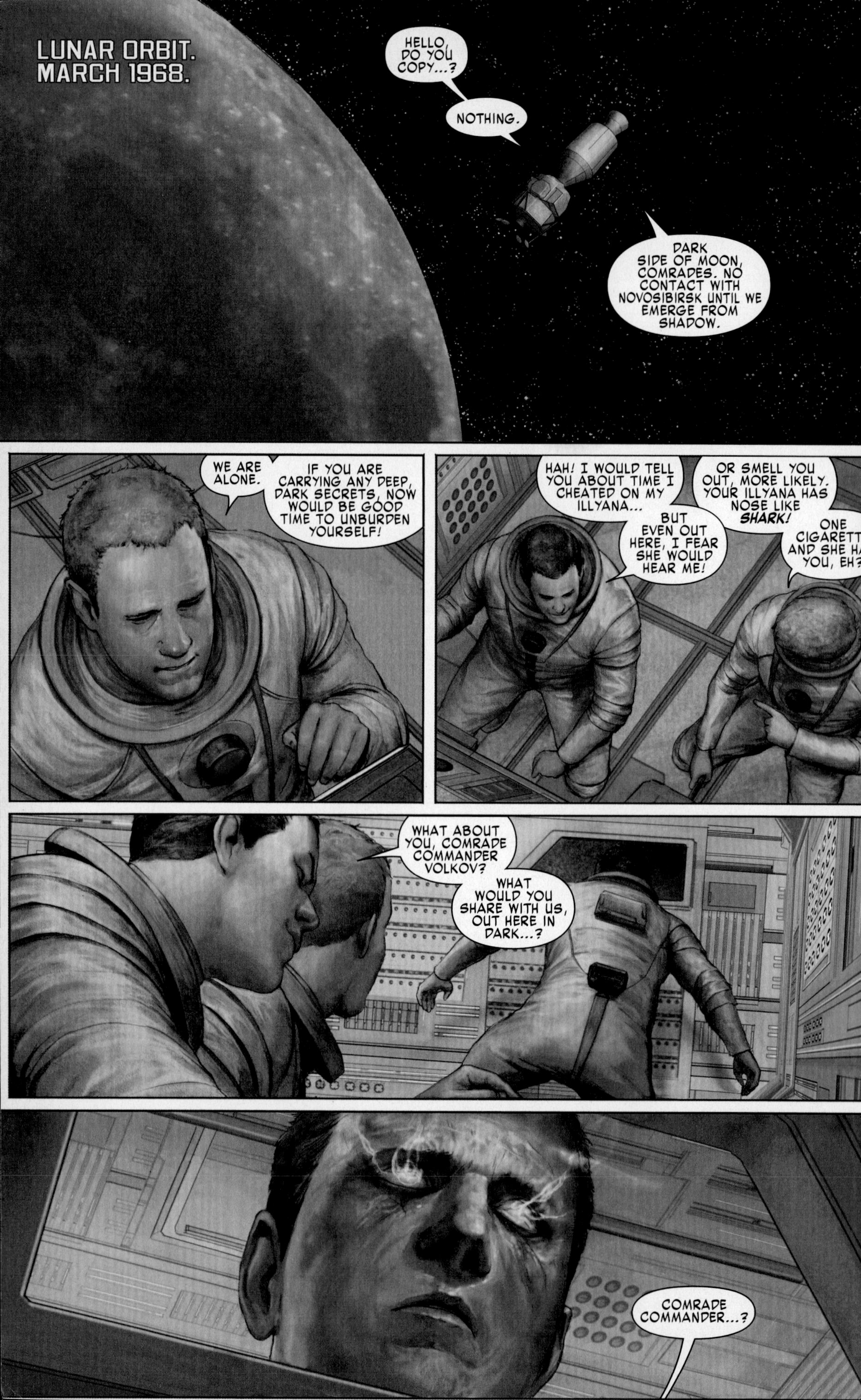
LUNAR ORBIT. MARCH 1968.
HELLO, DO YOU COPY...?
NOTHING.
DARK SIDE OF MOON, COMRADES. NO CONTACT WITH NOVOSIBIRSK UNTIL WE EMERGE FROM SHADOW.
WE ARE ALONE.
IF YOU ARE CARRYING ANY DEEP, DARK SECRETS, NOW WOULD BE GOOD TIME TO UNBURDEN YOURSELF!
HAH! I WOULD TELL YOU ABOUT TIME I CHEATED ON MY ILLYANA...
BUT EVEN OUT HERE, I FEAR SHE WOULD HEAR ME!
OR SMELL YOU OUT, MORE LIKELY. YOUR ILLYANA HAS NOSE LIKE SHARK!
WHAT ABOUT YOU, COMRADE COMMANDER VOLKOV?
WHAT WOULD YOU SHARE WITH US, OUT HERE IN DARK...?
COMRADE COMMANDER...?

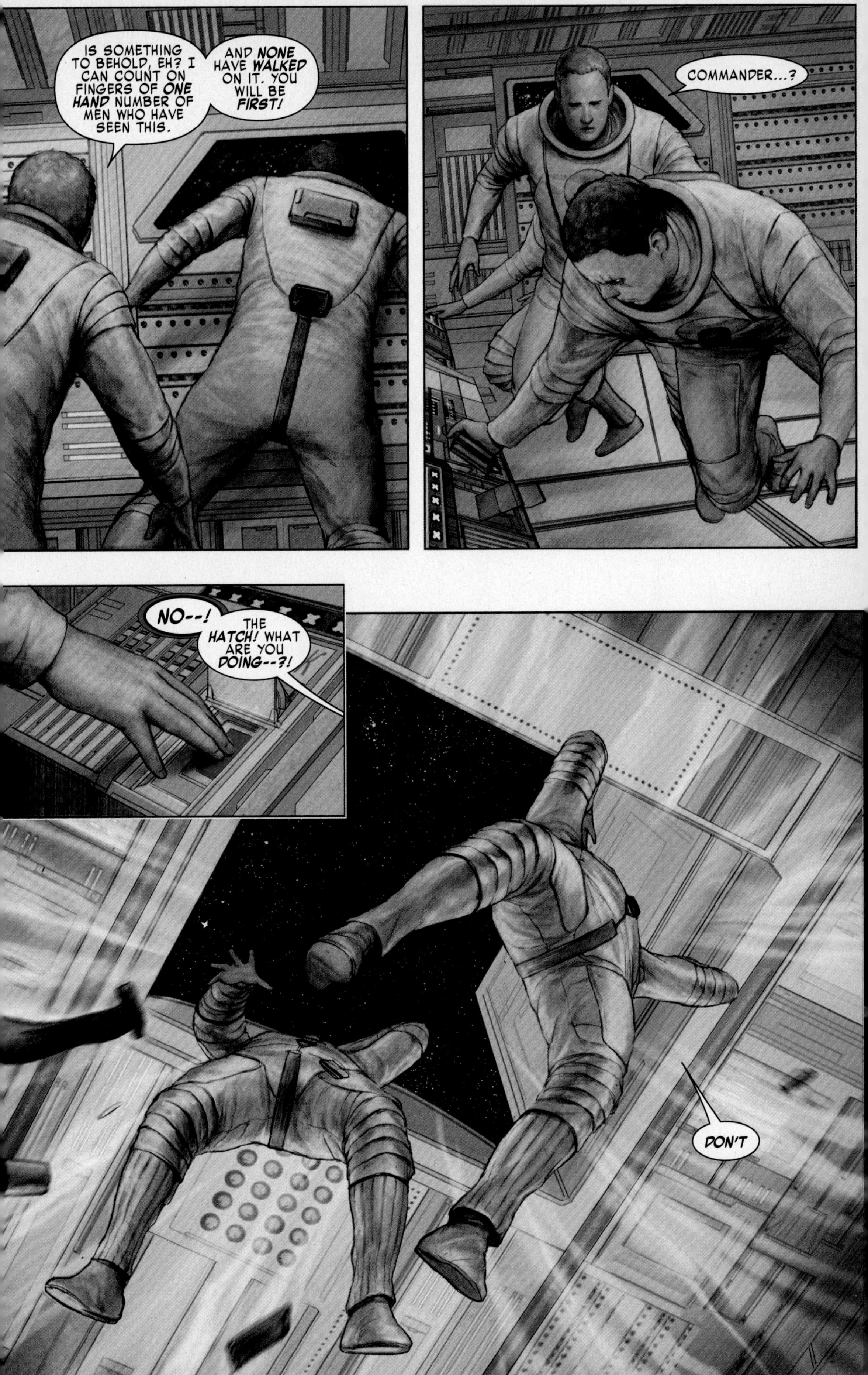
IS SOMETHING TO BEHOLD, EH? I CAN COUNT ON FINGERS OF ONE HAND NUMBER OF MEN WHO HAVE SEEN THIS.
AND NONE HAVE WALKED ON IT. YOU WILL BE FIRST!
COMMANDER...?
NO--!
THE HATCH! WHAT ARE YOU DOING--?!
DON'T

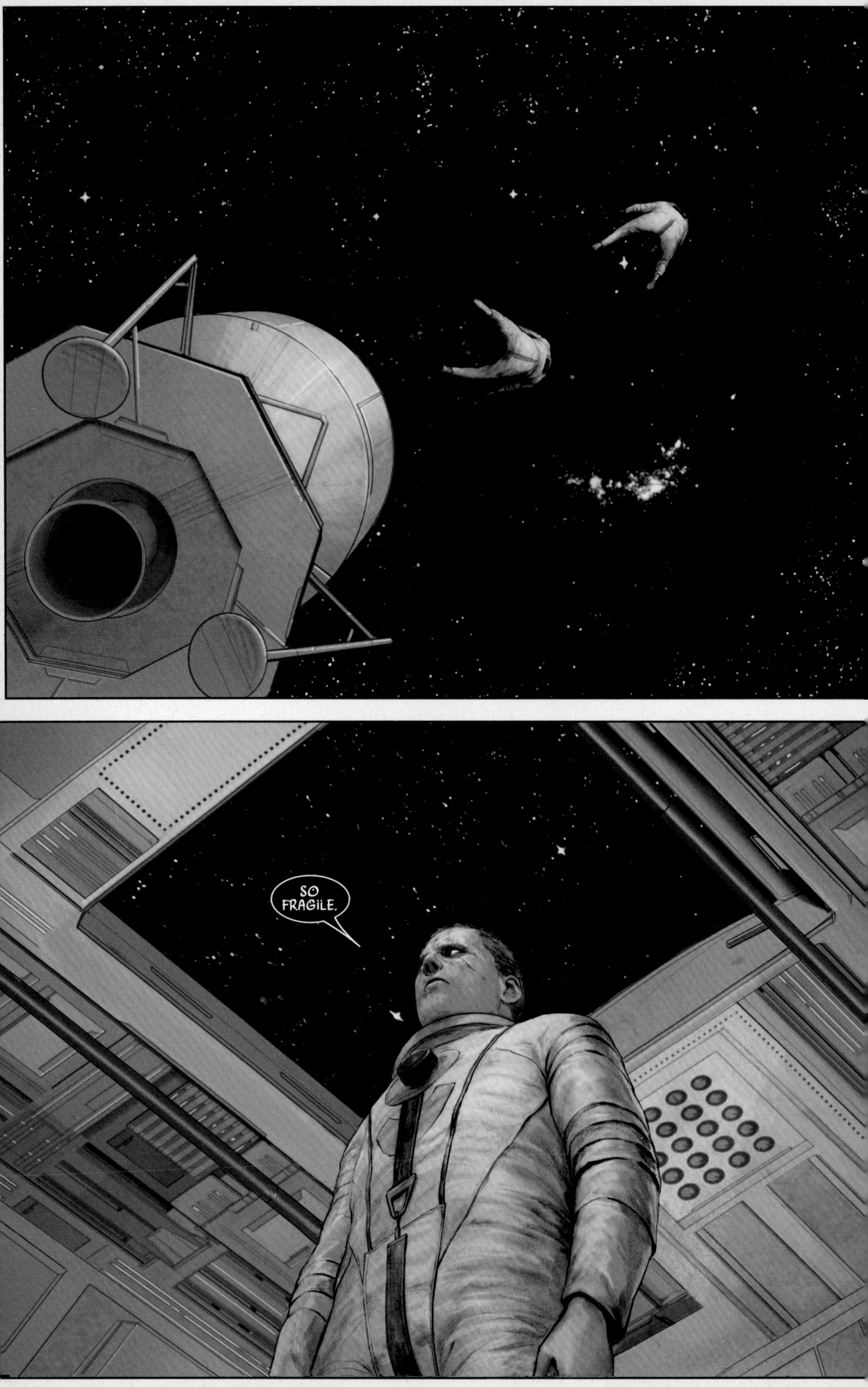
SO FRAGILE.

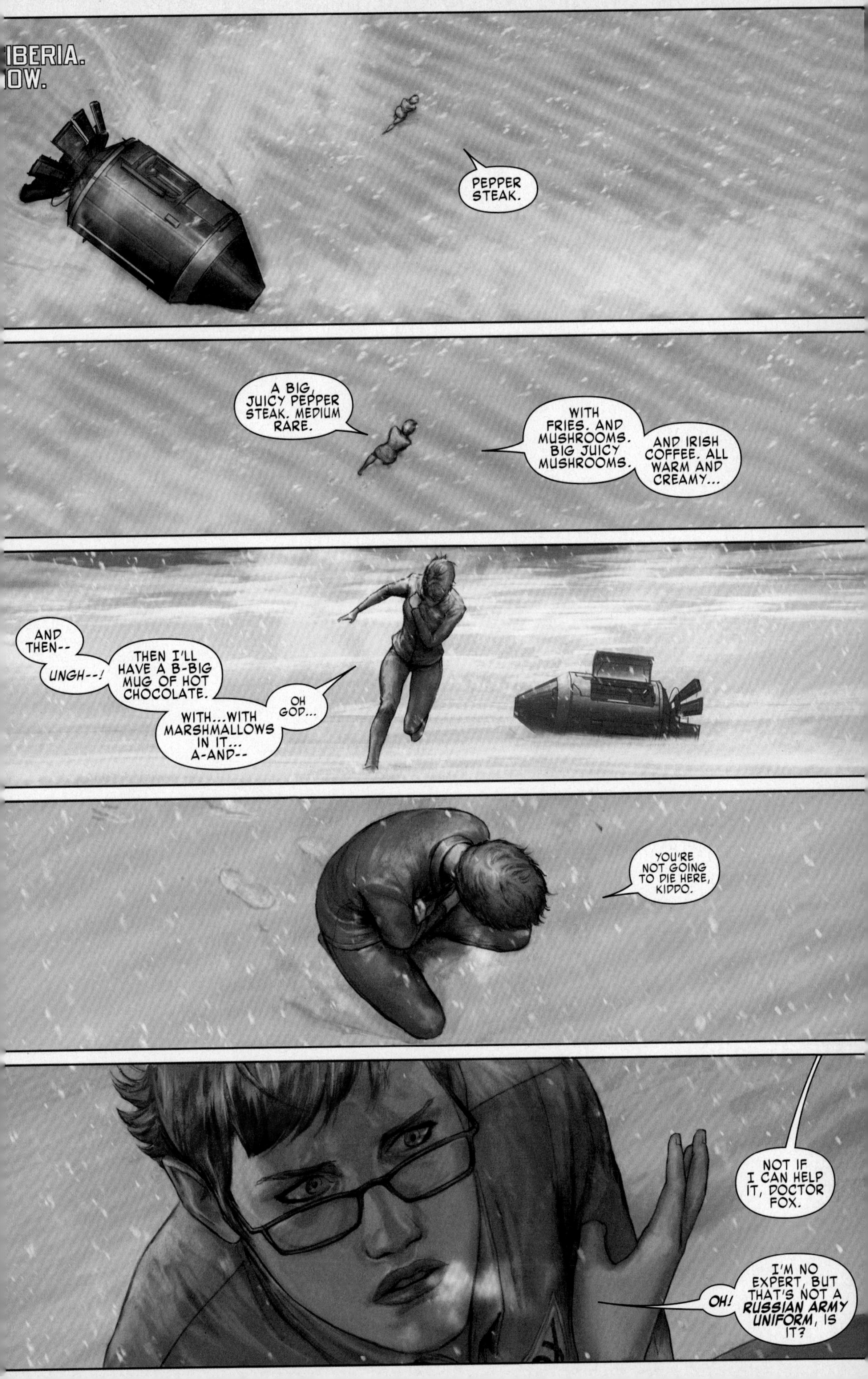
IBERIA.
OW.
PEPPER STEAK.
A BIG, JUICY PEPPER STEAK. MEDIUM RARE.
WITH FRIES. AND MUSHROOMS. BIG JUICY MUSHROOMS.
AND IRISH COFFEE. ALL WARM AND CREAMY...
AND THEN--
UNGH--!
THEN I'LL HAVE A B-BIG MUG OF HOT CHOCOLATE.
WITH...WITH MARSHMALLOWS IN IT... A-AND--
OH GOD...
YOU'RE NOT GOING TO DIE HERE, KIDDO.
NOT IF I CAN HELP IT, DOCTOR FOX.
OH!
I'M NO EXPERT, BUT THAT'S NOT A RUSSIAN ARMY UNIFORM, IS IT?

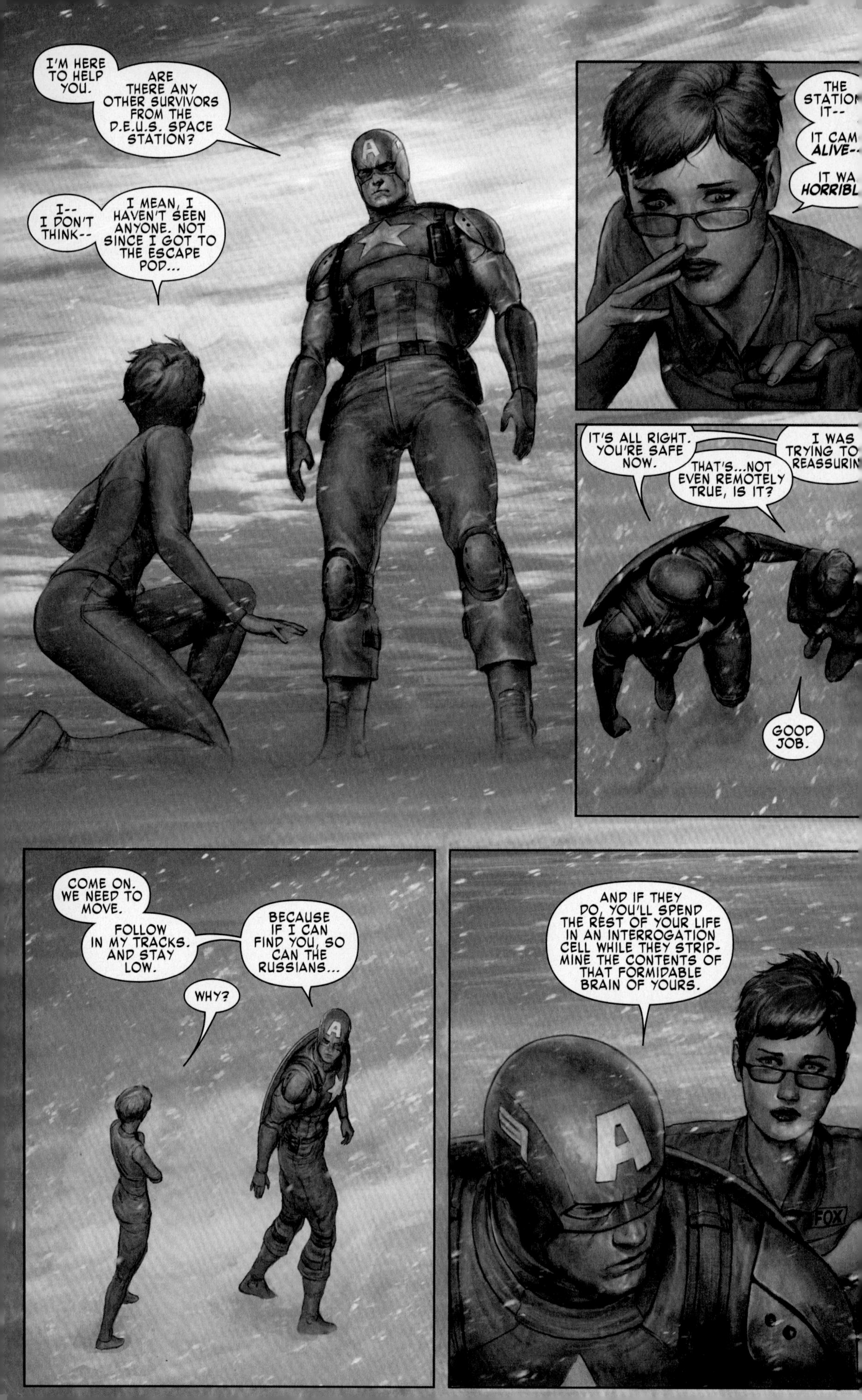

I'M HERE TO HELP YOU.
ARE THERE ANY OTHER SURVIVORS FROM THE D.E.U.S. SPACE STATION?
I-- I DON'T THINK--
I MEAN, I HAVEN'T SEEN ANYONE. NOT SINCE I GOT TO THE ESCAPE POD...
THE STATIO
IT--
IT CAM
ALIVE--
IT WA
HORRIBL
IT'S ALL RIGHT. YOU'RE SAFE NOW.
THAT'S...NOT EVEN REMOTELY TRUE, IS IT?
I WAS TRYING TO REASSURIN
GOOD JOB.
COME ON. WE NEED TO MOVE.
FOLLOW IN MY TRACKS. AND STAY LOW.
WHY?
BECAUSE IF I CAN FIND YOU, SO CAN THE RUSSIANS...
AND IF THEY DO, YOU'LL SPEND THE REST OF YOUR LIFE IN AN INTERROGATION CELL WHILE THEY STRIP-MINE THE CONTENTS OF THAT FORMIDABLE BRAIN OF YOURS.
FOX

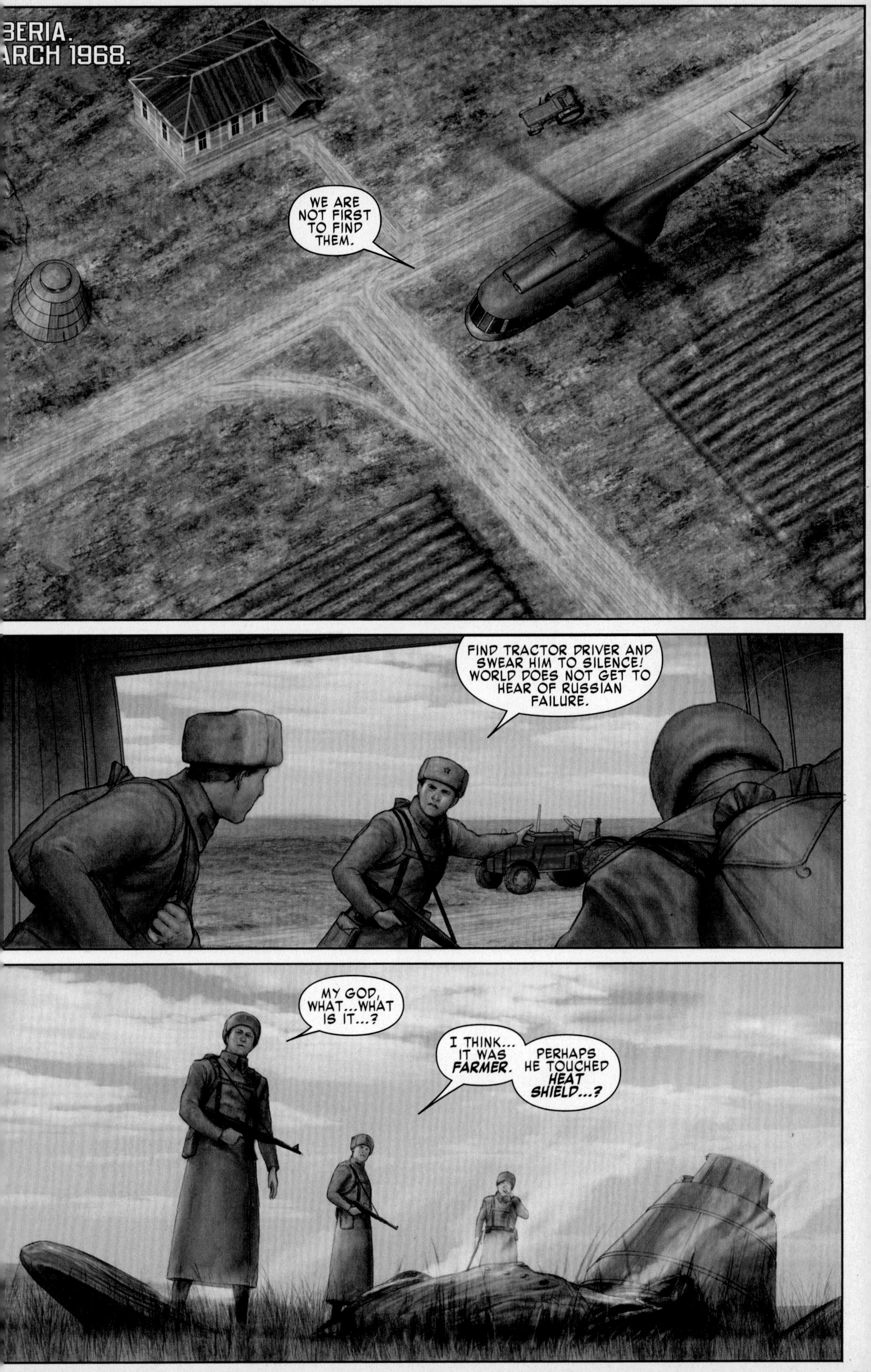
BERIA.
ARCH 1968.
WE ARE NOT FIRST TO FIND THEM.
FIND TRACTOR DRIVER AND SWEAR HIM TO SILENCE! WORLD DOES NOT GET TO HEAR OF RUSSIAN FAILURE.
MY GOD, WHAT...WHAT IS IT...?
I THINK... IT WAS FARMER.
PERHAPS HE TOUCHED HEAT SHIELD...?

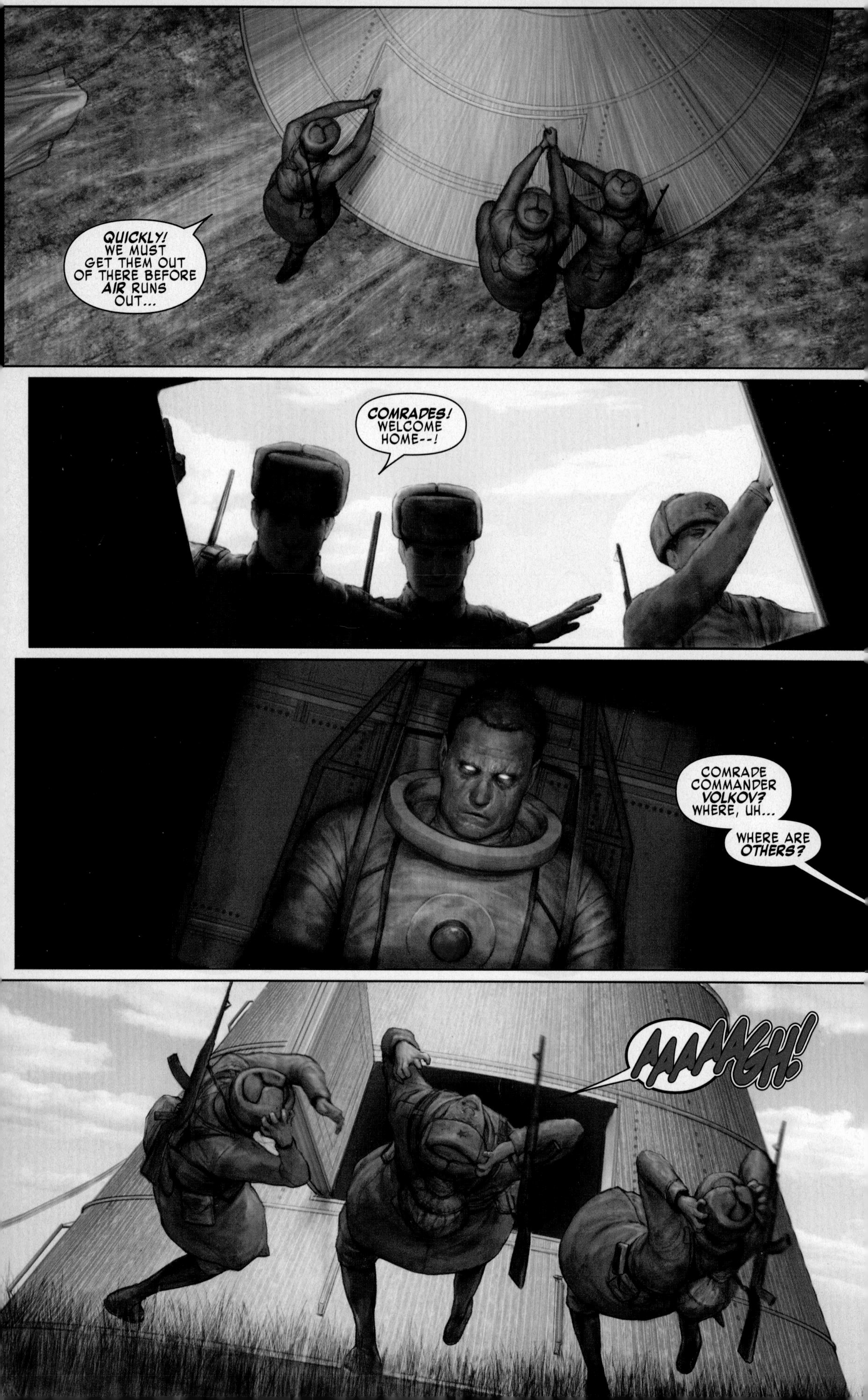
QUICKLY! WE MUST GET THEM OUT OF THERE BEFORE AIR RUNS OUT...
COMRADES! WELCOME HOME--!
COMRADE COMMANDER VOLKOV? WHERE, UH...
WHERE ARE OTHERS?
AAAAAGH!

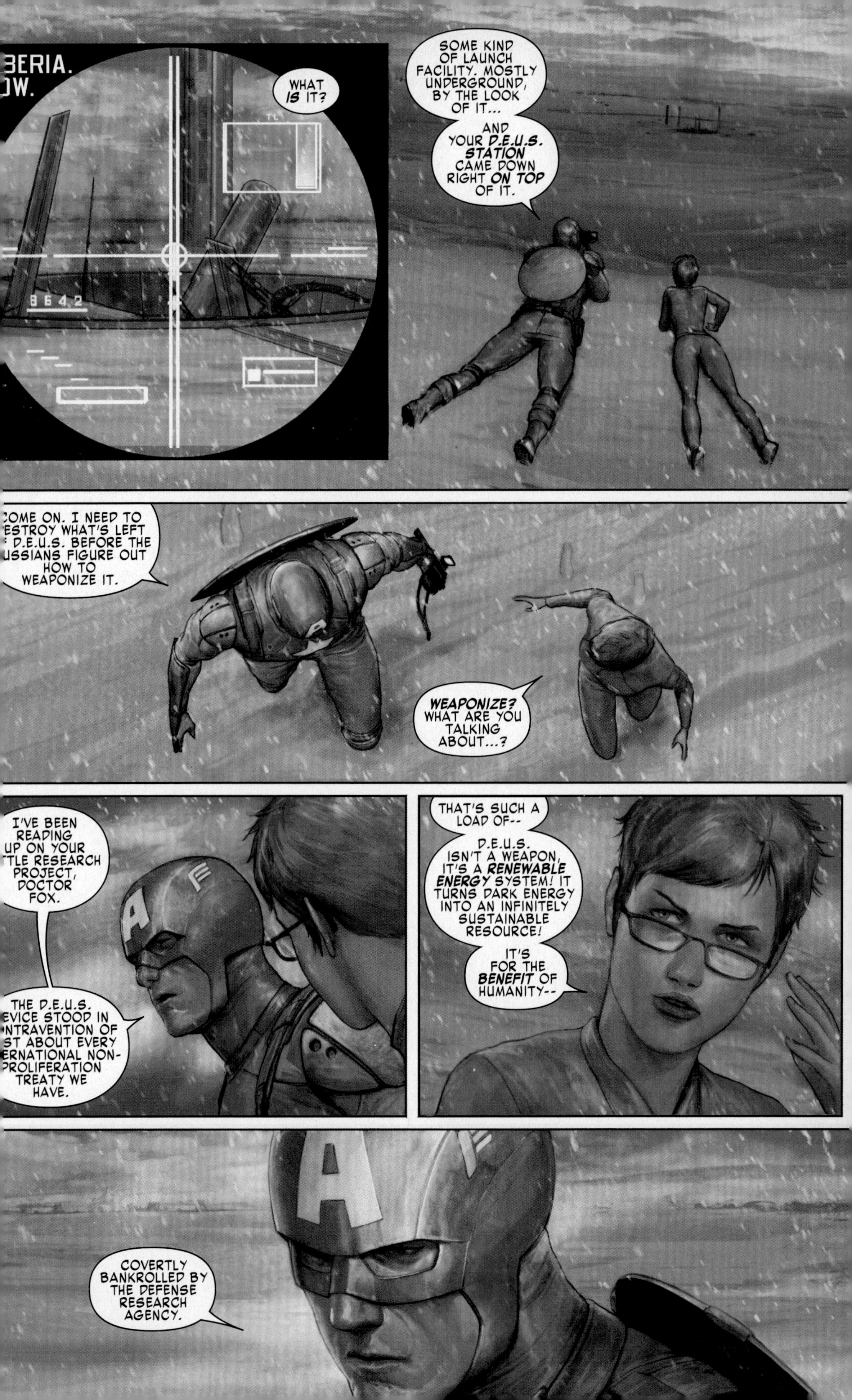

BERIA.
OW.
WHAT IS IT?
SOME KIND OF LAUNCH FACILITY. MOSTLY UNDERGROUND, BY THE LOOK OF IT...
AND YOUR D.E.U.S. STATION CAME DOWN RIGHT ON TOP OF IT.
OME ON. I NEED TO ESTROY WHAT'S LEFT D.E.U.S. BEFORE THE USSIANS FIGURE OUT HOW TO WEAPONIZE IT.
WEAPONIZE? WHAT ARE YOU TALKING ABOUT...?
I'VE BEEN READING UP ON YOUR TTLE RESEARCH PROJECT, DOCTOR FOX.
THE D.E.U.S. EVICE STOOD IN NTRAVENTION OF ST ABOUT EVERY ERNATIONAL NON-PROLIFERATION TREATY WE HAVE.
THAT'S SUCH A LOAD OF--
D.E.U.S. ISN'T A WEAPON, IT'S A RENEWABLE ENERGY SYSTEM! IT TURNS DARK ENERGY INTO AN INFINITELY SUSTAINABLE RESOURCE!
IT'S FOR THE BENEFIT OF HUMANITY--
COVERTLY BANKROLLED BY THE DEFENSE RESEARCH AGENCY.

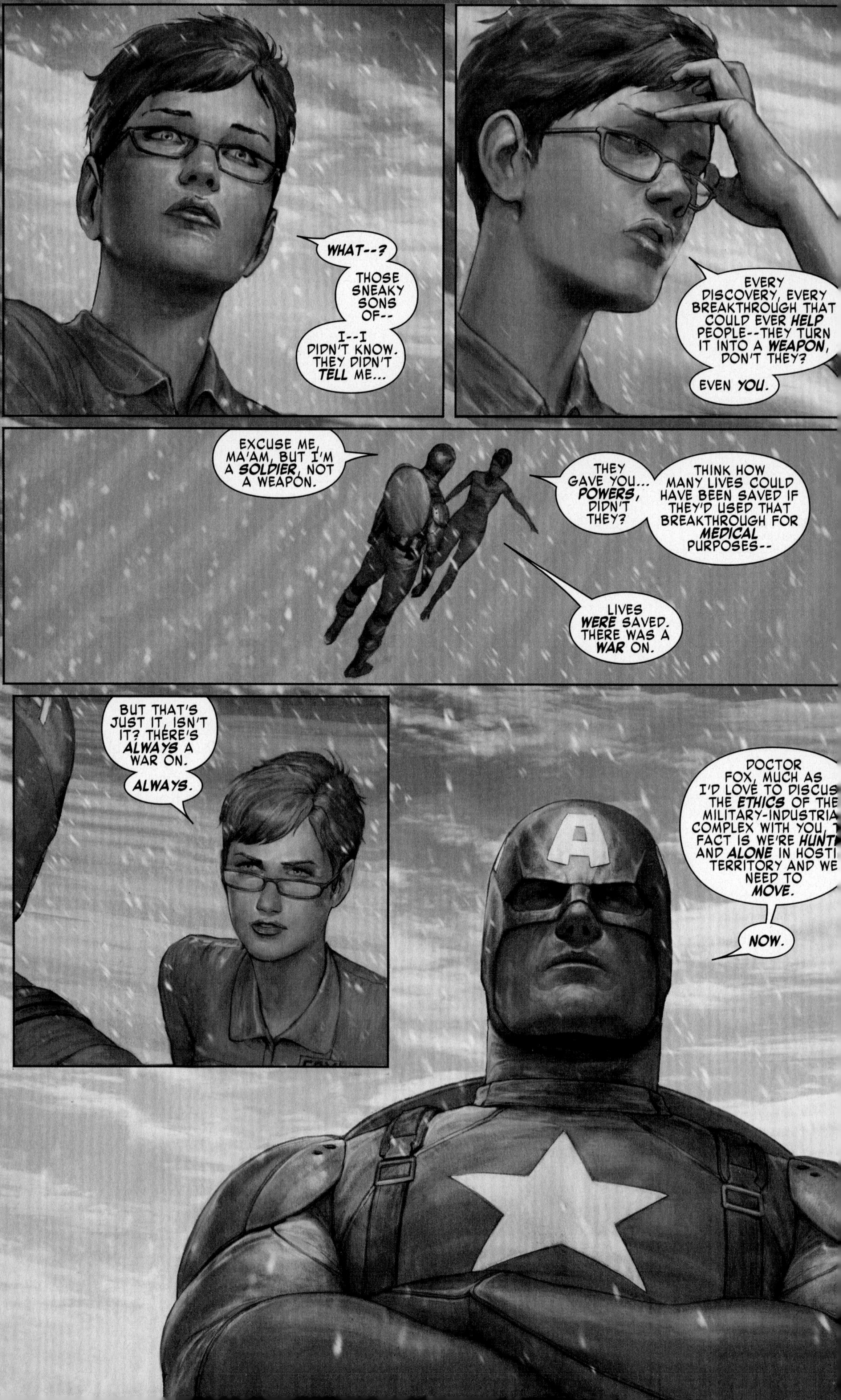
WHAT--?
THOSE SNEAKY SONS OF--
I--I DIDN'T KNOW. THEY DIDN'T TELL ME...
EVERY DISCOVERY, EVERY BREAKTHROUGH THAT COULD EVER HELP PEOPLE--THEY TURN IT INTO A WEAPON, DON'T THEY?
EVEN YOU.
THEY GAVE YOU... POWERS, DIDN'T THEY?
THINK HOW MANY LIVES COULD HAVE BEEN SAVED IF THEY'D USED THAT BREAKTHROUGH FOR MEDICAL PURPOSES--
EXCUSE ME, MA'AM, BUT I'M A SOLDIER, NOT A WEAPON.
LIVES WERE SAVED. THERE WAS A WAR ON.
BUT THAT'S JUST IT, ISN'T IT? THERE'S ALWAYS A WAR ON.
ALWAYS.
DOCTOR FOX, MUCH AS I'D LOVE TO DISCUS THE ETHICS OF THE MILITARY-INDUSTRIA COMPLEX WITH YOU, FACT IS WE'RE HUNT AND ALONE IN HOSTI TERRITORY AND WE NEED TO MOVE.
NOW.

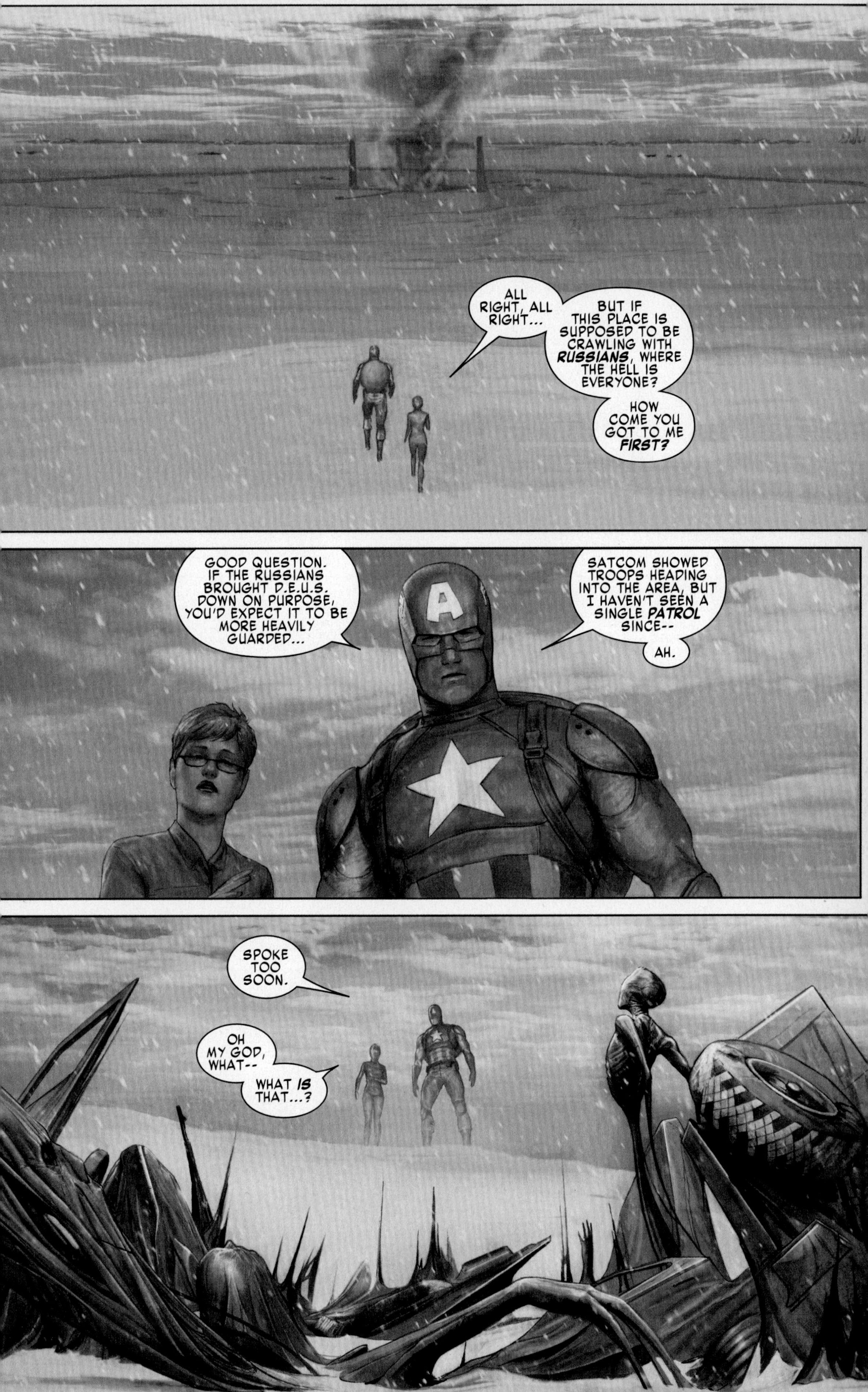
ALL RIGHT, ALL RIGHT...
BUT IF THIS PLACE IS SUPPOSED TO BE CRAWLING WITH RUSSIANS, WHERE THE HELL IS EVERYONE?
HOW COME YOU GOT TO ME FIRST?
GOOD QUESTION. IF THE RUSSIANS BROUGHT D.E.U.S. DOWN ON PURPOSE, YOU'D EXPECT IT TO BE MORE HEAVILY GUARDED...
SATCOM SHOWED TROOPS HEADING INTO THE AREA, BUT I HAVEN'T SEEN A SINGLE PATROL SINCE--
AH.
SPOKE TOO SOON.
OH MY GOD, WHAT--
WHAT IS THAT...?

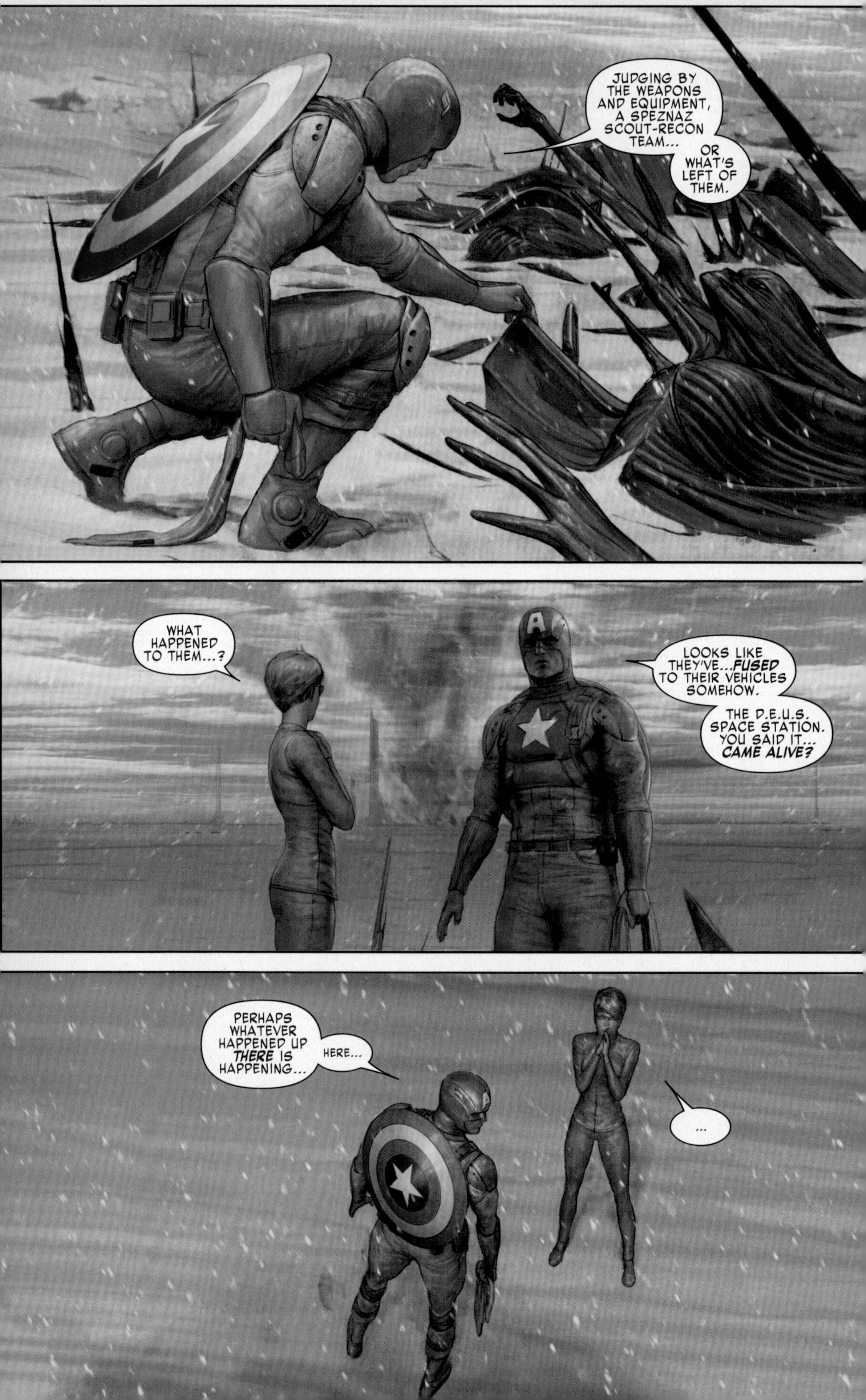
JUDGING BY THE WEAPONS AND EQUIPMENT, A SPEZNAZ SCOUT-RECON TEAM...
OR WHAT'S LEFT OF THEM.
WHAT HAPPENED TO THEM...?
LOOKS LIKE THEY'VE...FUSED TO THEIR VEHICLES SOMEHOW.
THE D.E.U.S. SPACE STATION. YOU SAID IT... CAME ALIVE?
PERHAPS WHATEVER HAPPENED UP THERE IS HAPPENING...
HERE...
...

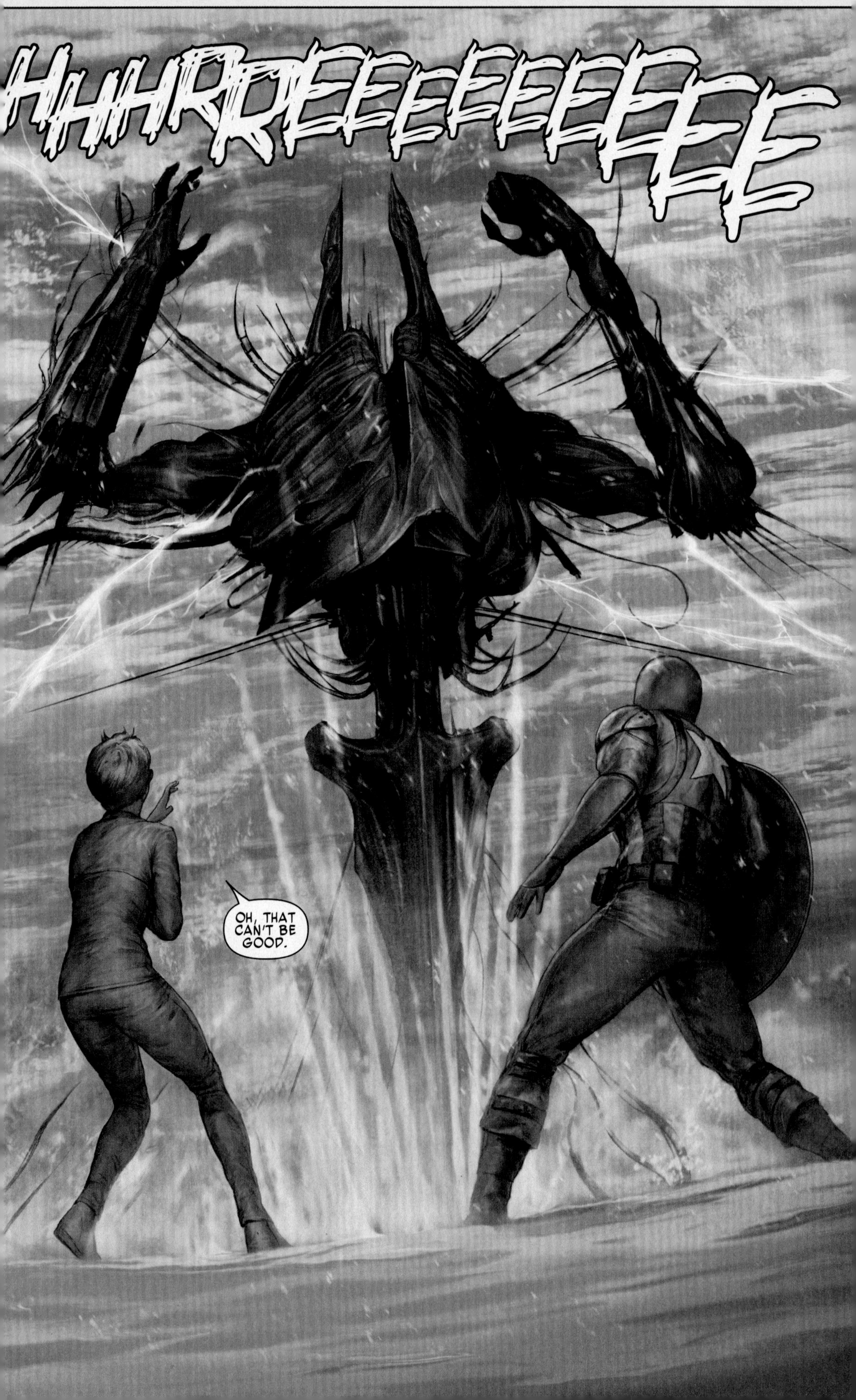
HHHRREEEEEEEEEEEEE
OH, THAT CAN'T BE GOOD.

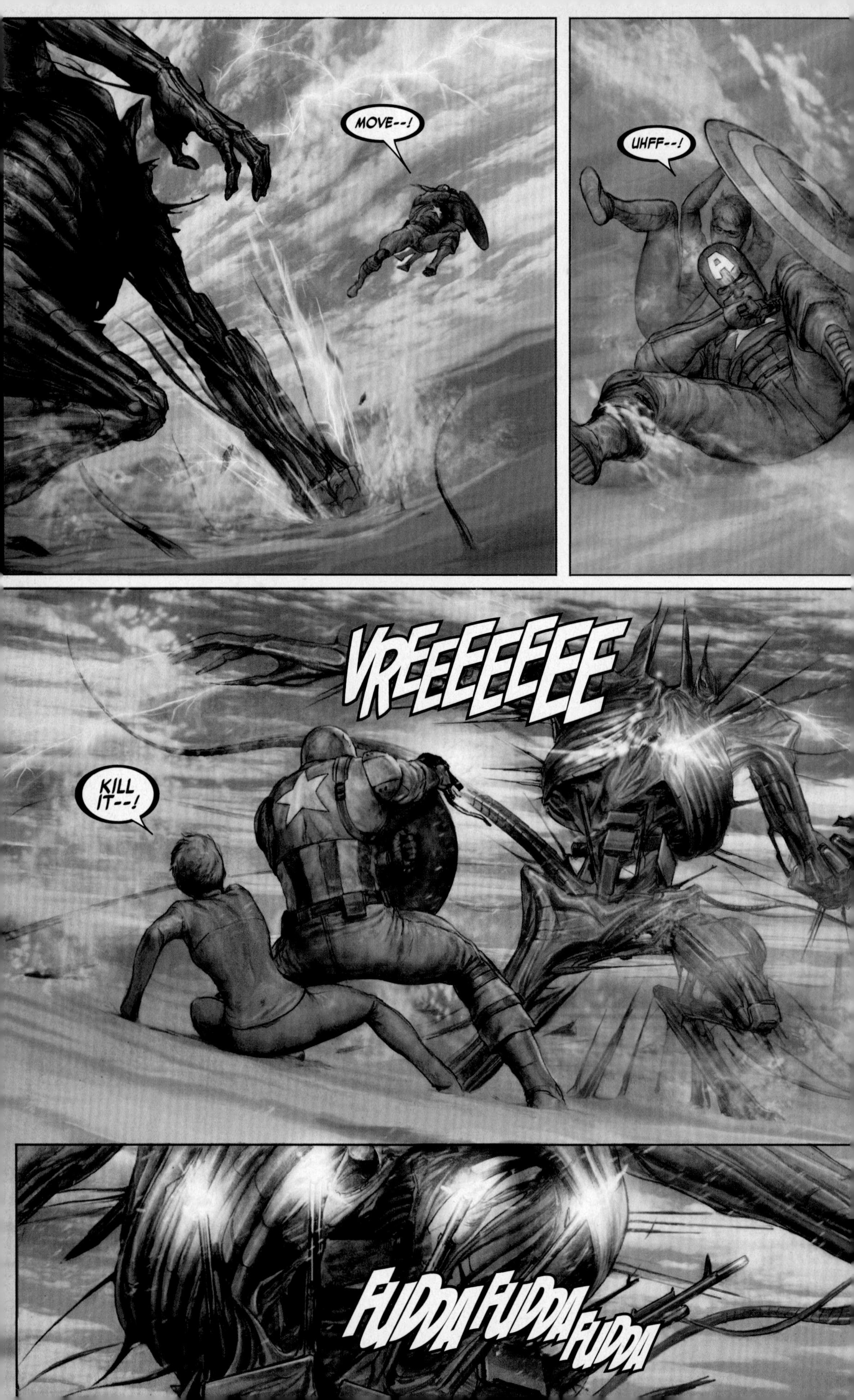
MOVE--!
UHFF--!
VREEEEEEE
KILL IT--!
FUDDA FUDDA FUDDA

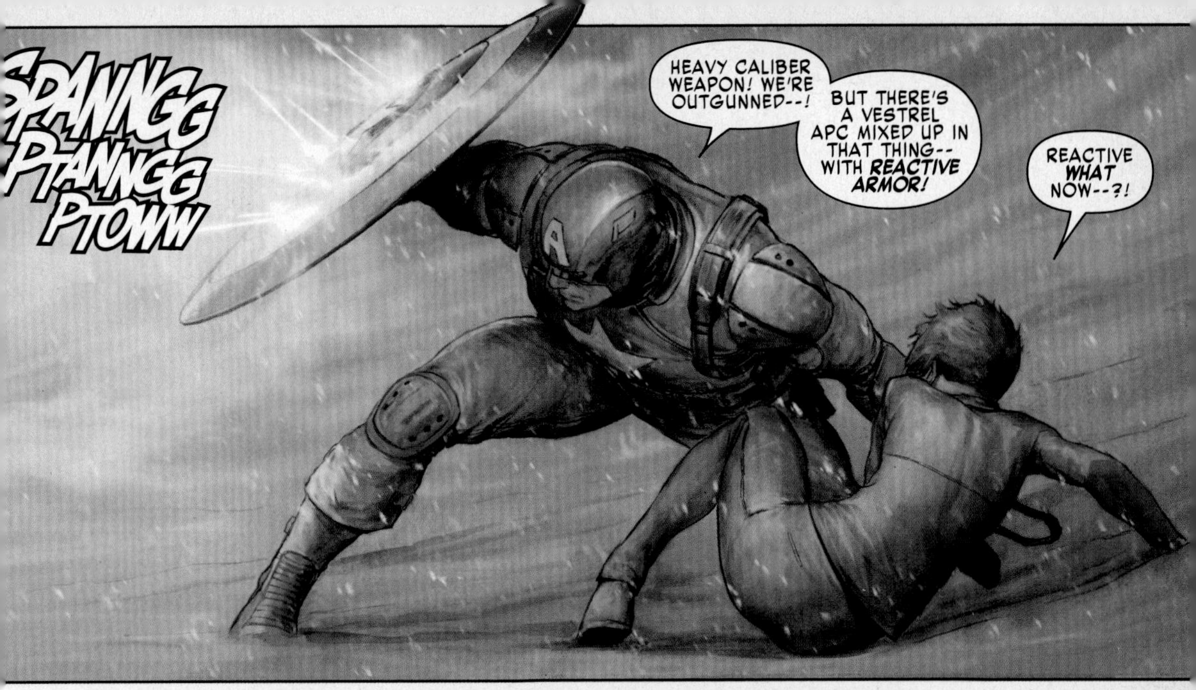
SPANNGG
PTANNGG
PTOWW
HEAVY CALIBER WEAPON! WE'RE OUTGUNNED--!
BUT THERE'S A VESTREL APC MIXED UP IN THAT THING-- WITH REACTIVE ARMOR!
REACTIVE WHAT NOW--?!

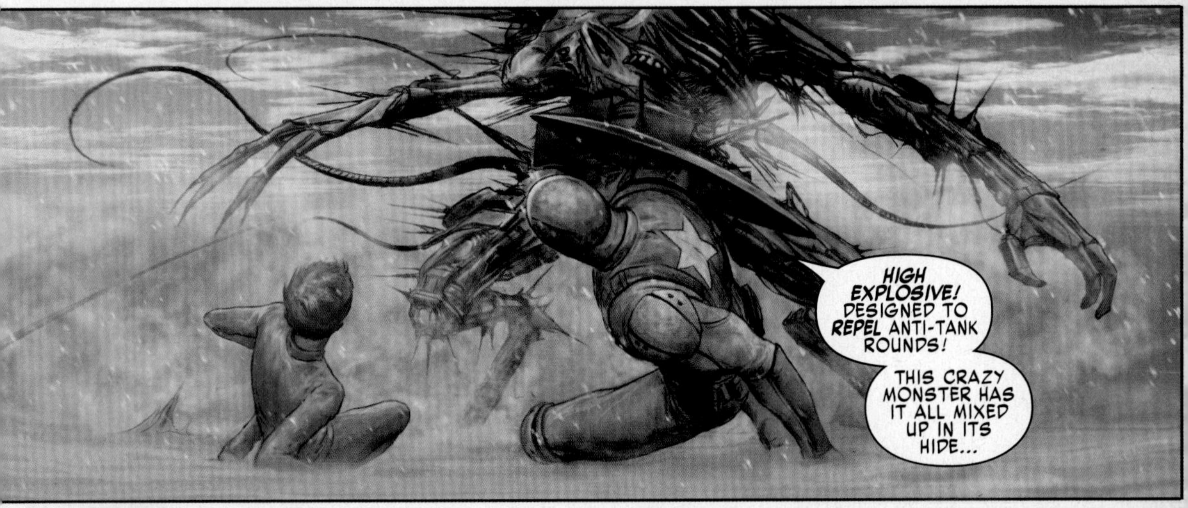
HIGH EXPLOSIVE! DESIGNED TO REPEL ANTI-TANK ROUNDS!
THIS CRAZY MONSTER HAS IT ALL MIXED UP IN ITS HIDE...

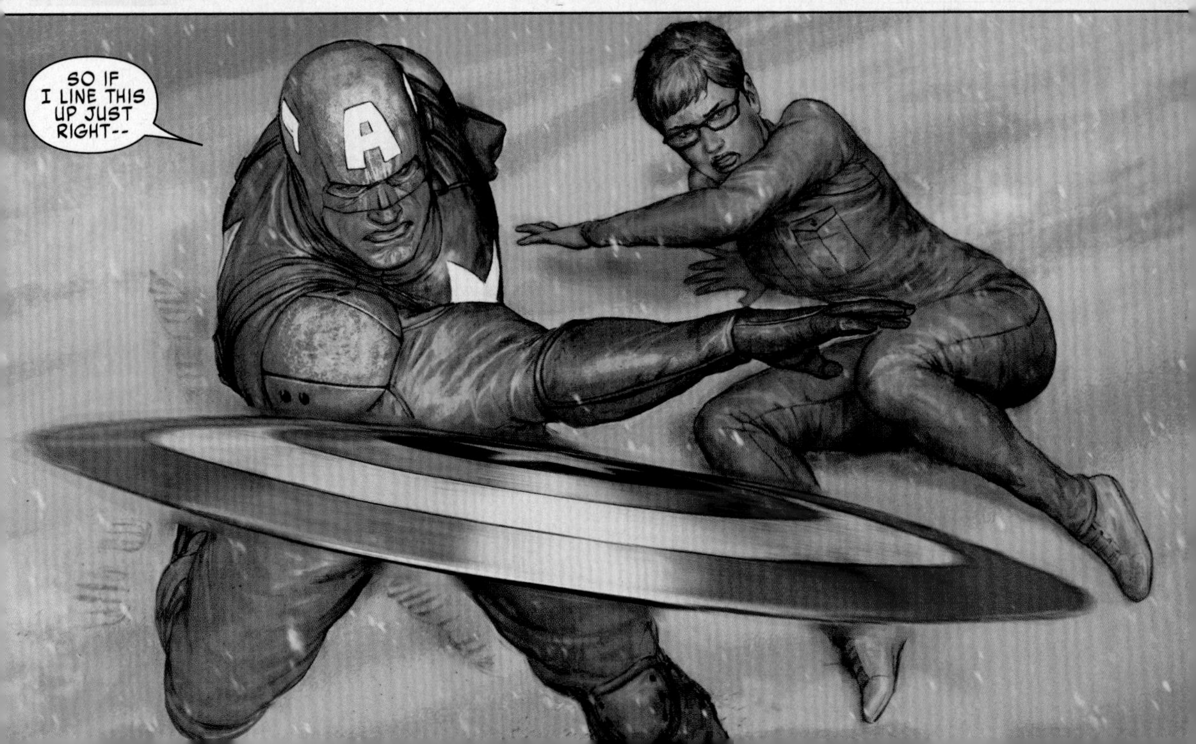
SO IF I LINE THIS UP JUST RIGHT--

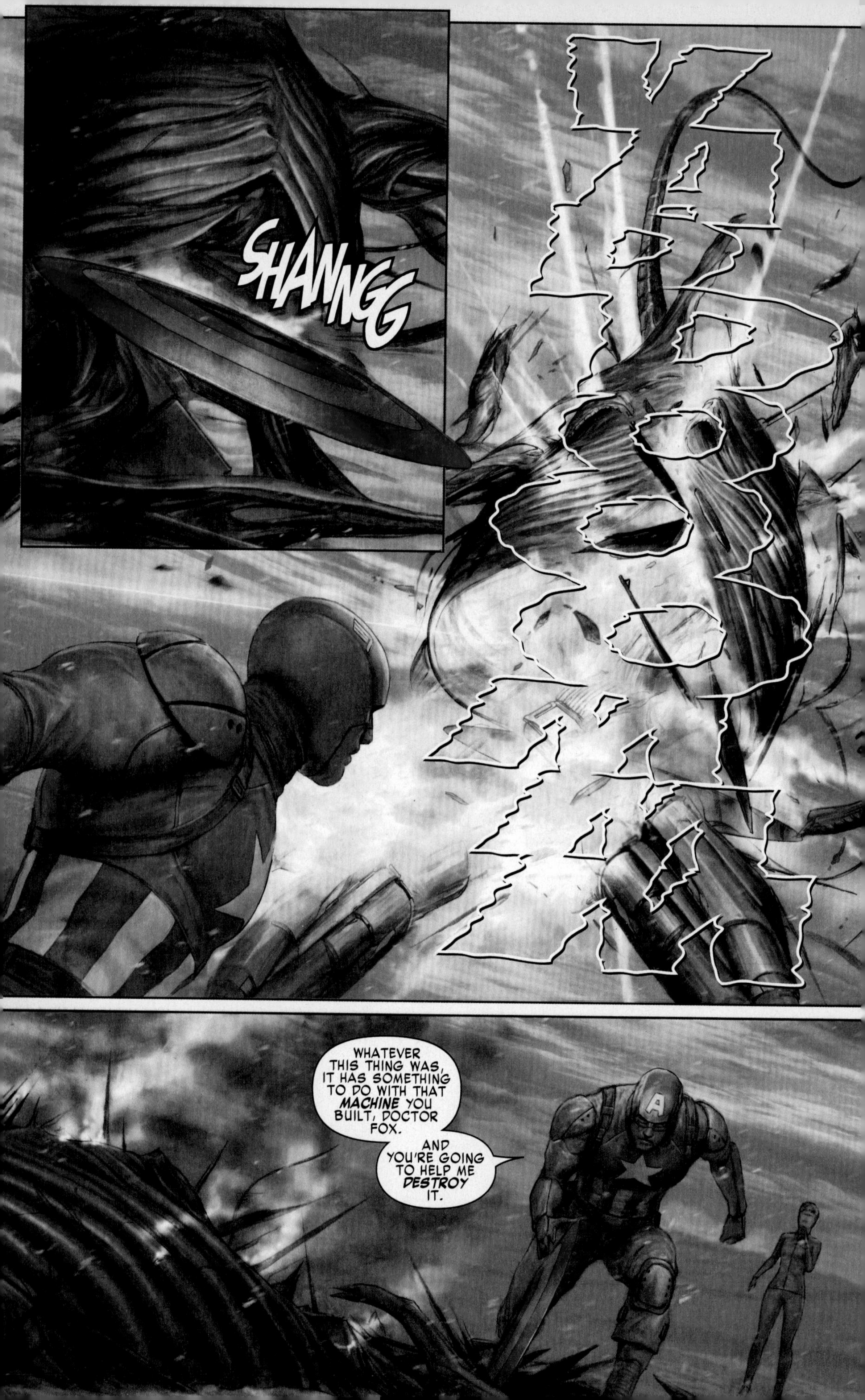
SHANNGG
WHATEVER THIS THING WAS, IT HAS SOMETHING TO DO WITH THAT MACHINE YOU BUILT, DOCTOR FOX.
AND YOU'RE GOING TO HELP ME DESTROY IT.

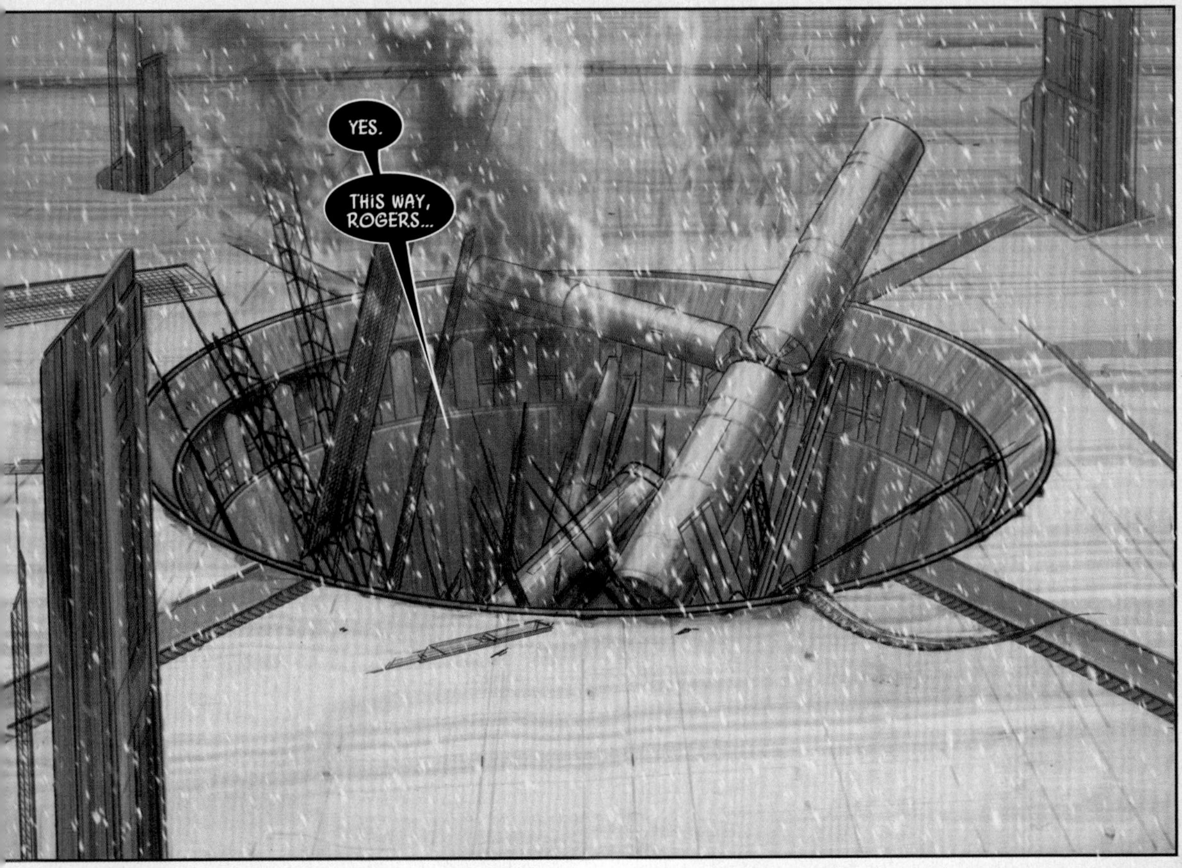
YES.
THIS WAY, ROGERS...

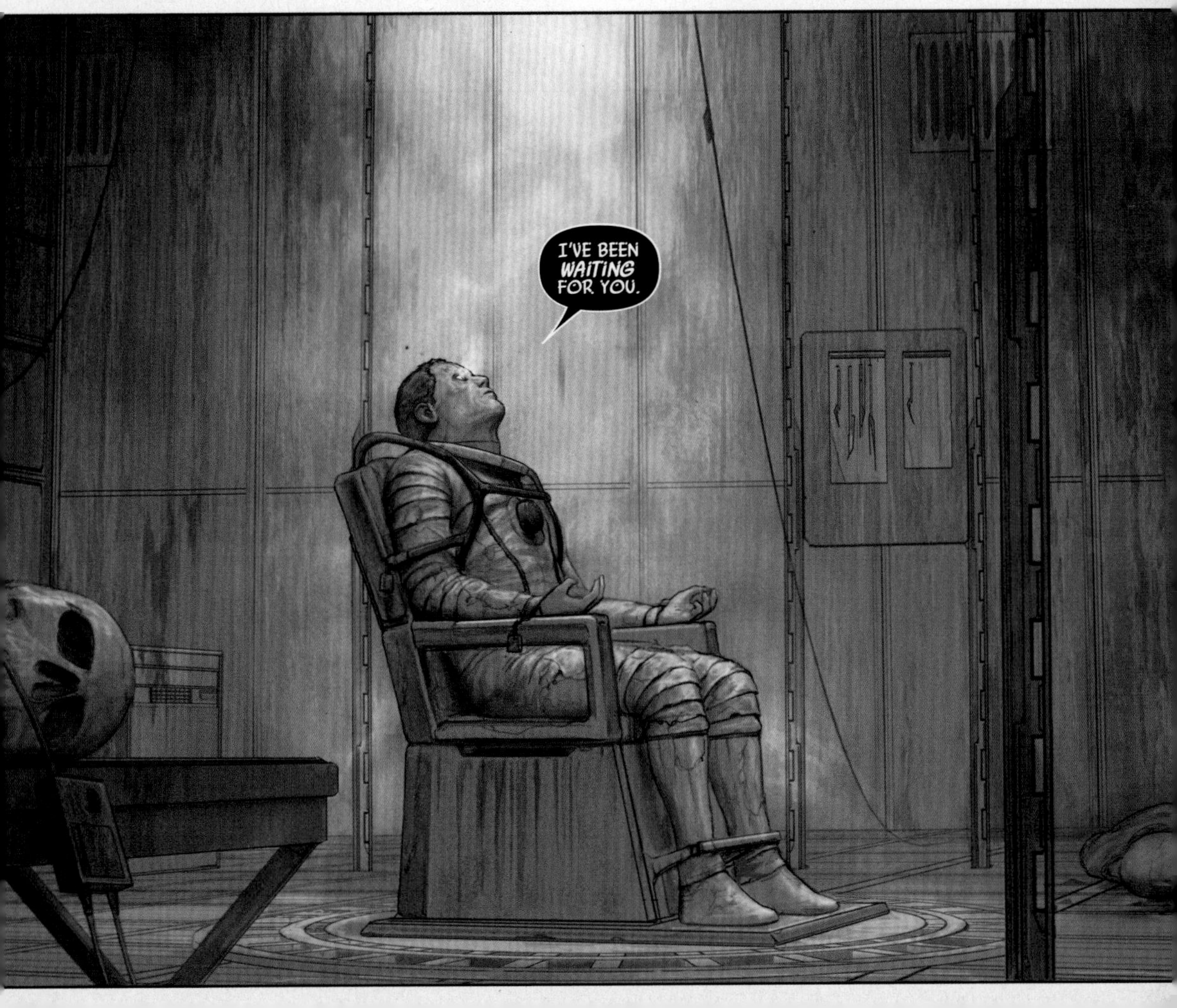
I'VE BEEN WAITING FOR YOU.

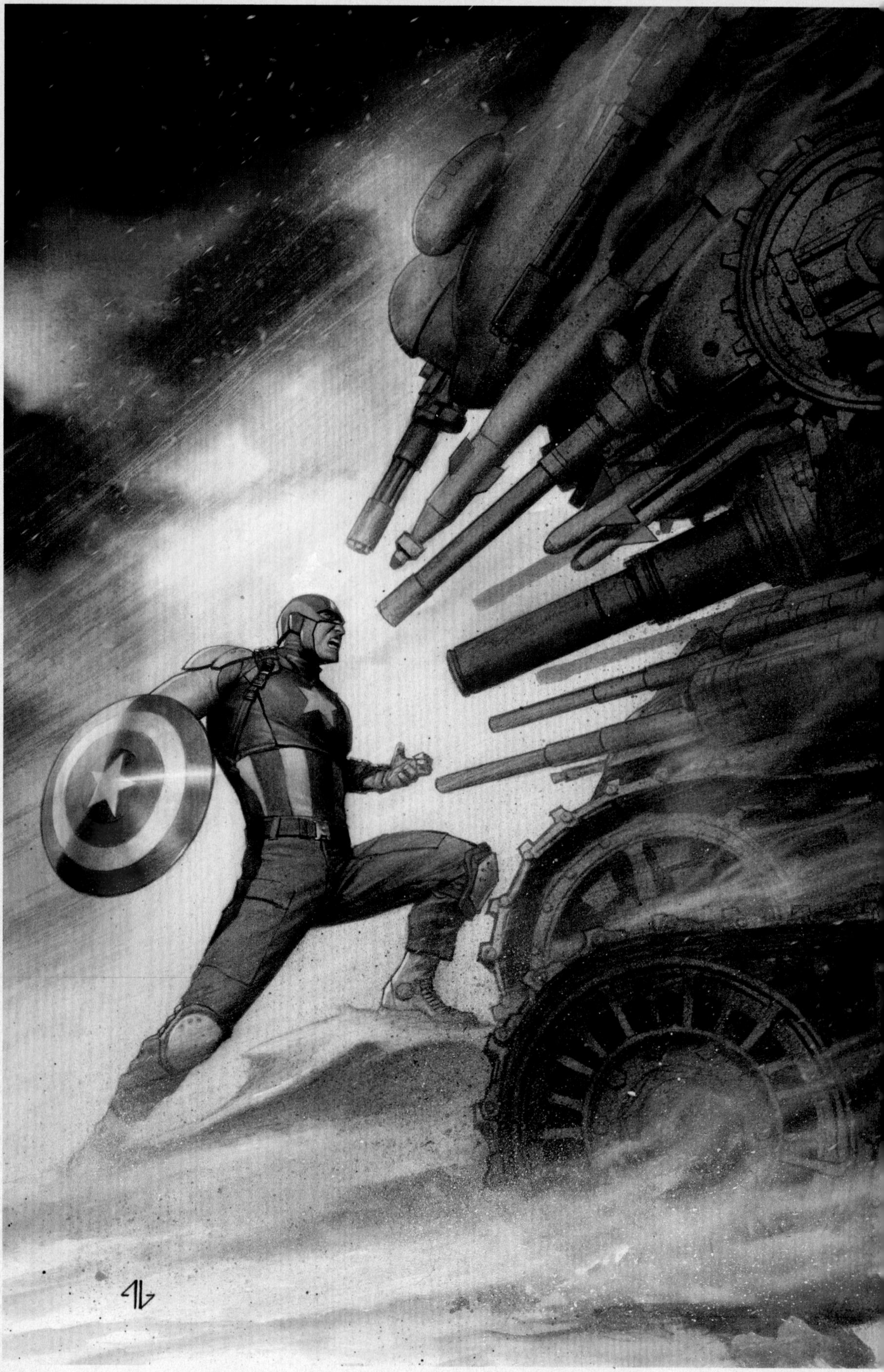

★ CHAPTER THREE ★

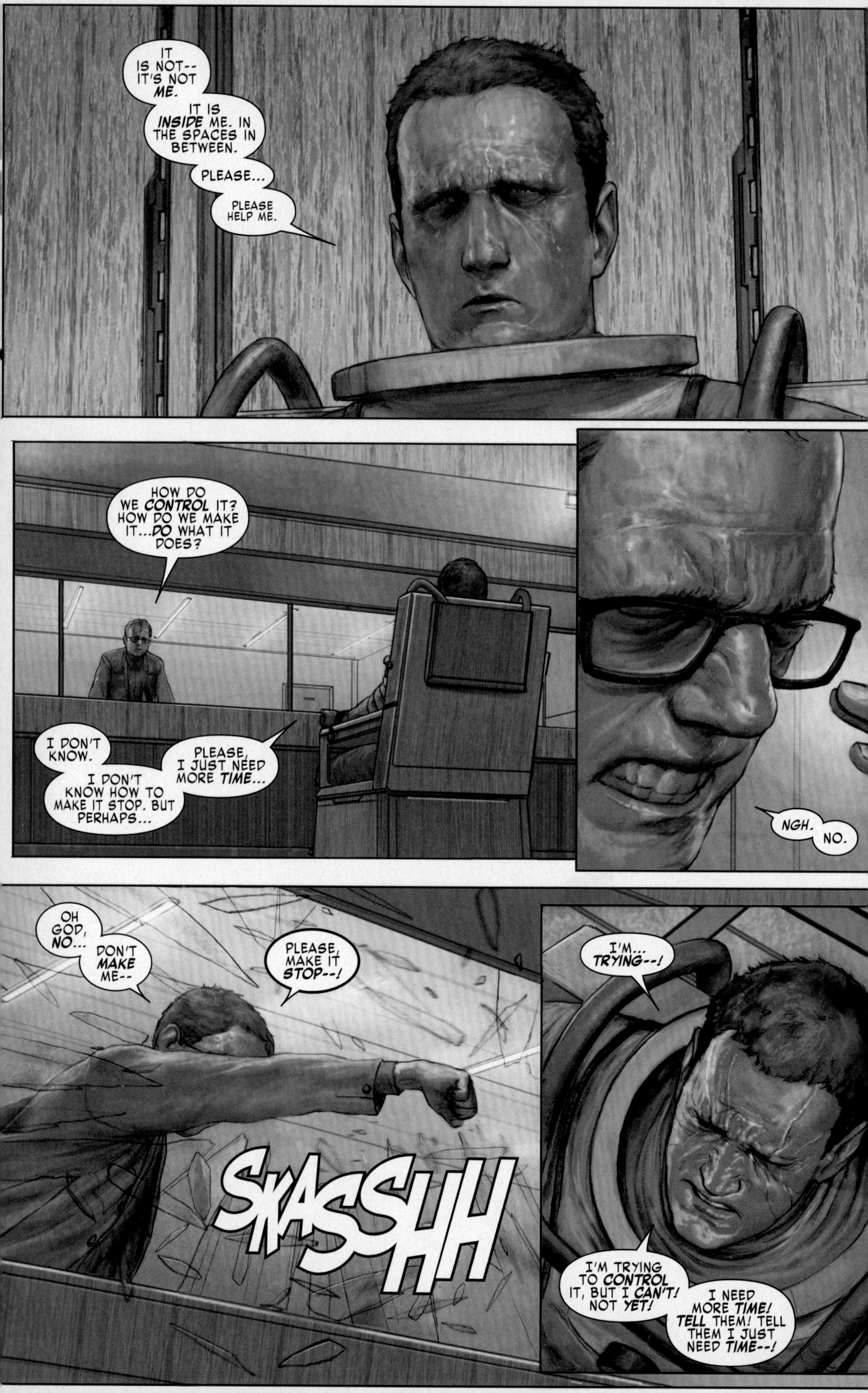
IT IS NOT-- IT'S NOT ME.
IT IS INSIDE ME. IN THE SPACES IN BETWEEN.
PLEASE...
PLEASE HELP ME.
HOW DO WE CONTROL IT? HOW DO WE MAKE IT...DO WHAT IT DOES?
I DON'T KNOW.
I DON'T KNOW HOW TO MAKE IT STOP. BUT PERHAPS...
PLEASE, I JUST NEED MORE TIME...
NGH.
NO.
OH GOD, NO...
DON'T MAKE ME--
PLEASE, MAKE IT STOP--!
SKASSHH
I'M... TRYING--!
I'M TRYING TO CONTROL IT, BUT I CAN'T! NOT YET!
I NEED MORE TIME! TELL THEM! TELL THEM I JUST NEED TIME--!

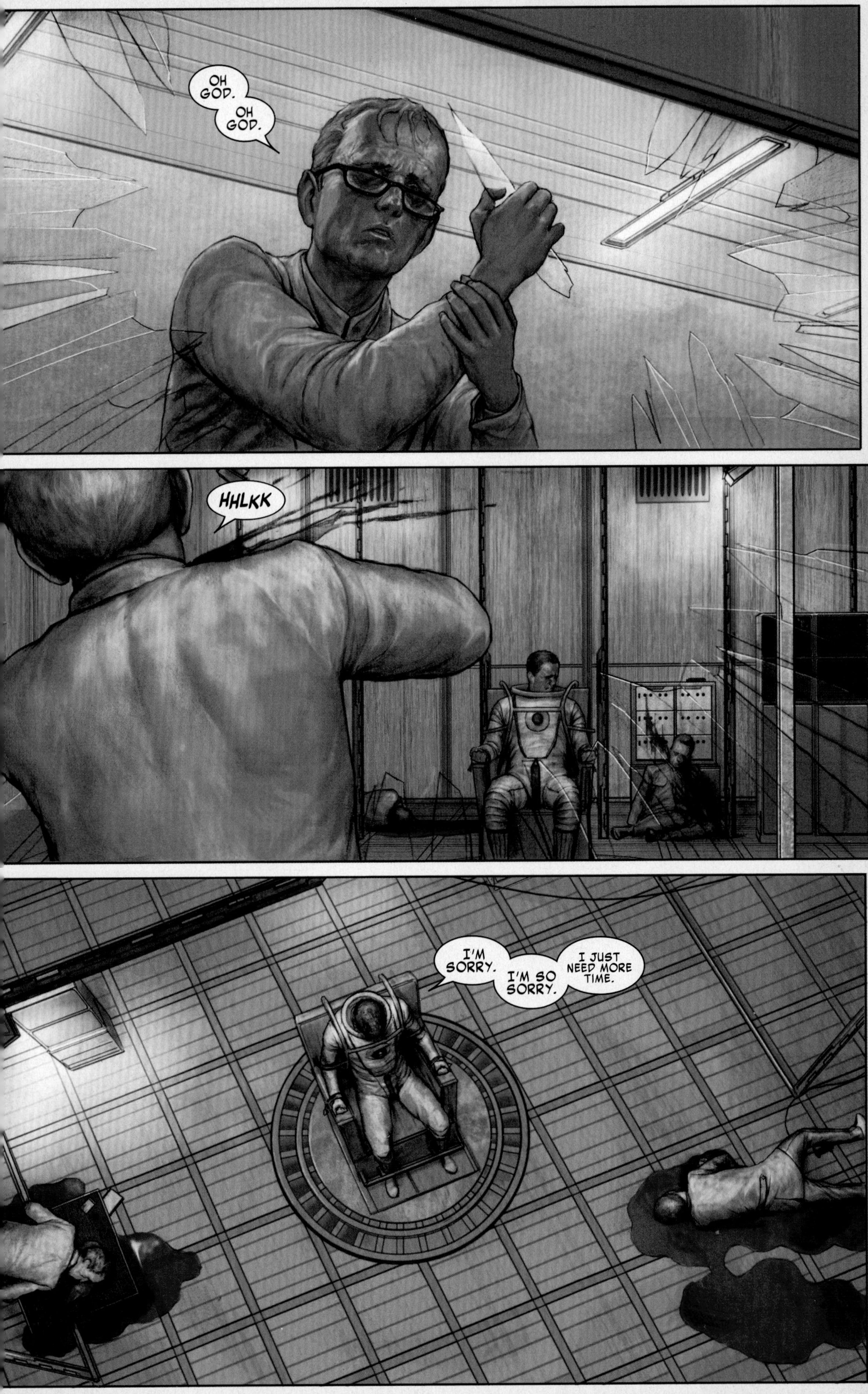
OH GOD.
OH GOD.
HHLKK
I'M SORRY.
I'M SO SORRY.
I JUST NEED MORE TIME.

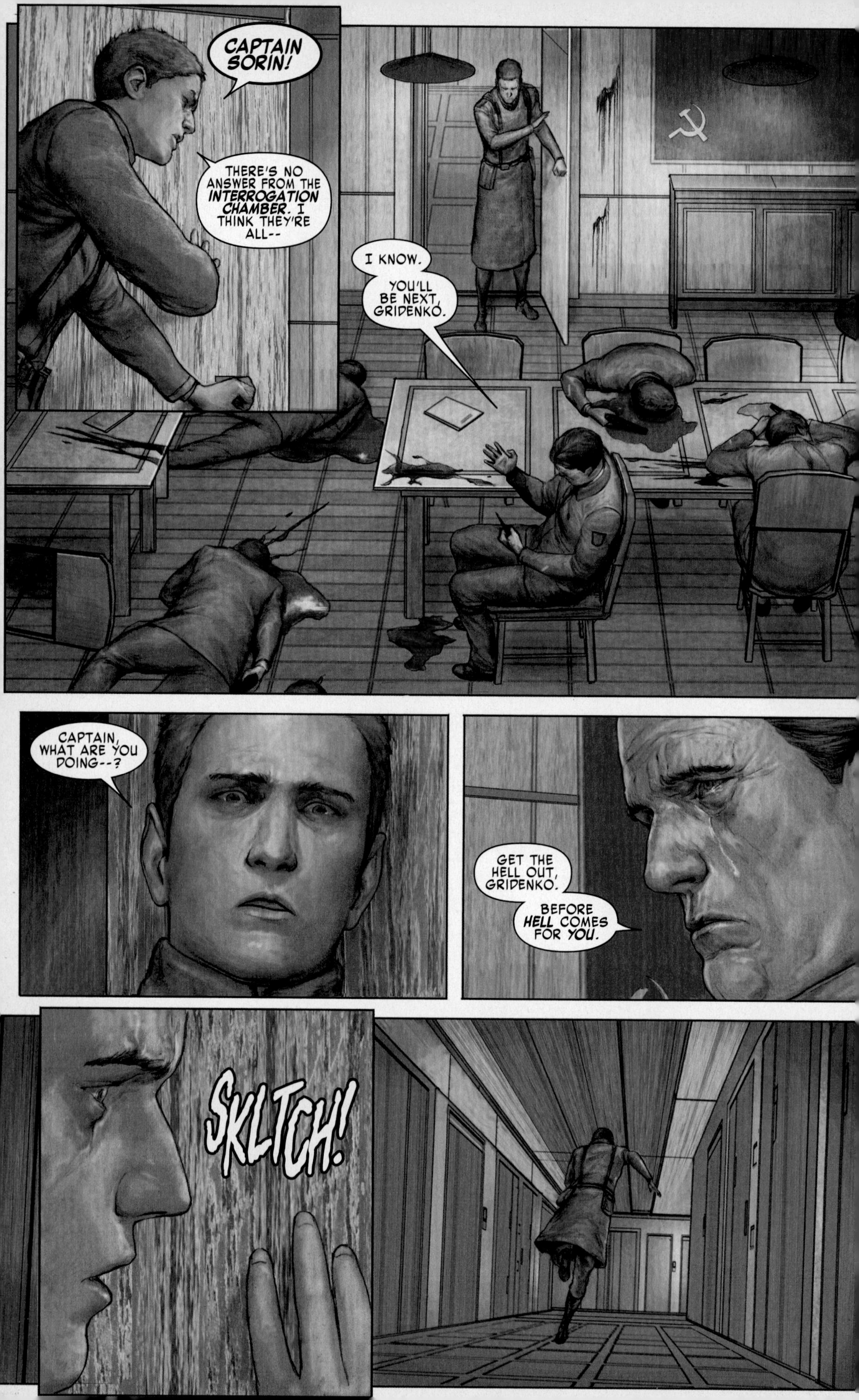
CAPTAIN SORIN!
THERE'S NO ANSWER FROM THE INTERROGATION CHAMBER. I THINK THEY'RE ALL--
I KNOW.
YOU'LL BE NEXT, GRIDENKO.
CAPTAIN, WHAT ARE YOU DOING--?
GET THE HELL OUT, GRIDENKO.
BEFORE HELL COMES FOR YOU.
SKLTCH!

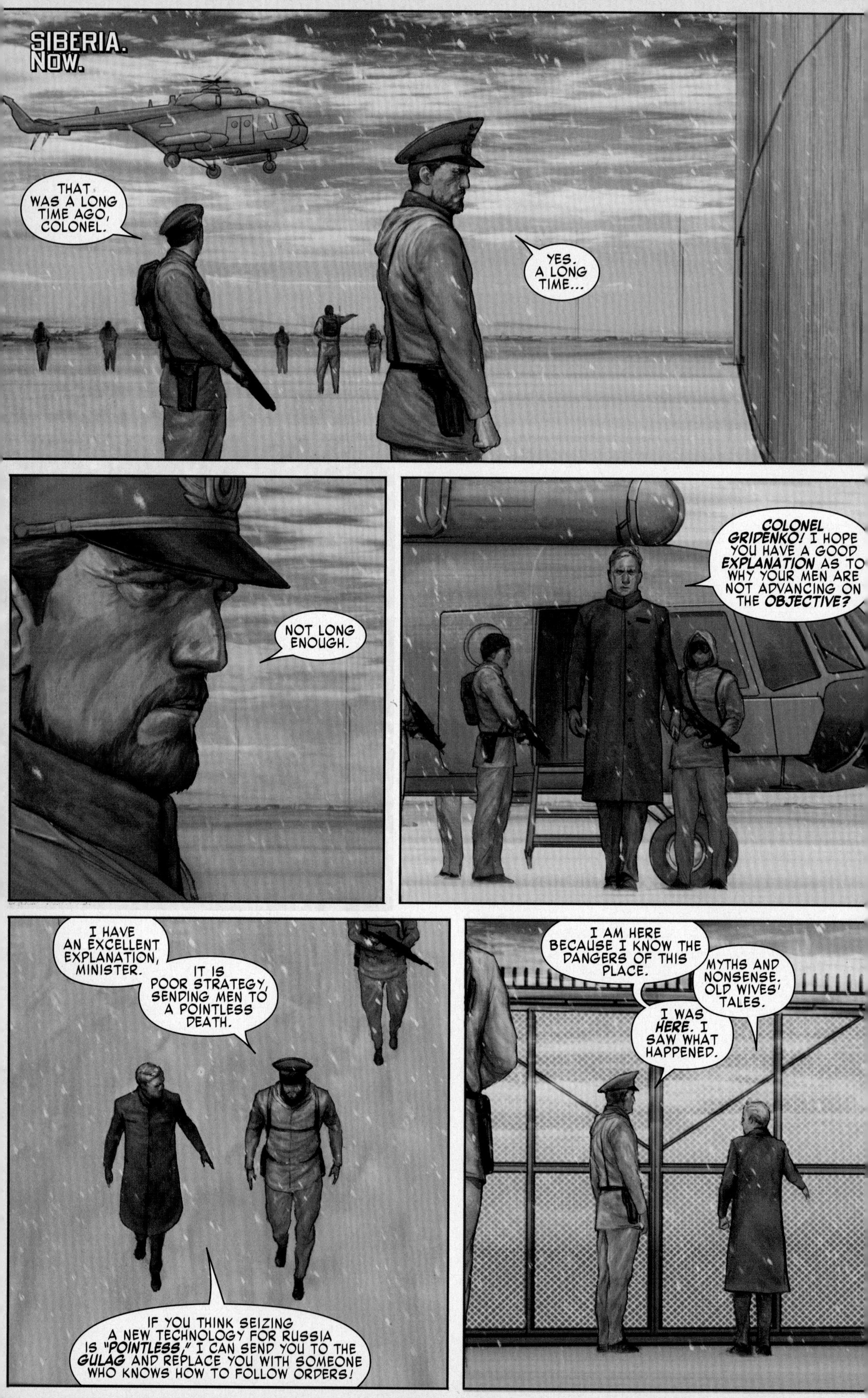
SIBERIA.
NOW.
THAT WAS A LONG TIME AGO, COLONEL.
YES. A LONG TIME...
NOT LONG ENOUGH.
COLONEL GRIDENKO! I HOPE YOU HAVE A GOOD EXPLANATION AS TO WHY YOUR MEN ARE NOT ADVANCING ON THE OBJECTIVE?
I HAVE AN EXCELLENT EXPLANATION, MINISTER.
IT IS POOR STRATEGY, SENDING MEN TO A POINTLESS DEATH.
IF YOU THINK SEIZING A NEW TECHNOLOGY FOR RUSSIA IS "POINTLESS," I CAN SEND YOU TO THE GULAG AND REPLACE YOU WITH SOMEONE WHO KNOWS HOW TO FOLLOW ORDERS!
I AM HERE BECAUSE I KNOW THE DANGERS OF THIS PLACE.
MYTHS AND NONSENSE. OLD WIVES' TALES.
I WAS HERE. I SAW WHAT HAPPENED.

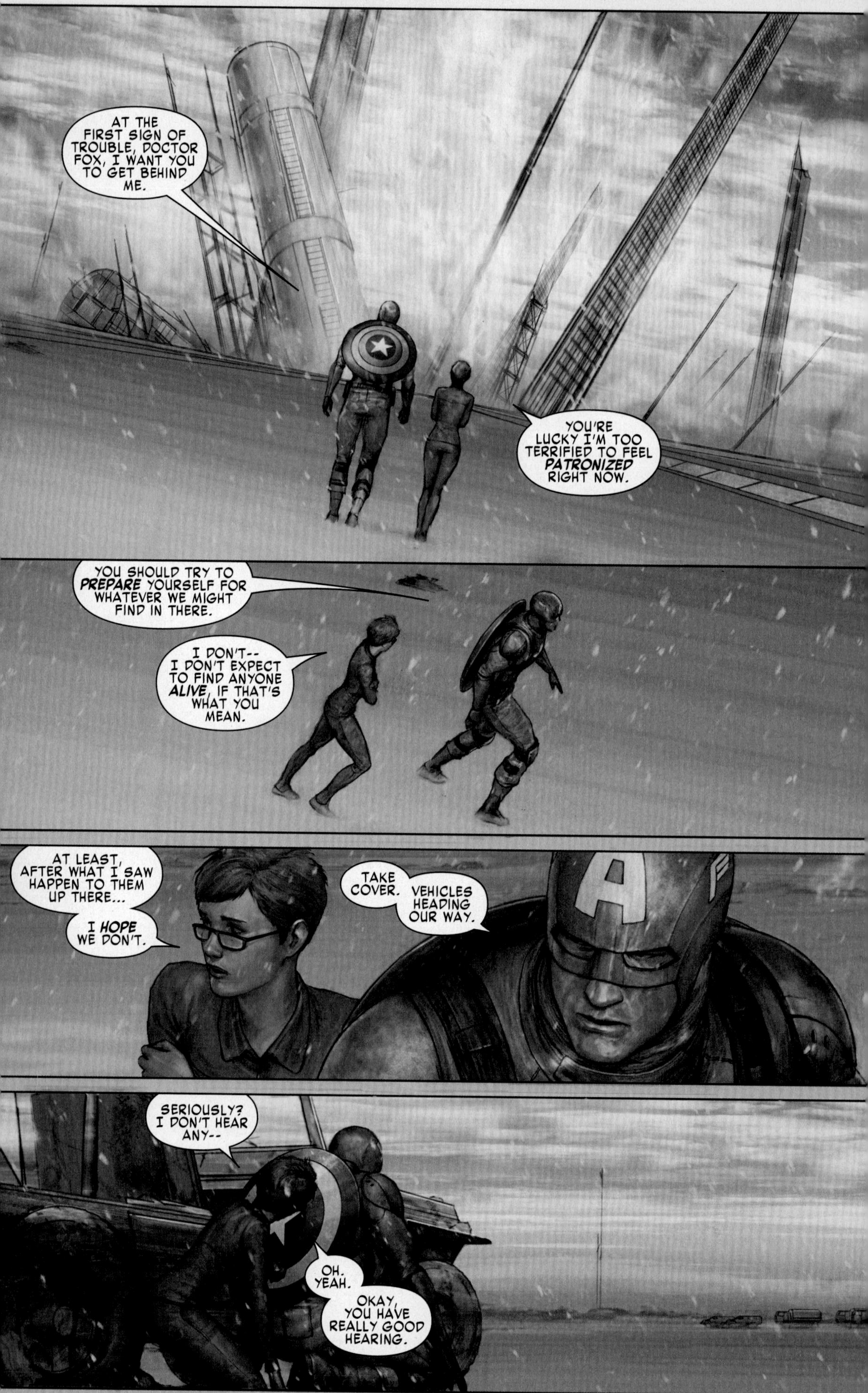
AT THE FIRST SIGN OF TROUBLE, DOCTOR FOX, I WANT YOU TO GET BEHIND ME.
YOU'RE LUCKY I'M TOO TERRIFIED TO FEEL *PATRONIZED* RIGHT NOW.
YOU SHOULD TRY TO *PREPARE* YOURSELF FOR WHATEVER WE MIGHT FIND IN THERE.
I DON'T-- I DON'T EXPECT TO FIND ANYONE *ALIVE*, IF THAT'S WHAT YOU MEAN.
AT LEAST, AFTER WHAT I SAW HAPPEN TO THEM UP THERE...
I *HOPE* WE DON'T.
TAKE COVER.
VEHICLES HEADING OUR WAY.
SERIOUSLY? I DON'T HEAR ANY--
OH. YEAH.
OKAY, YOU HAVE REALLY GOOD HEARING.

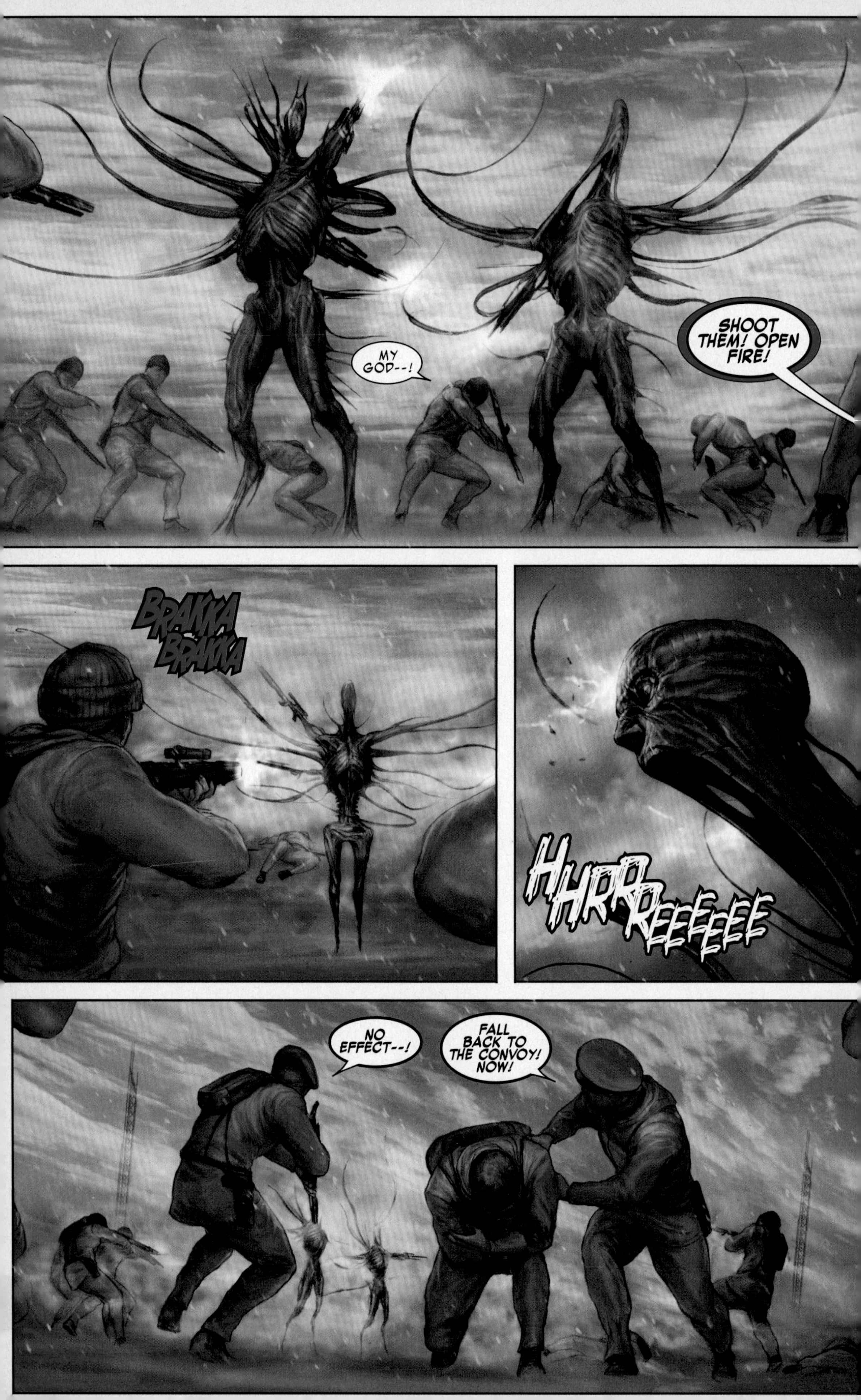
MY GOD--!
SHOOT THEM! OPEN FIRE!
BRAKKA BRAKKA
HHRRREEEEEEE
NO EFFECT--!
FALL BACK TO THE CONVOY! NOW!

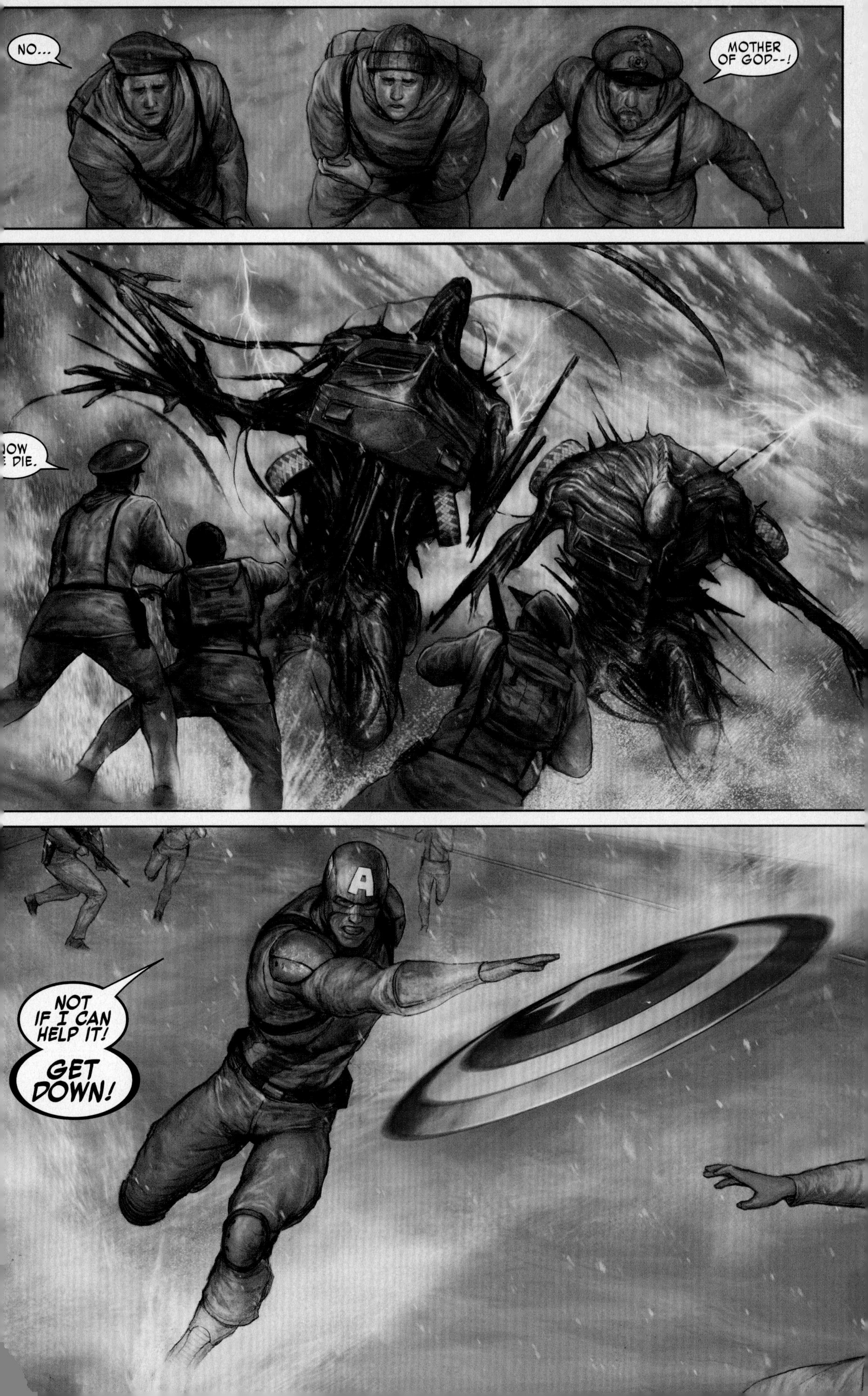
NO...
MOTHER OF GOD--!
NOW E DIE.
NOT IF I CAN HELP IT!
GET DOWN!

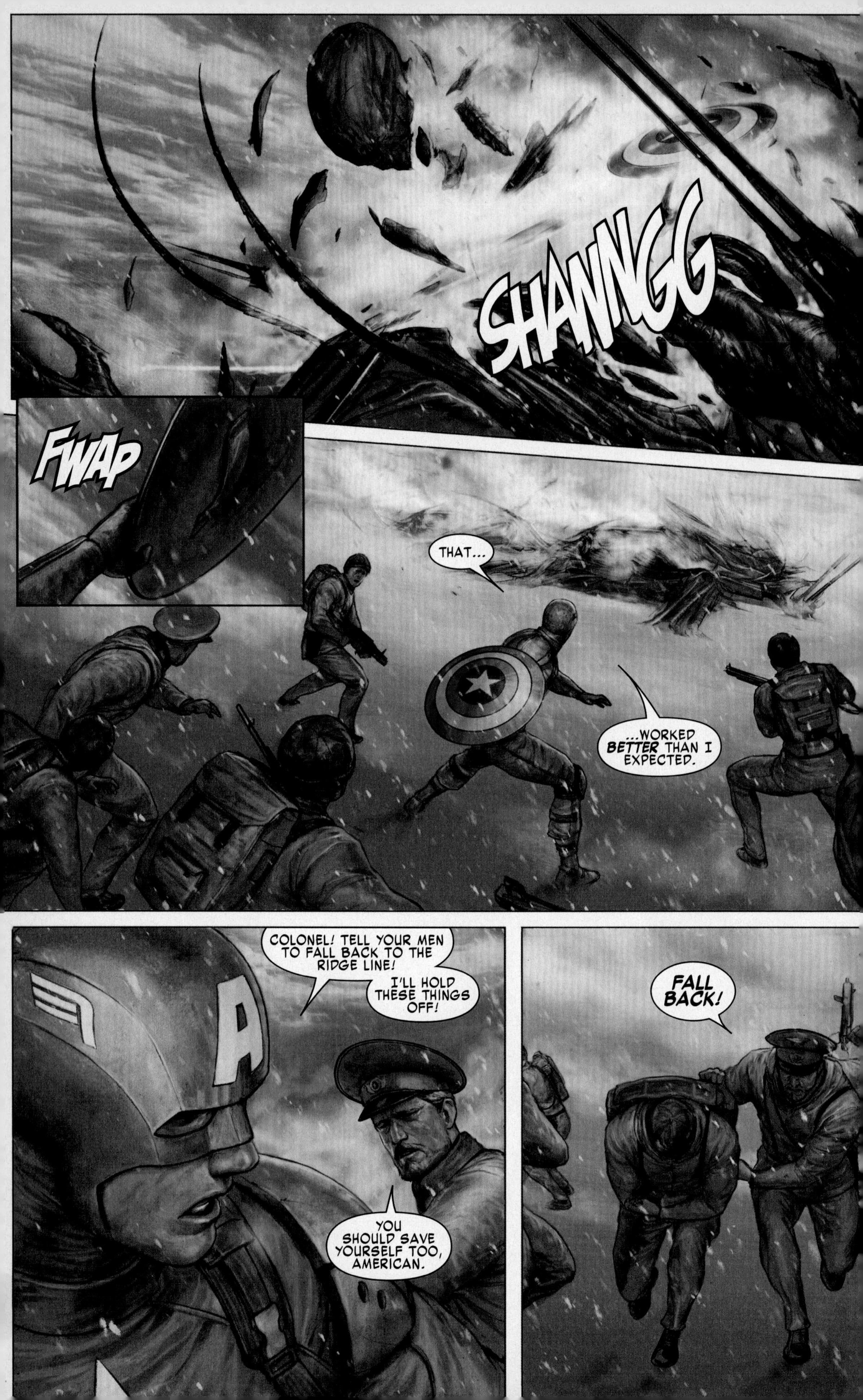
SHANNGG
FWAP
THAT...
...WORKED BETTER THAN I EXPECTED.
COLONEL! TELL YOUR MEN TO FALL BACK TO THE RIDGE LINE!
I'LL HOLD THESE THINGS OFF!
YOU SHOULD SAVE YOURSELF TOO, AMERICAN.
FALL BACK!

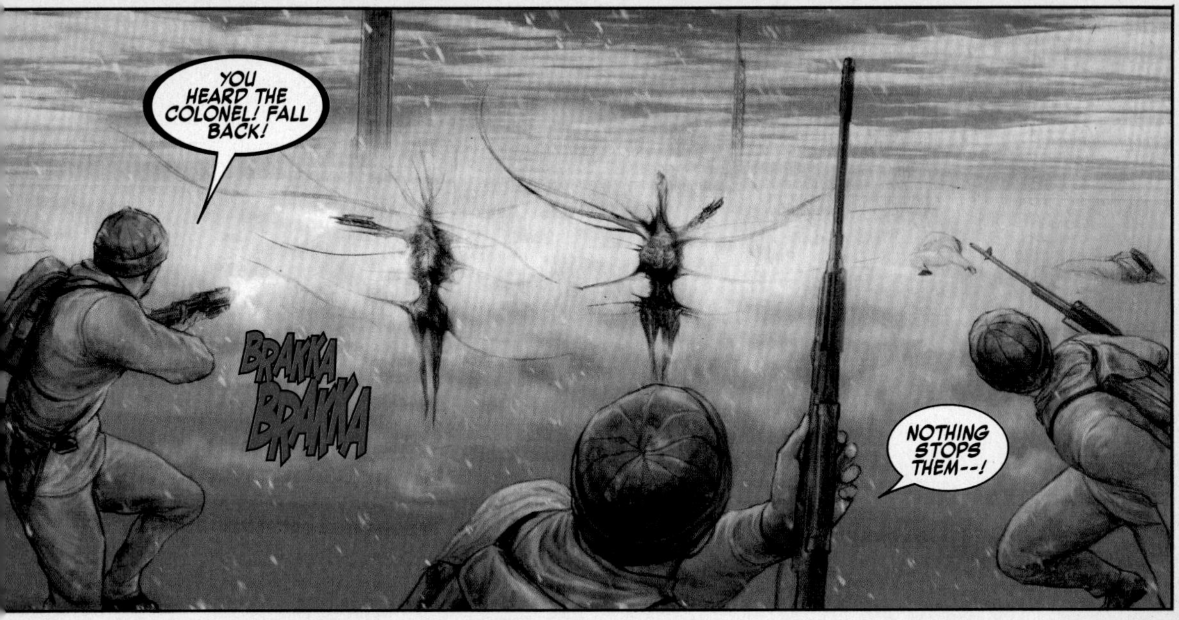
YOU HEARD THE COLONEL! FALL BACK!
BRAKKA BRAKKA
NOTHING STOPS THEM--!

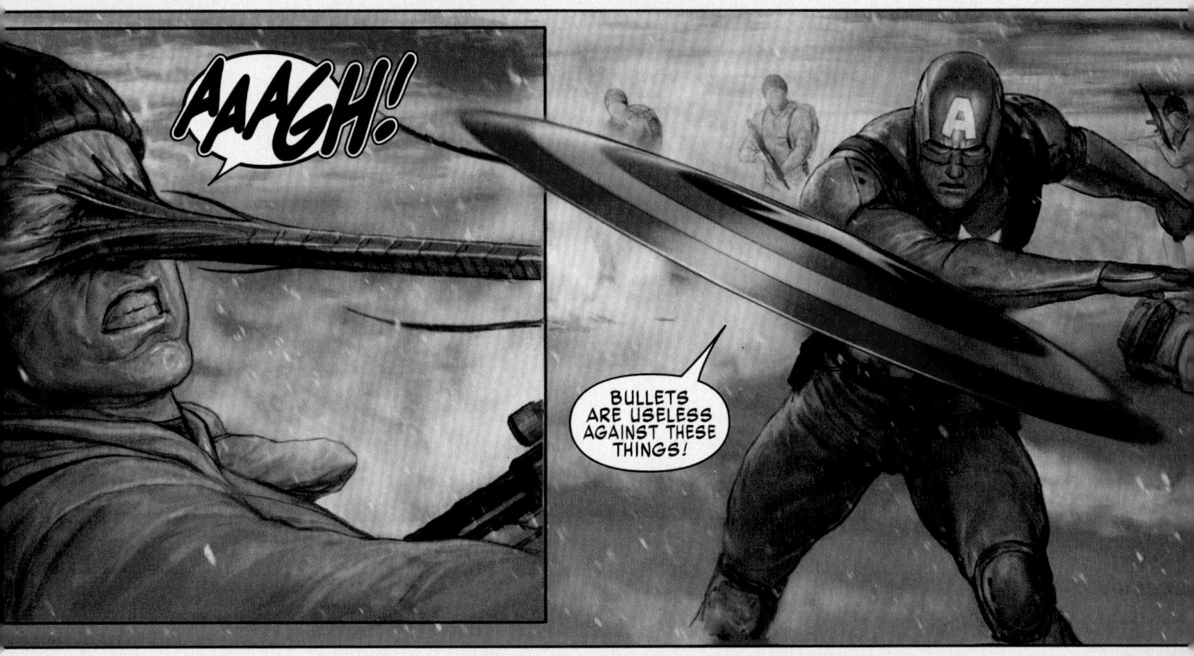
AAAGH!
BULLETS ARE USELESS AGAINST THESE THINGS!

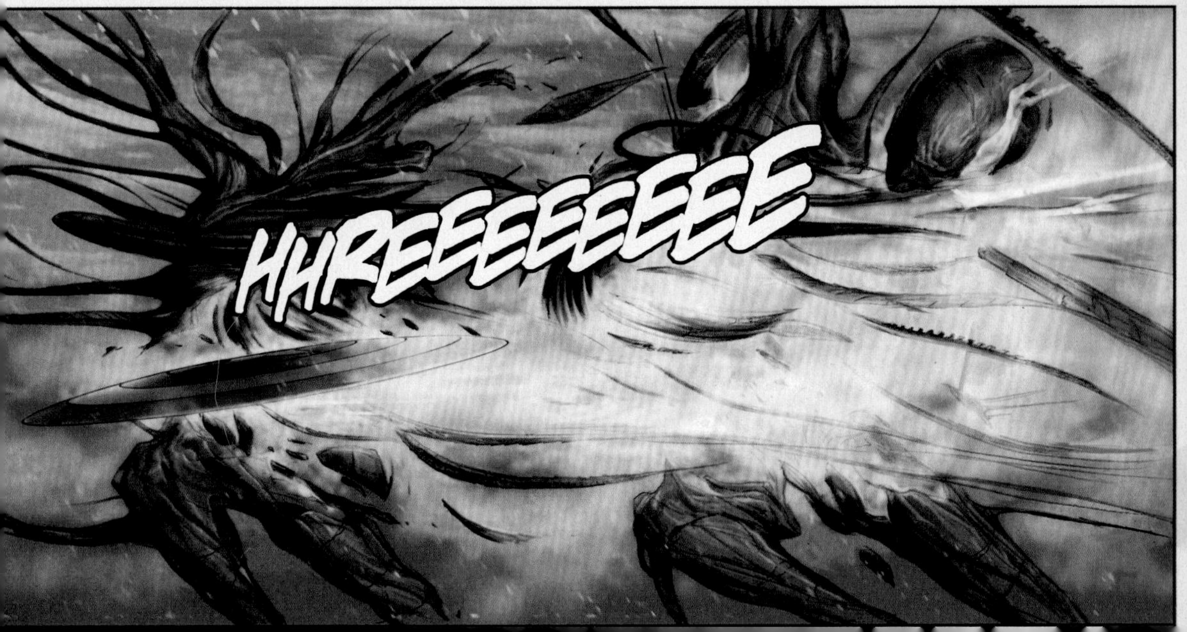
HHREEEEEEEEEE

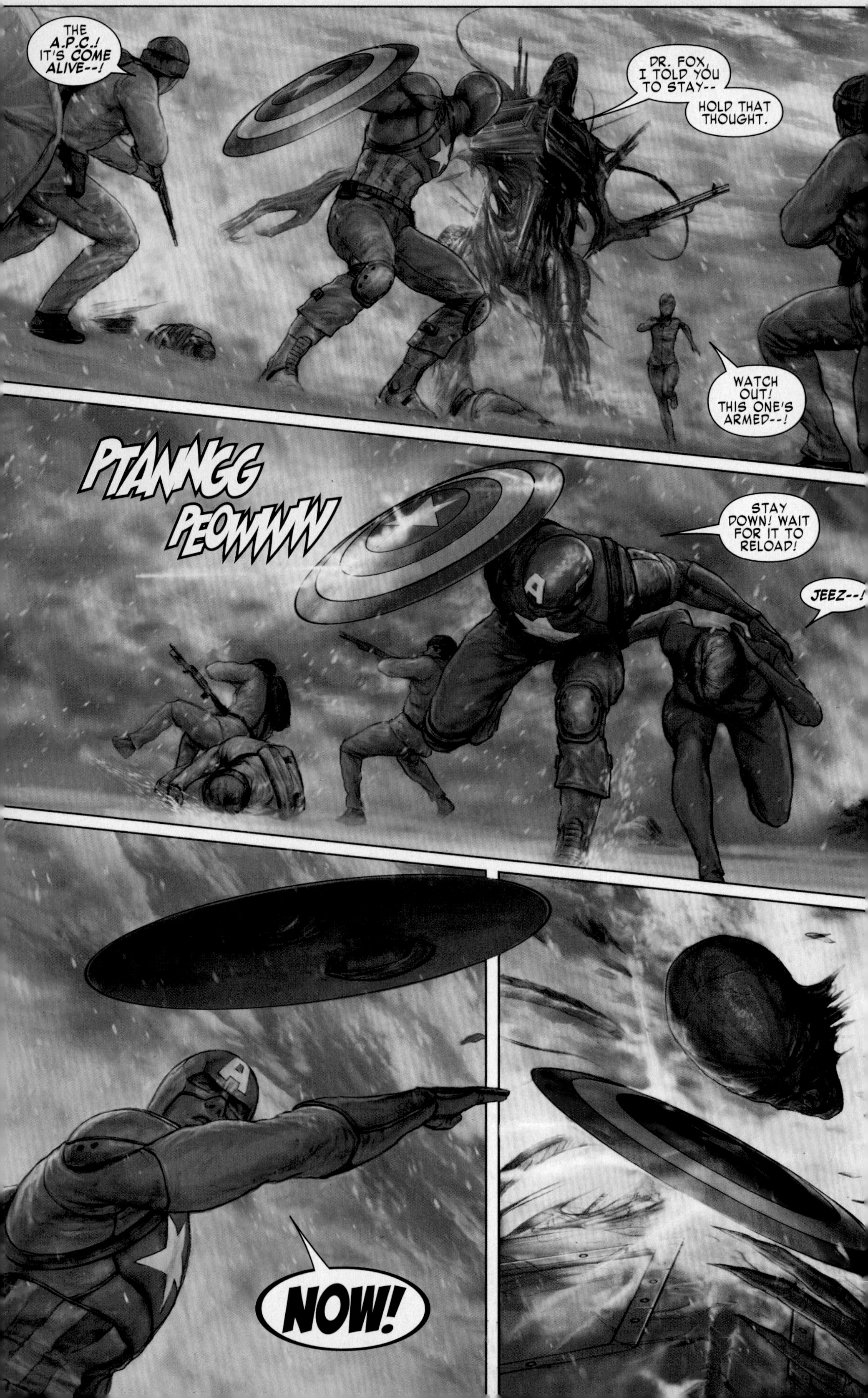

THE A.P.C.! IT'S COME ALIVE--!
DR. FOX, I TOLD YOU TO STAY--
HOLD THAT THOUGHT.
WATCH OUT! THIS ONE'S ARMED--!
PTANNGG
PEOWWW
STAY DOWN! WAIT FOR IT TO RELOAD!
JEEZ--!
NOW!

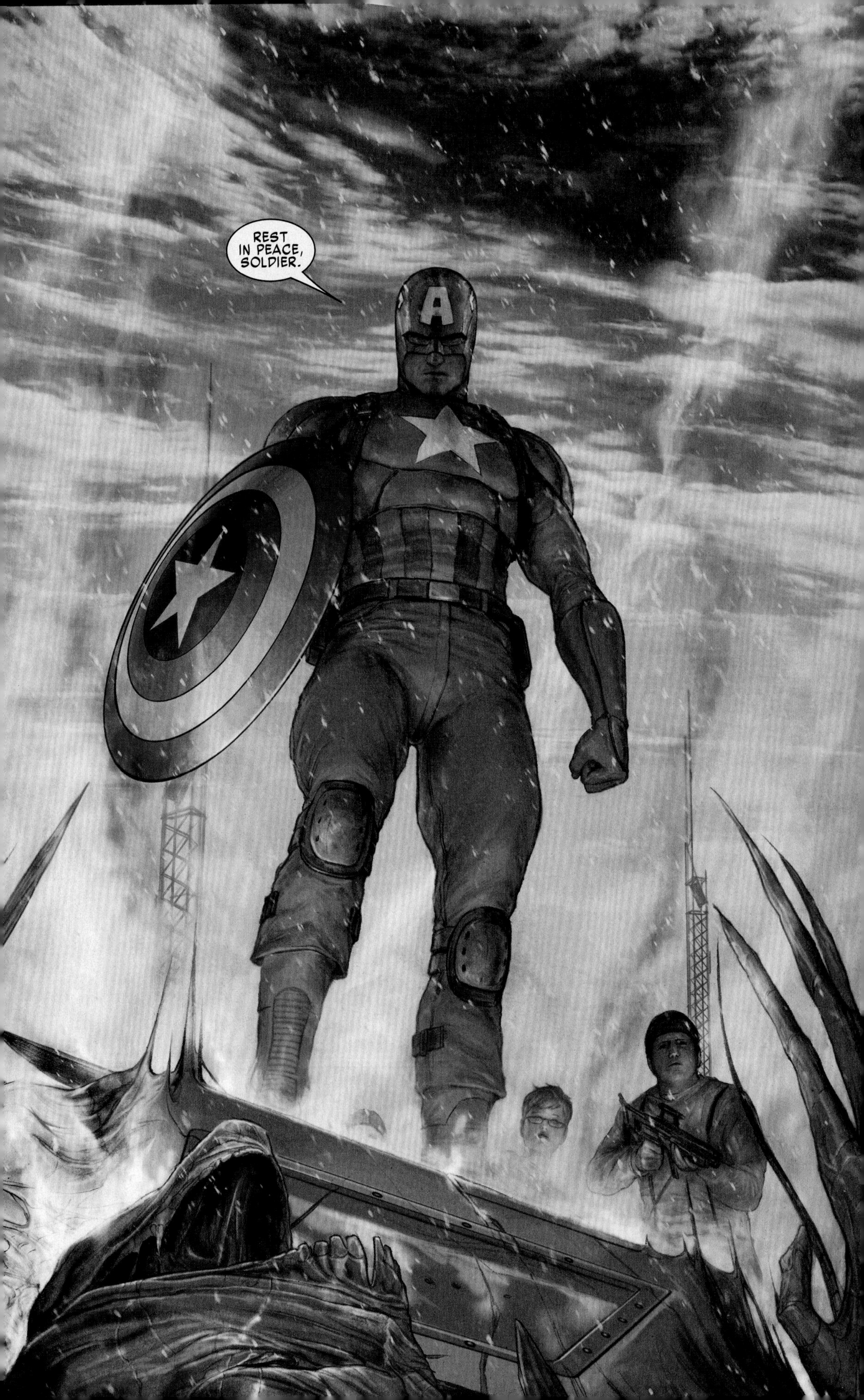
REST IN PEACE, SOLDIER.

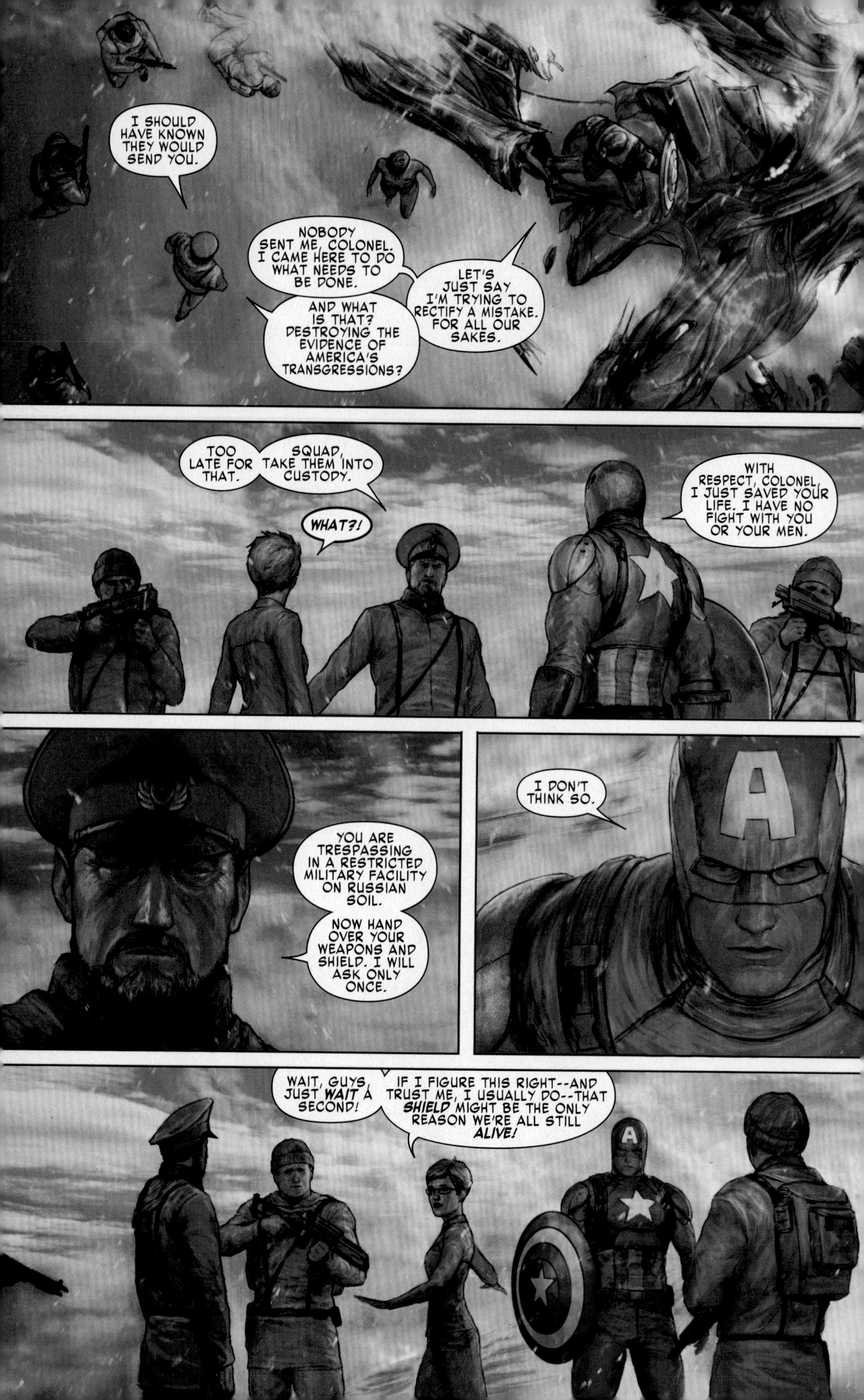
I SHOULD HAVE KNOWN THEY WOULD SEND YOU.
NOBODY SENT ME, COLONEL. I CAME HERE TO DO WHAT NEEDS TO BE DONE.
AND WHAT IS THAT? DESTROYING THE EVIDENCE OF AMERICA'S TRANSGRESSIONS?
LET'S JUST SAY I'M TRYING TO RECTIFY A MISTAKE. FOR ALL OUR SAKES.
TOO LATE FOR THAT.
SQUAD, TAKE THEM INTO CUSTODY.
WHAT?!
WITH RESPECT, COLONEL, I JUST SAVED YOUR LIFE. I HAVE NO FIGHT WITH YOU OR YOUR MEN.
YOU ARE TRESPASSING IN A RESTRICTED MILITARY FACILITY ON RUSSIAN SOIL.
NOW HAND OVER YOUR WEAPONS AND SHIELD. I WILL ASK ONLY ONCE.
I DON'T THINK SO.
WAIT, GUYS, JUST WAIT A SECOND!
IF I FIGURE THIS RIGHT--AND TRUST ME, I USUALLY DO--THAT SHIELD MIGHT BE THE ONLY REASON WE'RE ALL STILL ALIVE!

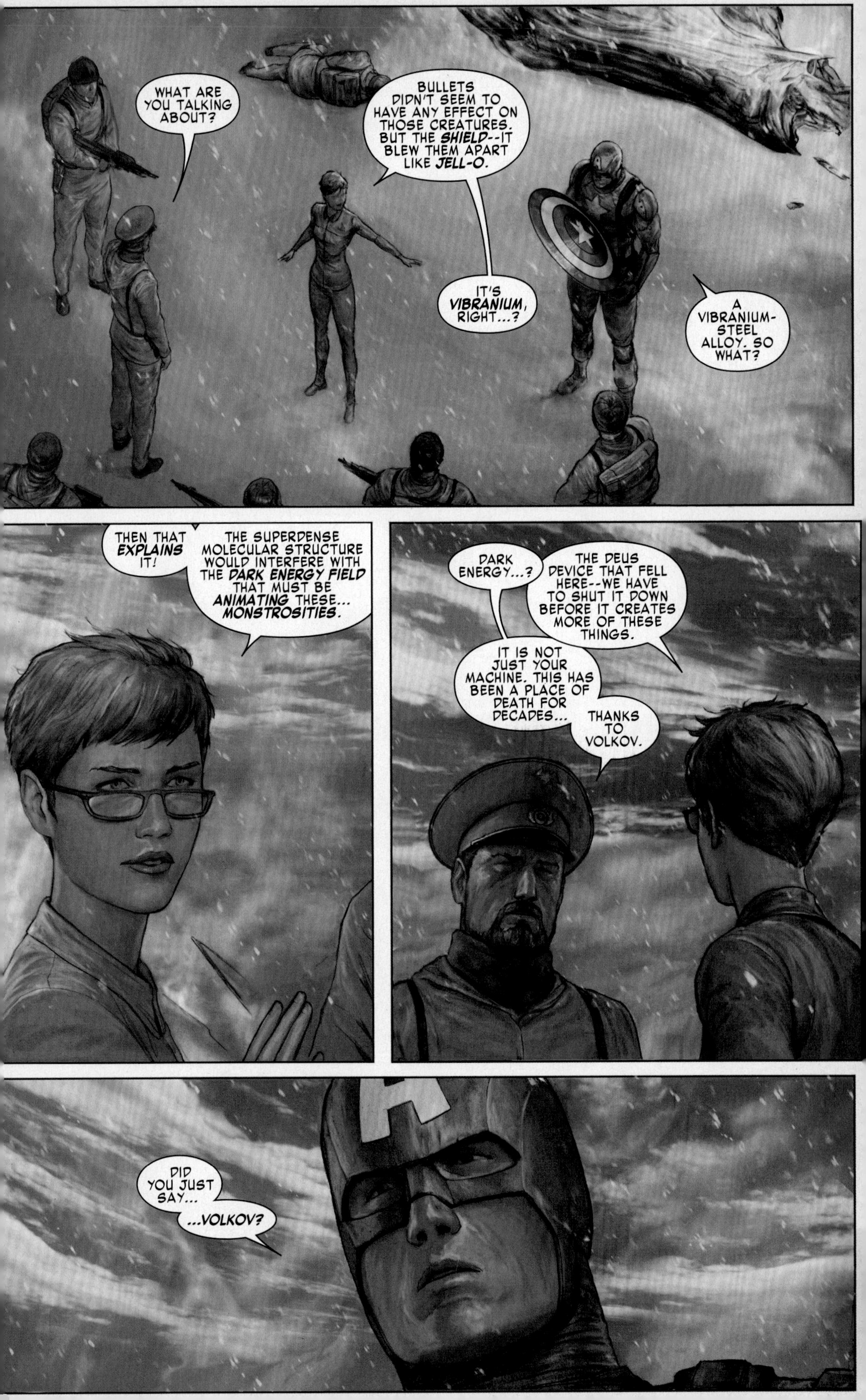
WHAT ARE YOU TALKING ABOUT?
BULLETS DIDN'T SEEM TO HAVE ANY EFFECT ON THOSE CREATURES. BUT THE SHIELD--IT BLEW THEM APART LIKE JELL-O.
IT'S VIBRANIUM, RIGHT...?
A VIBRANIUM-STEEL ALLOY. SO WHAT?
THEN THAT EXPLAINS IT!
THE SUPERDENSE MOLECULAR STRUCTURE WOULD INTERFERE WITH THE DARK ENERGY FIELD THAT MUST BE ANIMATING THESE... MONSTROSITIES.
DARK ENERGY...?
THE DEUS DEVICE THAT FELL HERE--WE HAVE TO SHUT IT DOWN BEFORE IT CREATES MORE OF THESE THINGS.
IT IS NOT JUST YOUR MACHINE. THIS HAS BEEN A PLACE OF DEATH FOR DECADES...
THANKS TO VOLKOV.
DID YOU JUST SAY...
...VOLKOV?

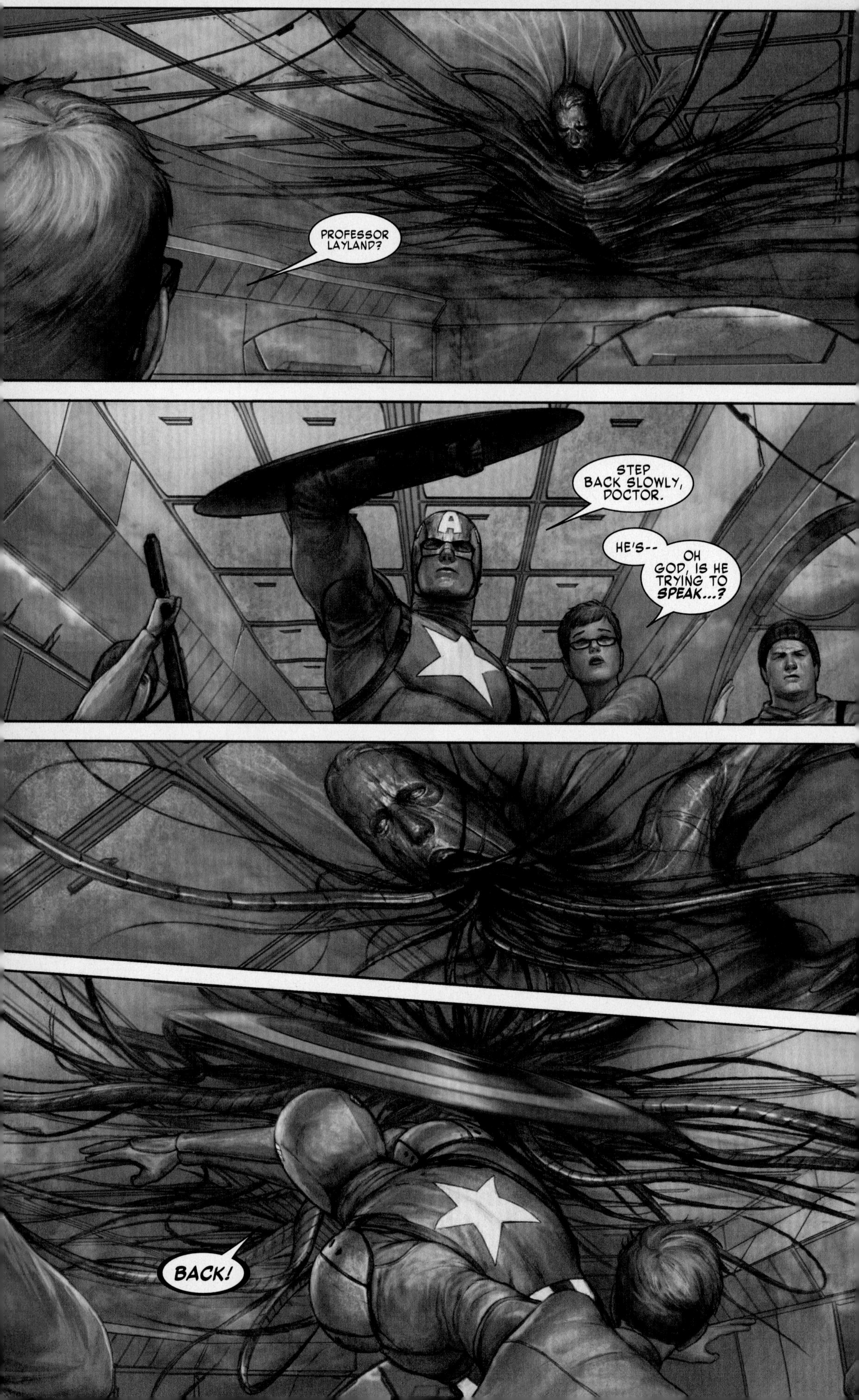
PROFESSOR LAYLAND?
STEP BACK SLOWLY, DOCTOR.
HE'S--
OH GOD, IS HE TRYING TO SPEAK...?
BACK!

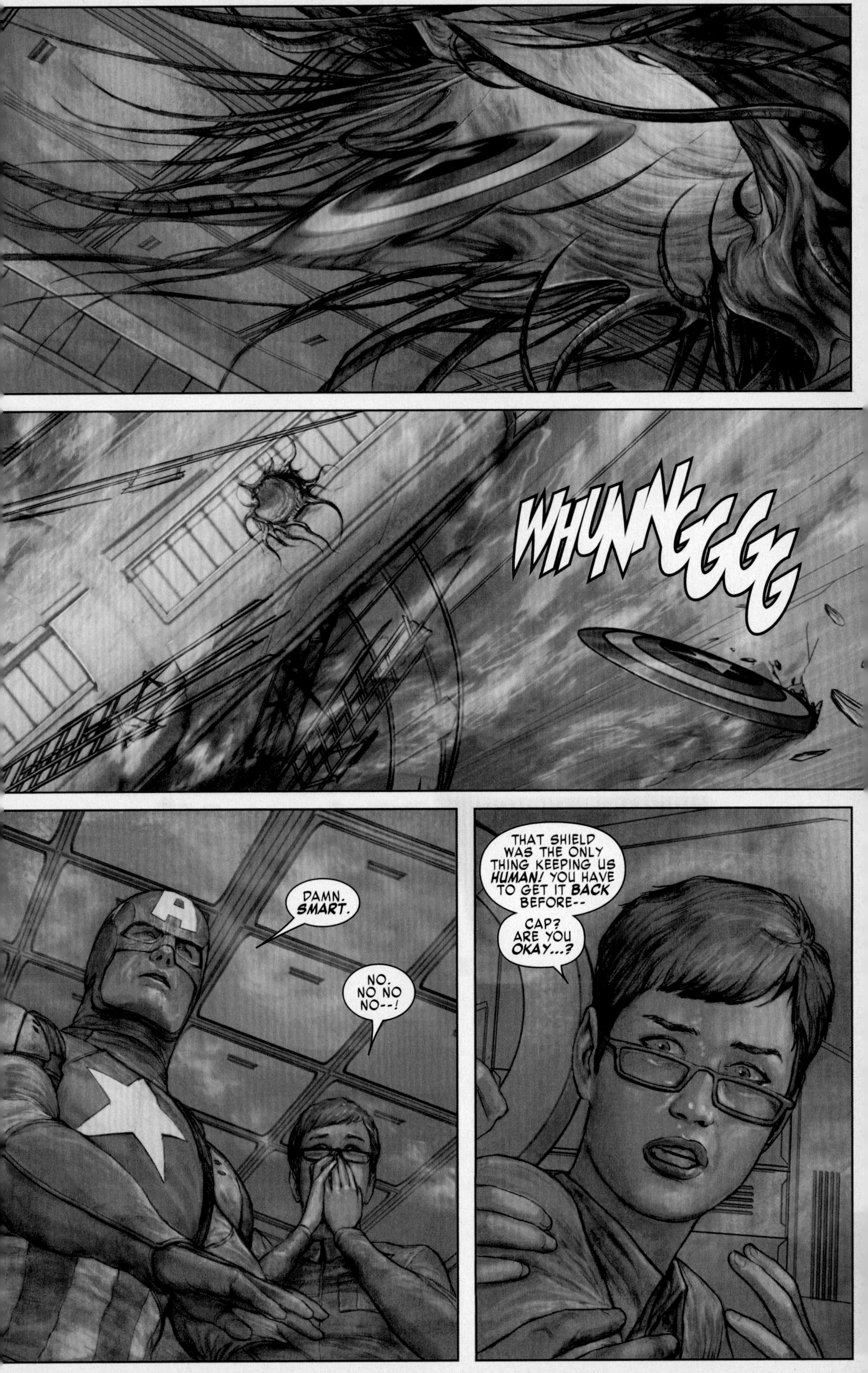

WHUNNGGGG
DAMN. SMART.
NO. NO NO NO--!
THAT SHIELD WAS THE ONLY THING KEEPING US HUMAN! YOU HAVE TO GET IT BACK BEFORE--
CAP? ARE YOU OKAY...?

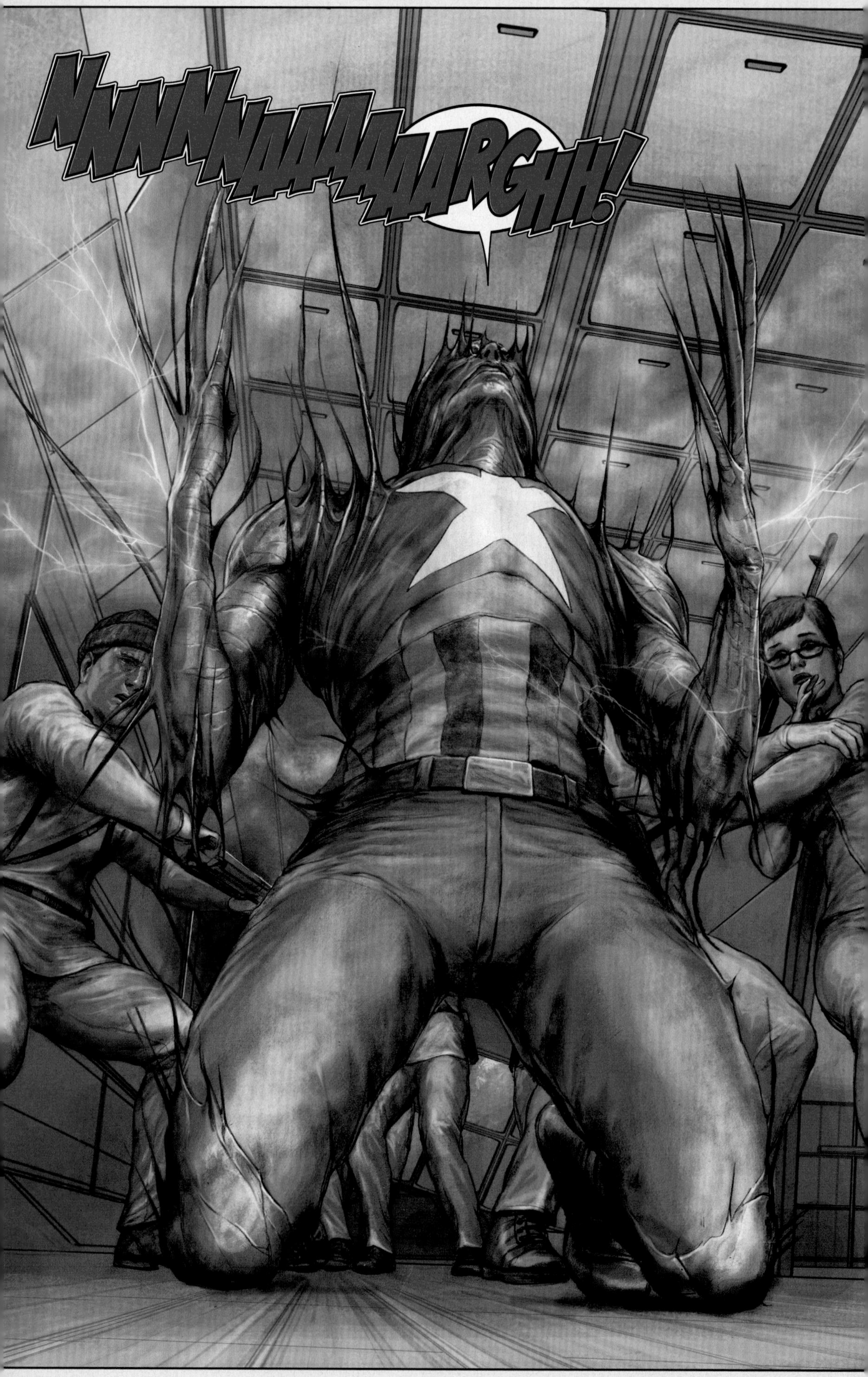
NNNNNAAAAAAARGHH!

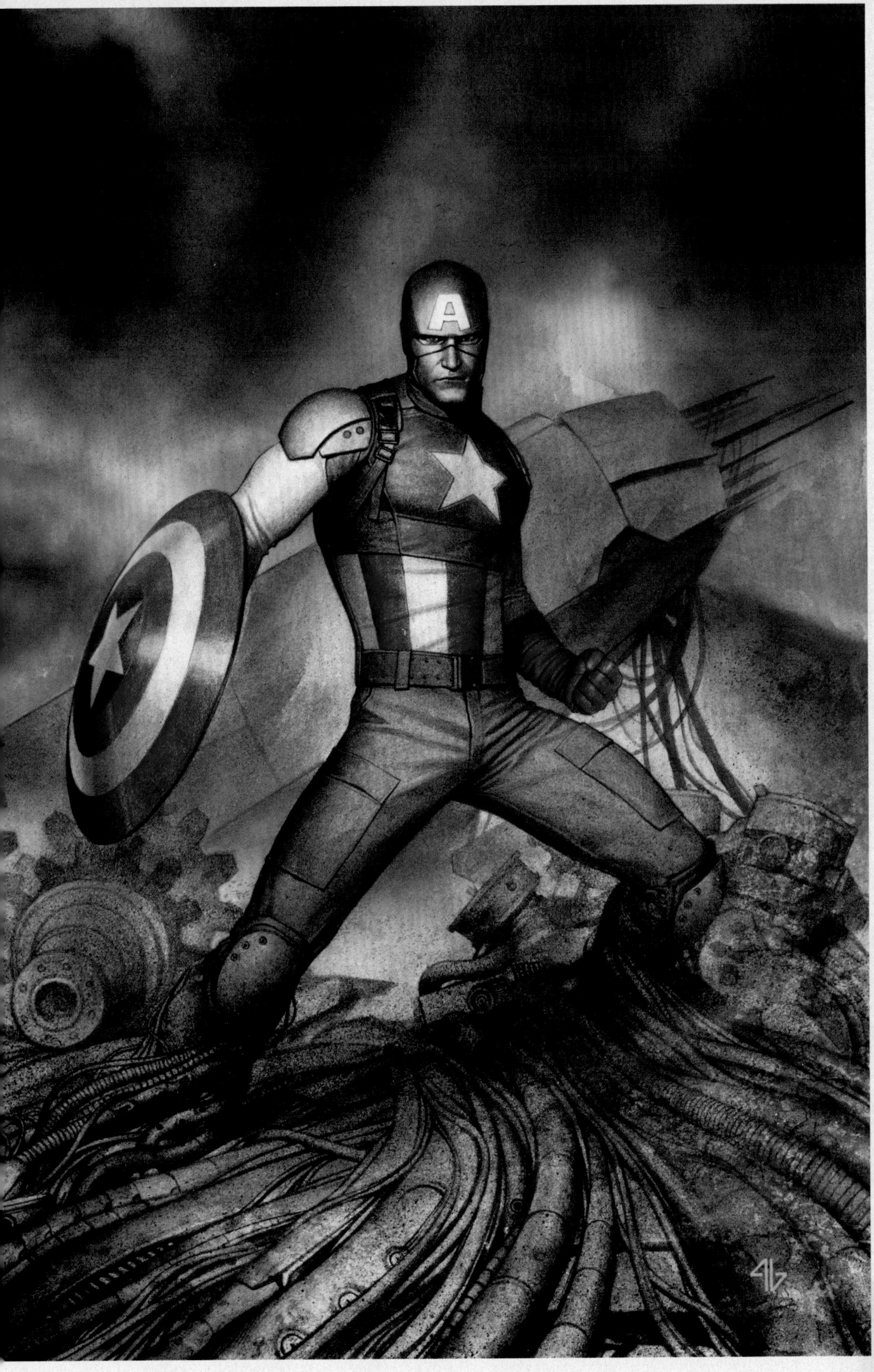

★ CHAPTER FOUR ★

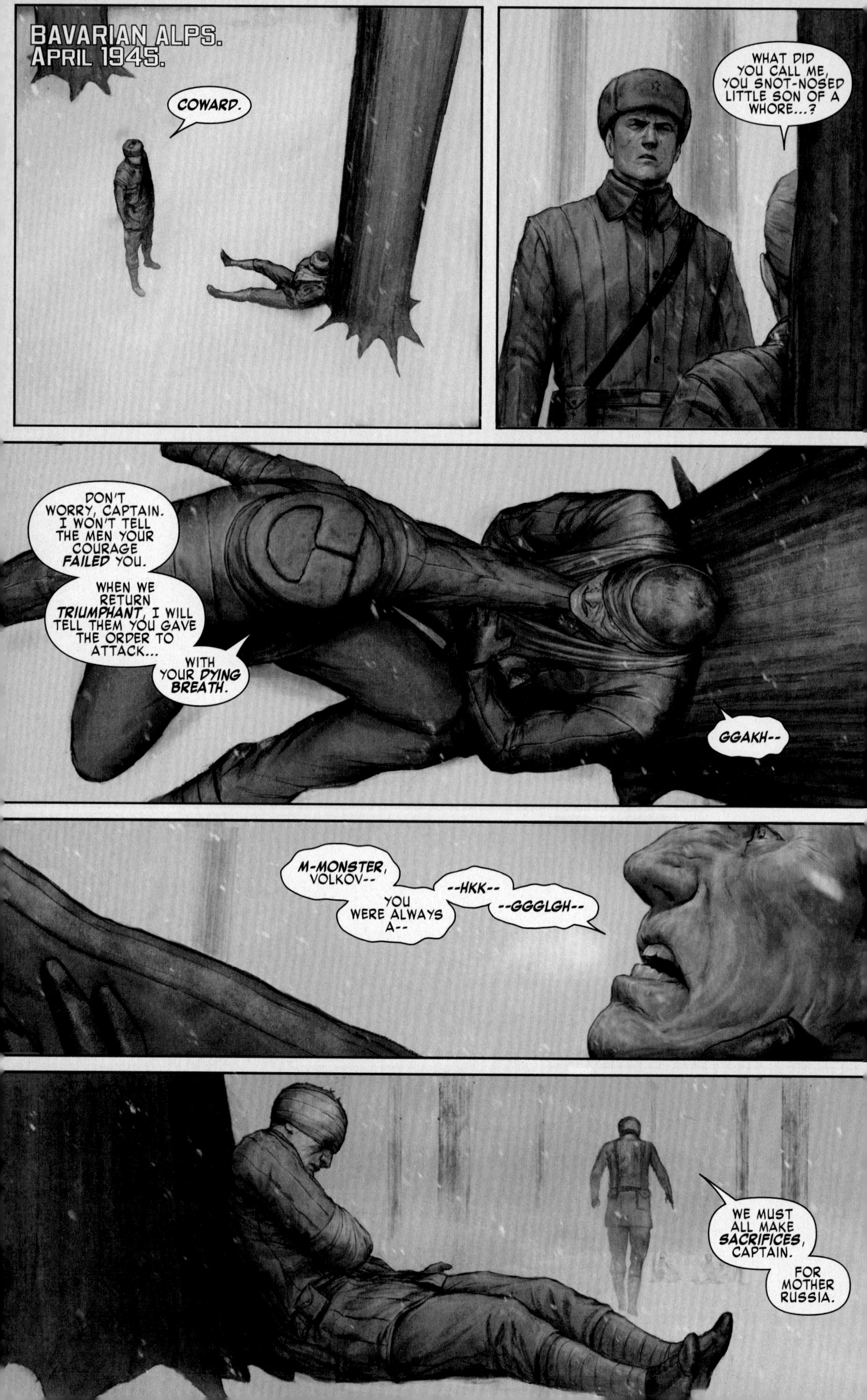
BAVARIAN ALPS.
APRIL 1945.
COWARD.
WHAT DID YOU CALL ME, YOU SNOT-NOSED LITTLE SON OF A WHORE...?
DON'T WORRY, CAPTAIN. I WON'T TELL THE MEN YOUR COURAGE FAILED YOU.
WHEN WE RETURN TRIUMPHANT, I WILL TELL THEM YOU GAVE THE ORDER TO ATTACK...
WITH YOUR DYING BREATH.
GGAKH--
M-MONSTER, VOLKOV--
YOU WERE ALWAYS A--
--HKK--
--GGGLGH--
WE MUST ALL MAKE SACRIFICES, CAPTAIN.
FOR MOTHER RUSSIA.

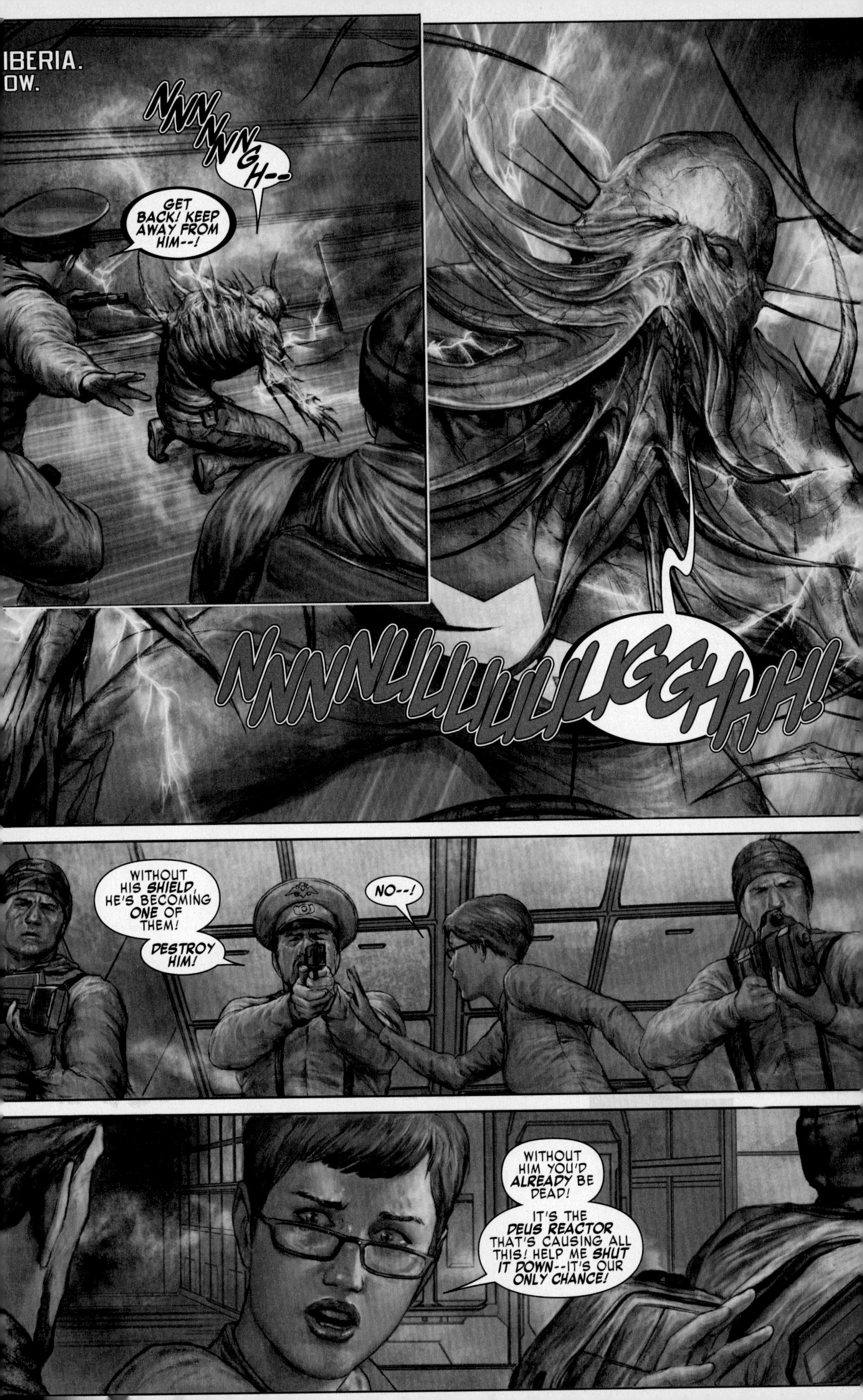
IBERIA.
OW.
NNNNNNGH--
GET BACK! KEEP AWAY FROM HIM--!
NNNNUUUUUUGGHHH!
WITHOUT HIS SHIELD, HE'S BECOMING ONE OF THEM!
DESTROY HIM!
NO--!
WITHOUT HIM YOU'D ALREADY BE DEAD!
IT'S THE DEUS REACTOR THAT'S CAUSING ALL THIS! HELP ME SHUT IT DOWN--IT'S OUR ONLY CHANCE!

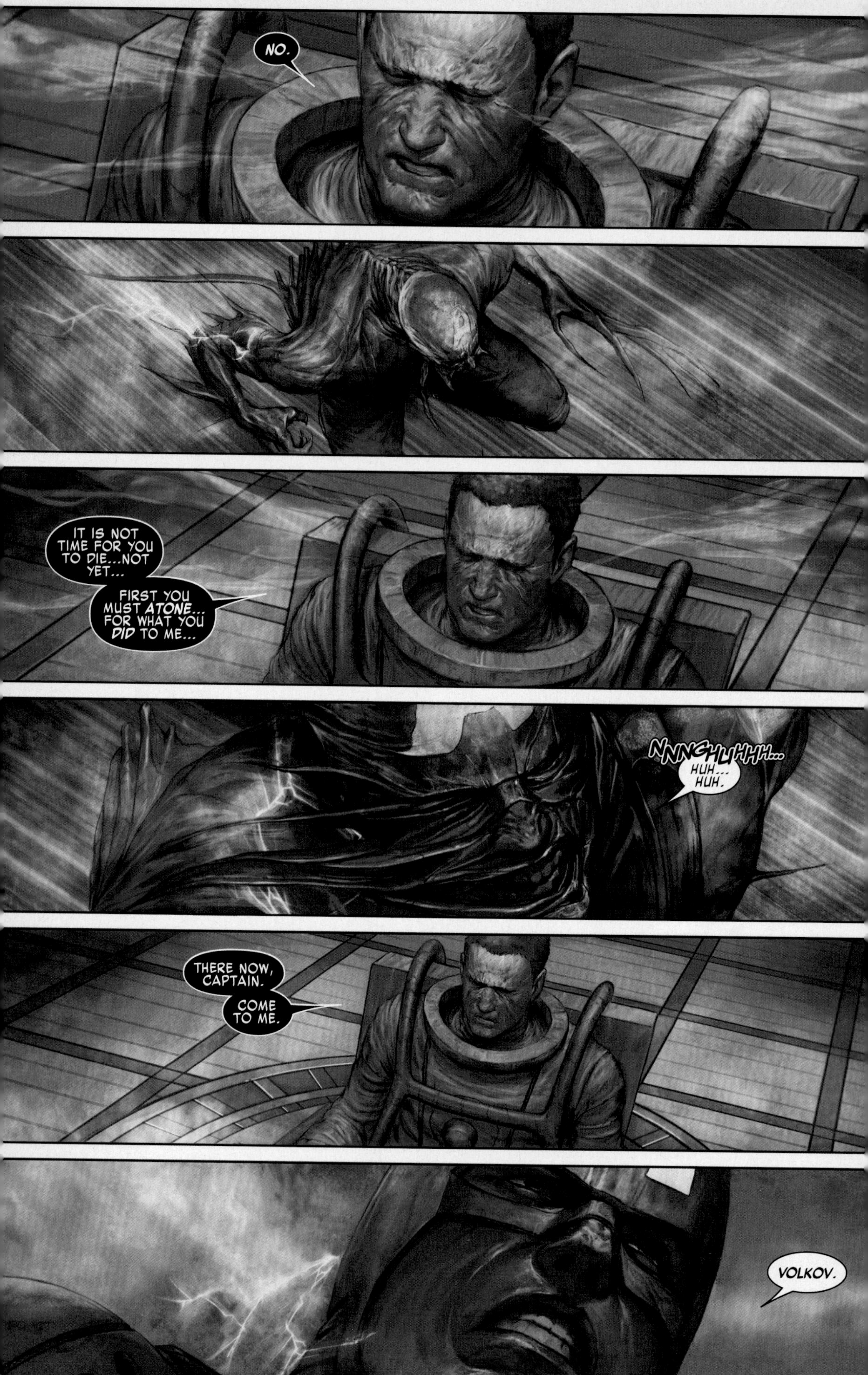
NO.
IT IS NOT TIME FOR YOU TO DIE...NOT YET...
FIRST YOU MUST ATONE... FOR WHAT YOU DID TO ME...
NNNGHUHHH...
HUH... HUH.
THERE NOW, CAPTAIN.
COME TO ME.
VOLKOV.

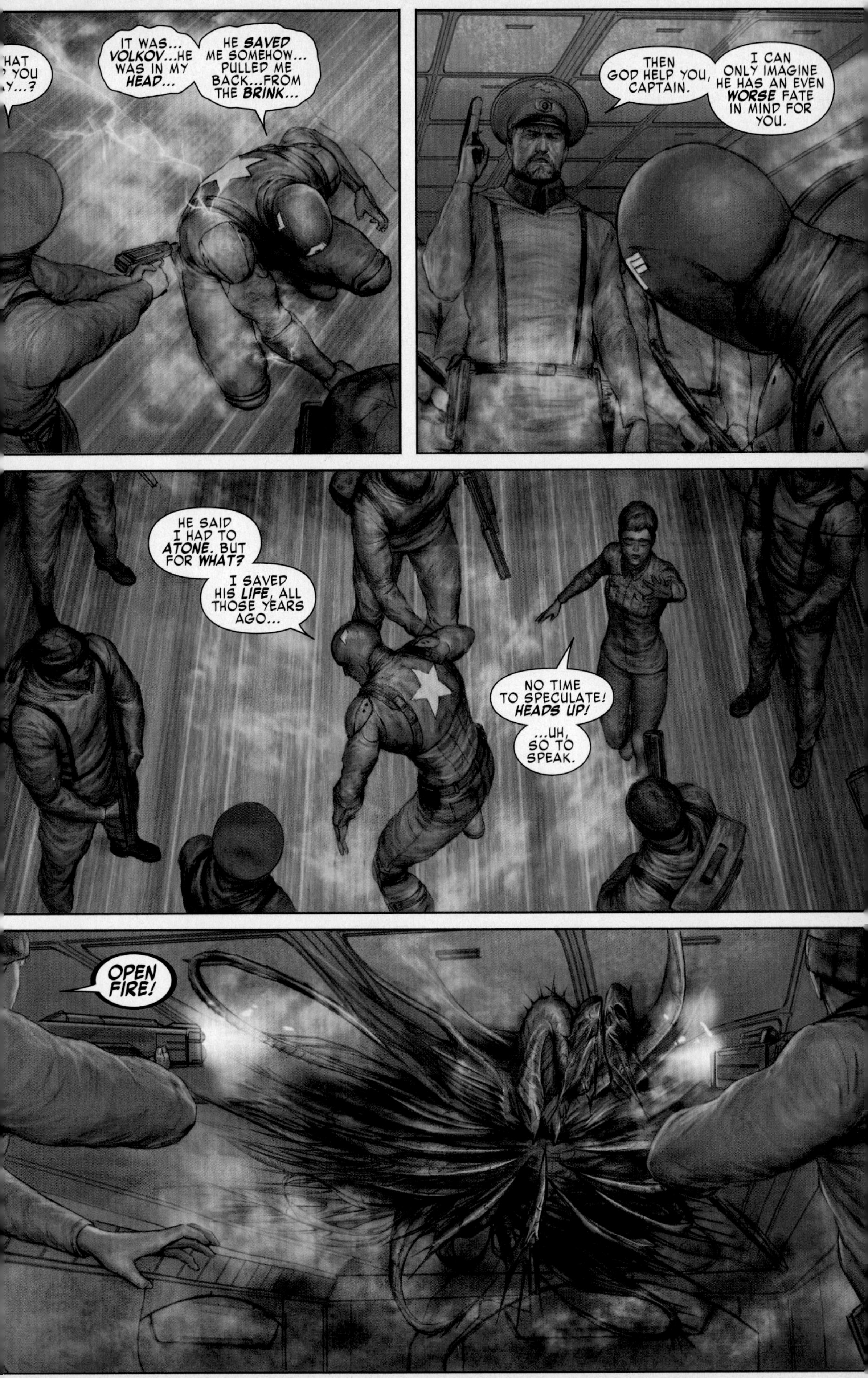
IT WAS... VOLKOV...HE WAS IN MY HEAD...
HE SAVED ME SOMEHOW... PULLED ME BACK...FROM THE BRINK...
THEN GOD HELP YOU, CAPTAIN.
I CAN ONLY IMAGINE HE HAS AN EVEN WORSE FATE IN MIND FOR YOU.
HE SAID I HAD TO ATONE. BUT FOR WHAT?
I SAVED HIS LIFE, ALL THOSE YEARS AGO...
NO TIME TO SPECULATE! HEADS UP!
...UH, SO TO SPEAK.
OPEN FIRE!

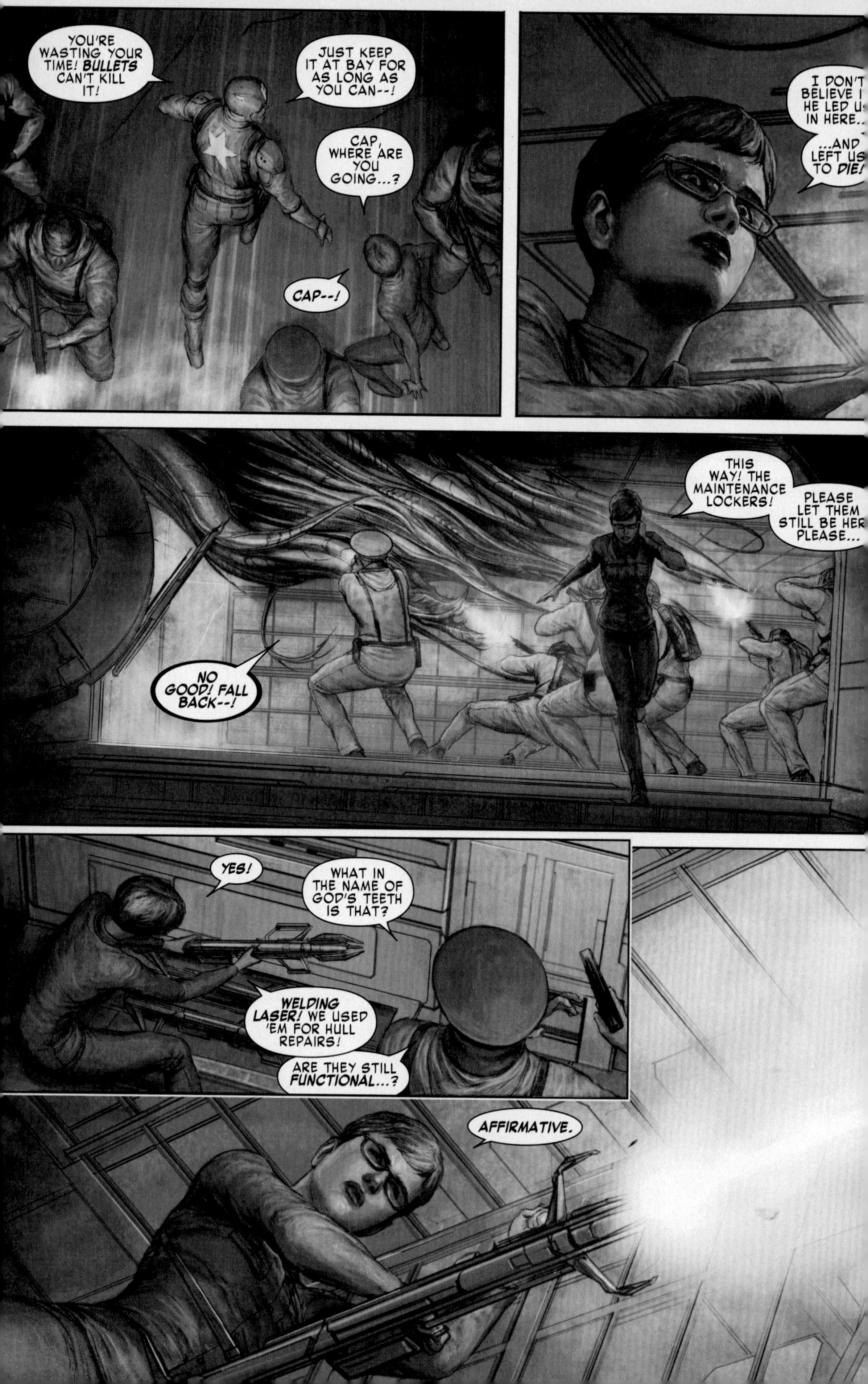
YOU'RE WASTING YOUR TIME! BULLETS CAN'T KILL IT!
JUST KEEP IT AT BAY FOR AS LONG AS YOU CAN--!
CAP, WHERE ARE YOU GOING...?
CAP--!
I DON'T BELIEVE I HE LED U IN HERE...
...AND LEFT US TO DIE!
THIS WAY! THE MAINTENANCE LOCKERS!
PLEASE LET THEM STILL BE HER PLEASE...
NO GOOD! FALL BACK--!
YES!
WHAT IN THE NAME OF GOD'S TEETH IS THAT?
WELDING LASER! WE USED 'EM FOR HULL REPAIRS!
ARE THEY STILL FUNCTIONAL...?
AFFIRMATIVE.

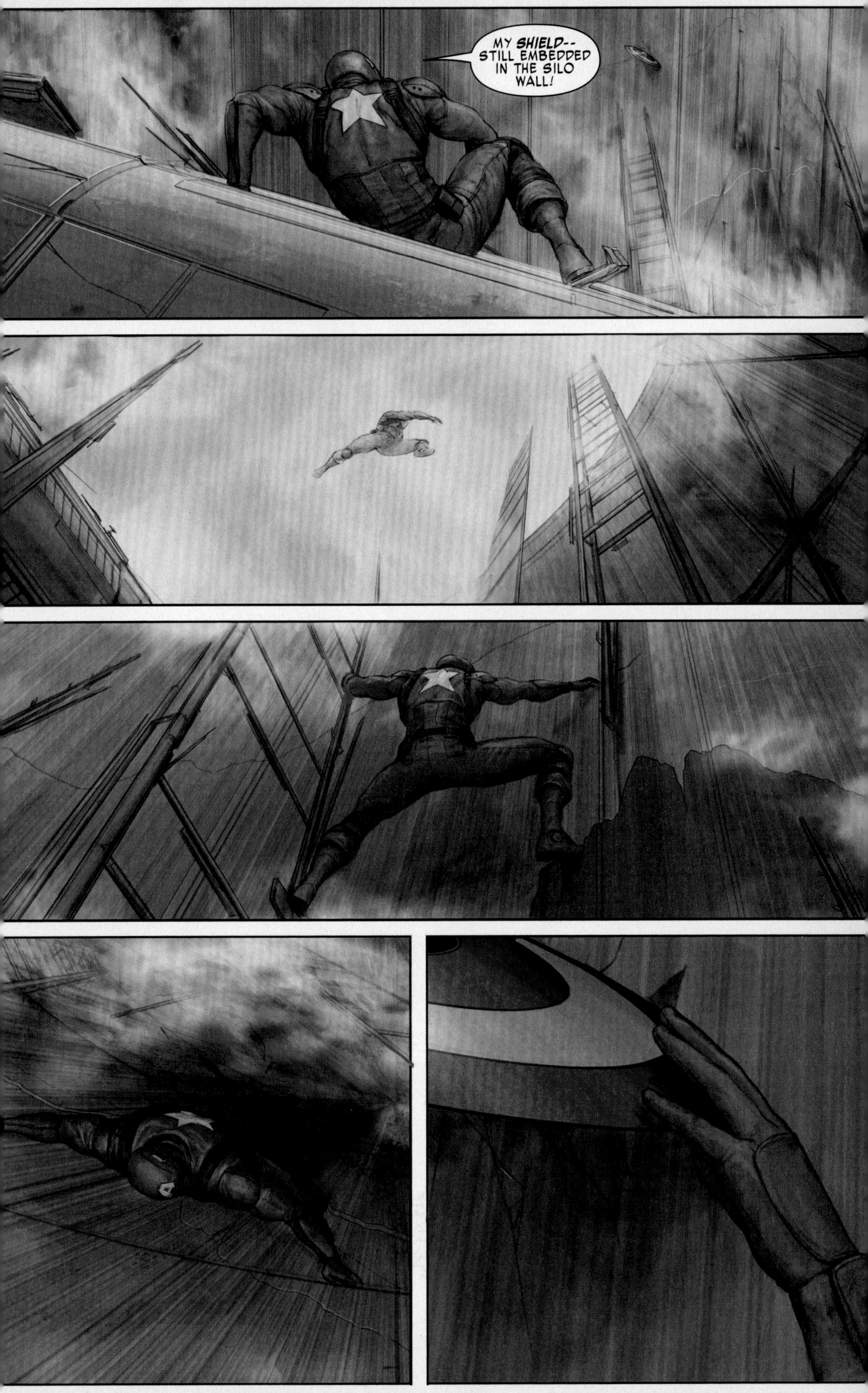
MY SHIELD--
STILL EMBEDDED
IN THE SILO
WALL!

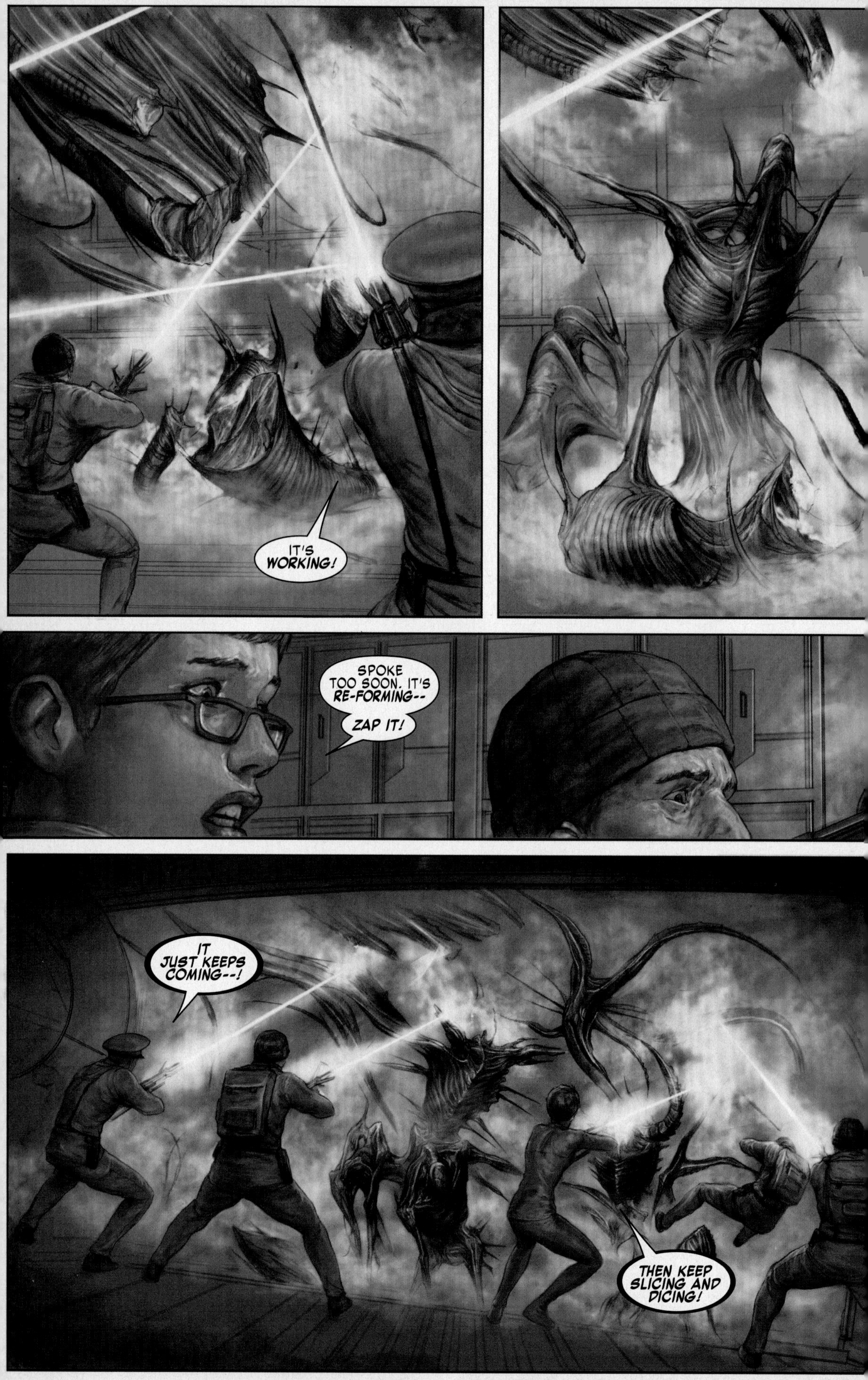
IT'S WORKING!
SPOKE TOO SOON. IT'S RE-FORMING--
ZAP IT!
IT JUST KEEPS COMING--!
THEN KEEP SLICING AND DICING!

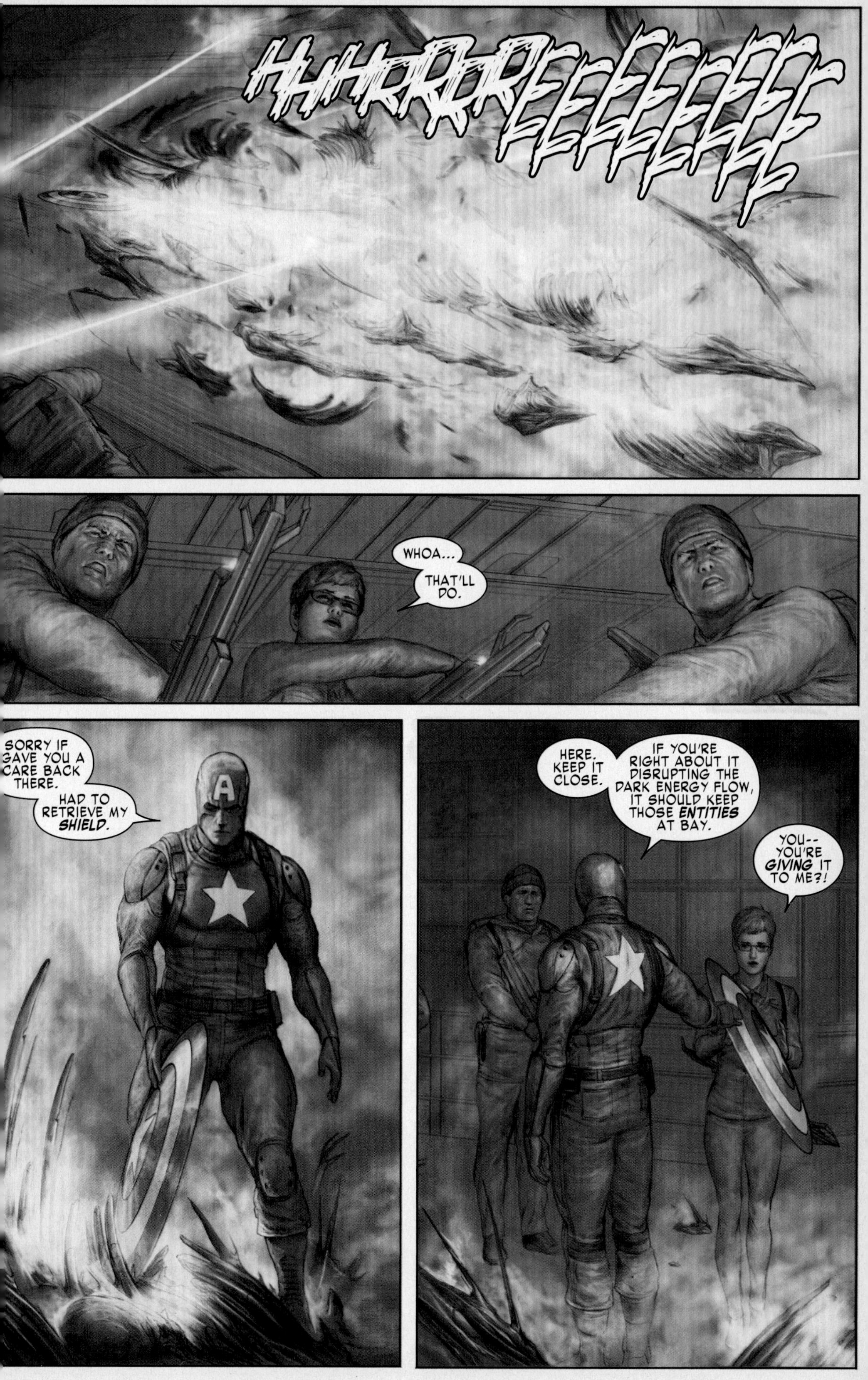

HHHRRREEEEEEEEEE
WHOA... THAT'LL DO.
SORRY IF GAVE YOU A CARE BACK THERE.
HAD TO RETRIEVE MY *SHIELD*.
HERE. KEEP IT CLOSE.
IF YOU'RE RIGHT ABOUT IT DISRUPTING THE DARK ENERGY FLOW, IT SHOULD KEEP THOSE *ENTITIES* AT BAY.
YOU-- YOU'RE *GIVING* IT TO ME?!

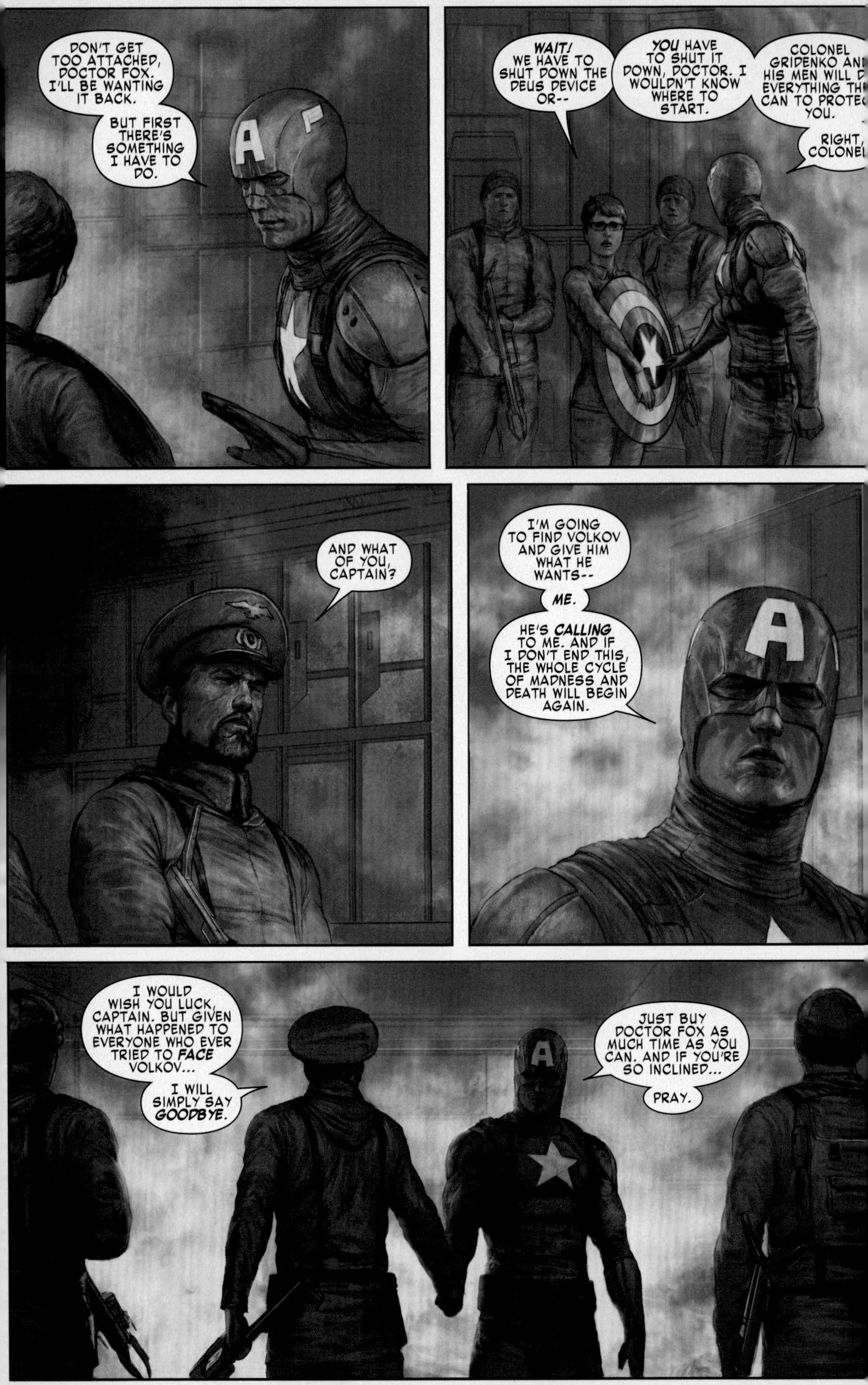
DON'T GET TOO ATTACHED, DOCTOR FOX. I'LL BE WANTING IT BACK.
BUT FIRST THERE'S SOMETHING I HAVE TO DO.
WAIT! WE HAVE TO SHUT DOWN THE DEUS DEVICE OR--
YOU HAVE TO SHUT IT DOWN, DOCTOR. I WOULDN'T KNOW WHERE TO START.
AND WHAT OF YOU, CAPTAIN?
I'M GOING TO FIND VOLKOV AND GIVE HIM WHAT HE WANTS--
ME.
HE'S CALLING TO ME. AND IF I DON'T END THIS, THE WHOLE CYCLE OF MADNESS AND DEATH WILL BEGIN AGAIN.
I WOULD WISH YOU LUCK, CAPTAIN. BUT GIVEN WHAT HAPPENED TO EVERYONE WHO EVER TRIED TO FACE VOLKOV...
I WILL SIMPLY SAY GOODBYE.
JUST BUY DOCTOR FOX AS MUCH TIME AS YOU CAN. AND IF YOU'RE SO INCLINED...
PRAY.

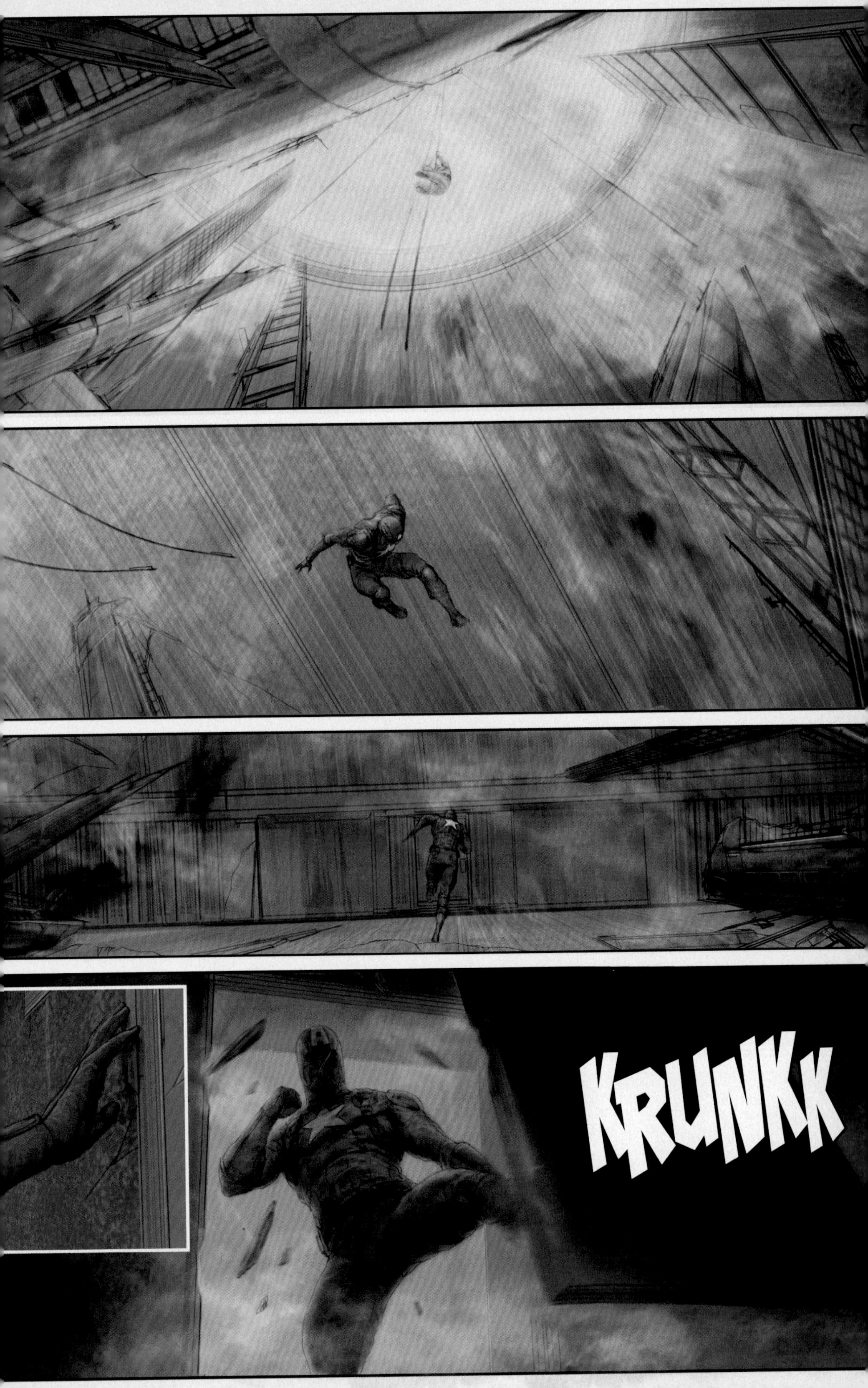
KRUNKK

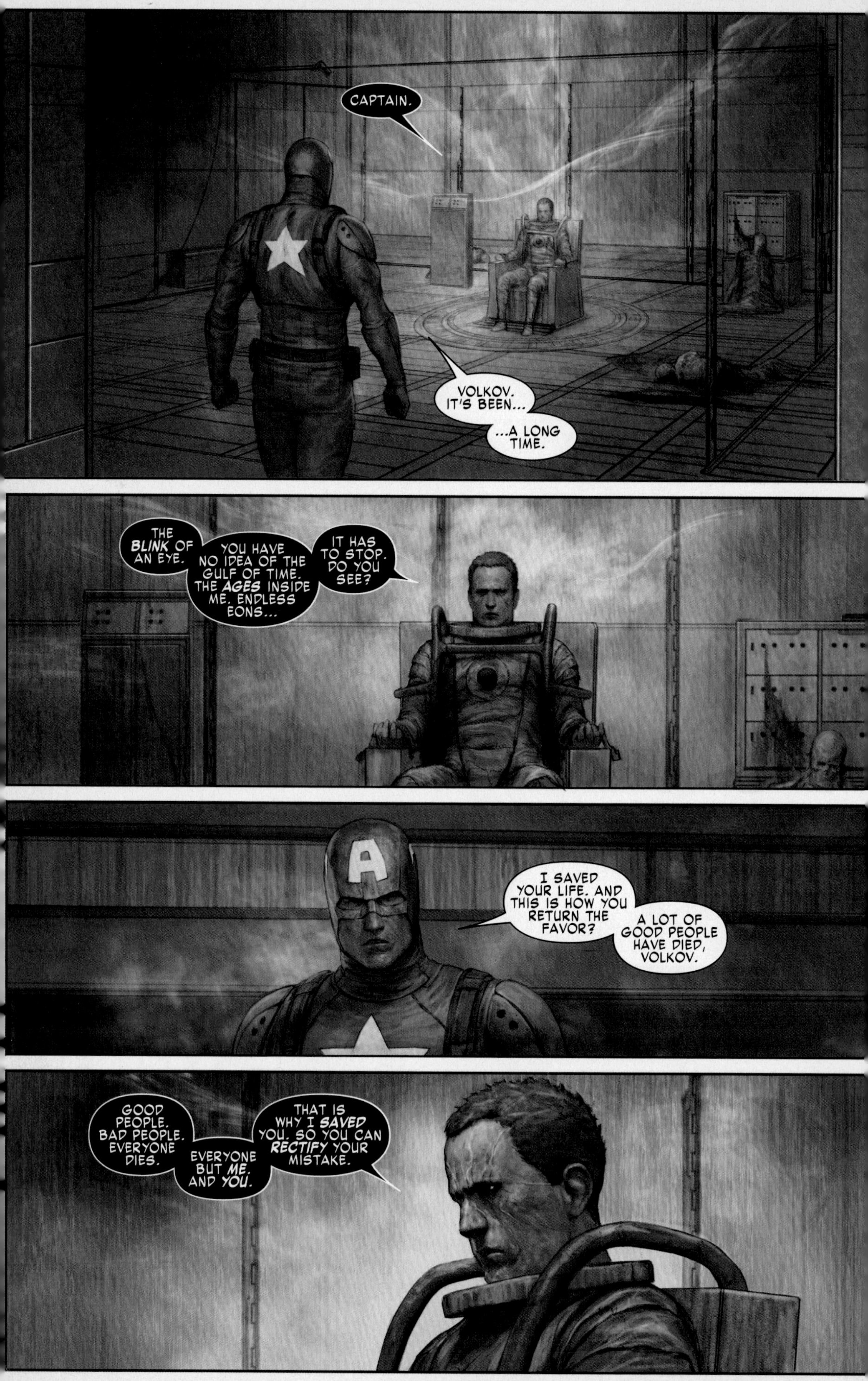
CAPTAIN.
VOLKOV. IT'S BEEN...
...A LONG TIME.
THE BLINK OF AN EYE.
YOU HAVE NO IDEA OF THE GULF OF TIME. THE AGES INSIDE ME. ENDLESS EONS...
IT HAS TO STOP. DO YOU SEE?
I SAVED YOUR LIFE. AND THIS IS HOW YOU RETURN THE FAVOR?
A LOT OF GOOD PEOPLE HAVE DIED, VOLKOV.
GOOD PEOPLE. BAD PEOPLE. EVERYONE DIES.
EVERYONE BUT ME. AND YOU.
THAT IS WHY I SAVED YOU. SO YOU CAN RECTIFY YOUR MISTAKE.

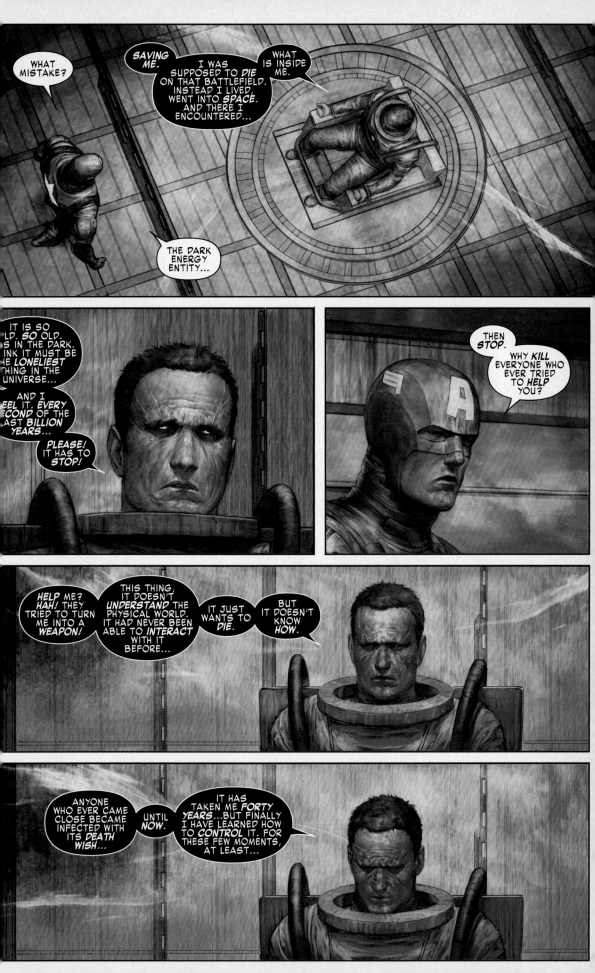

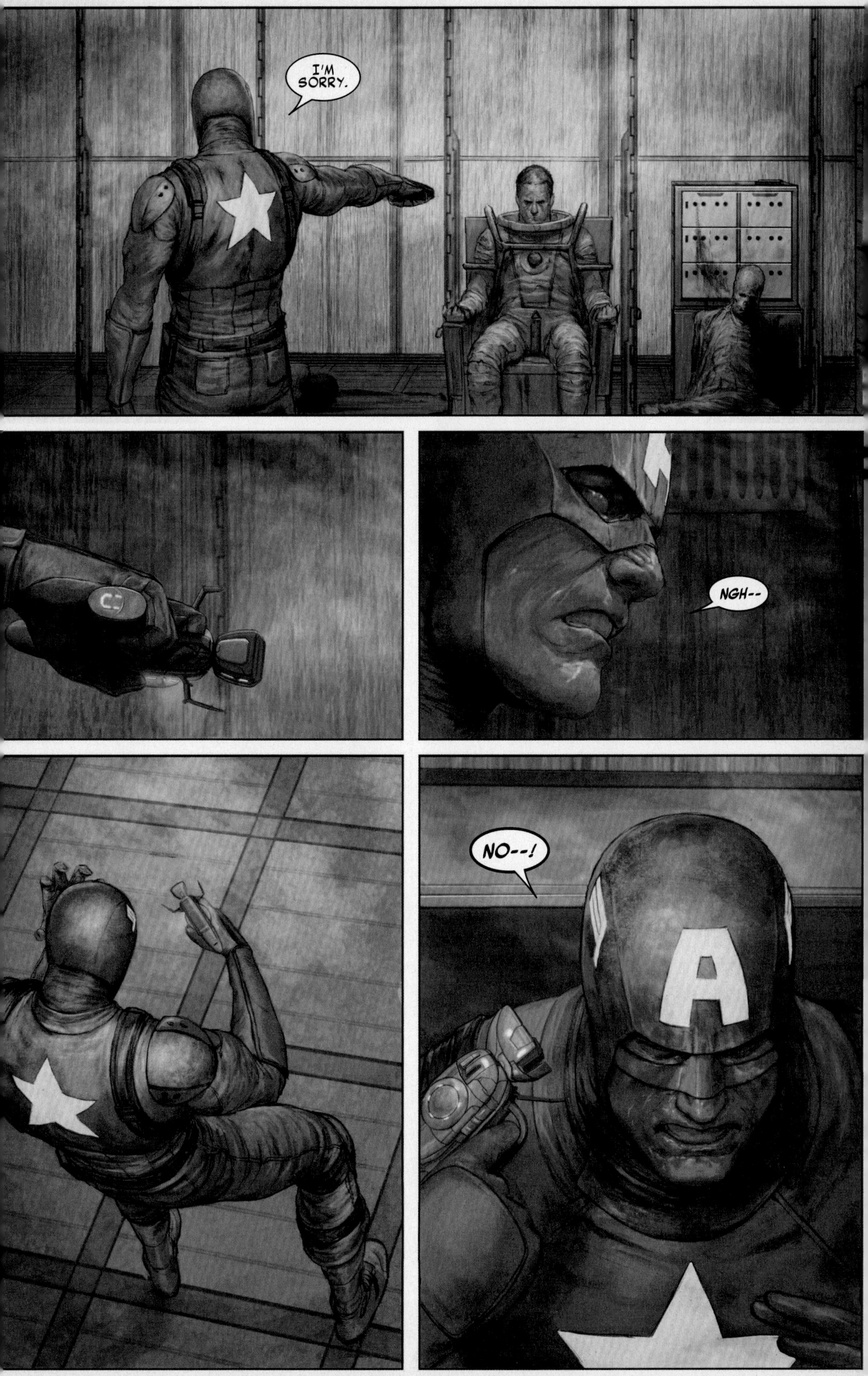
I'M SORRY.
NGH--
NO--!

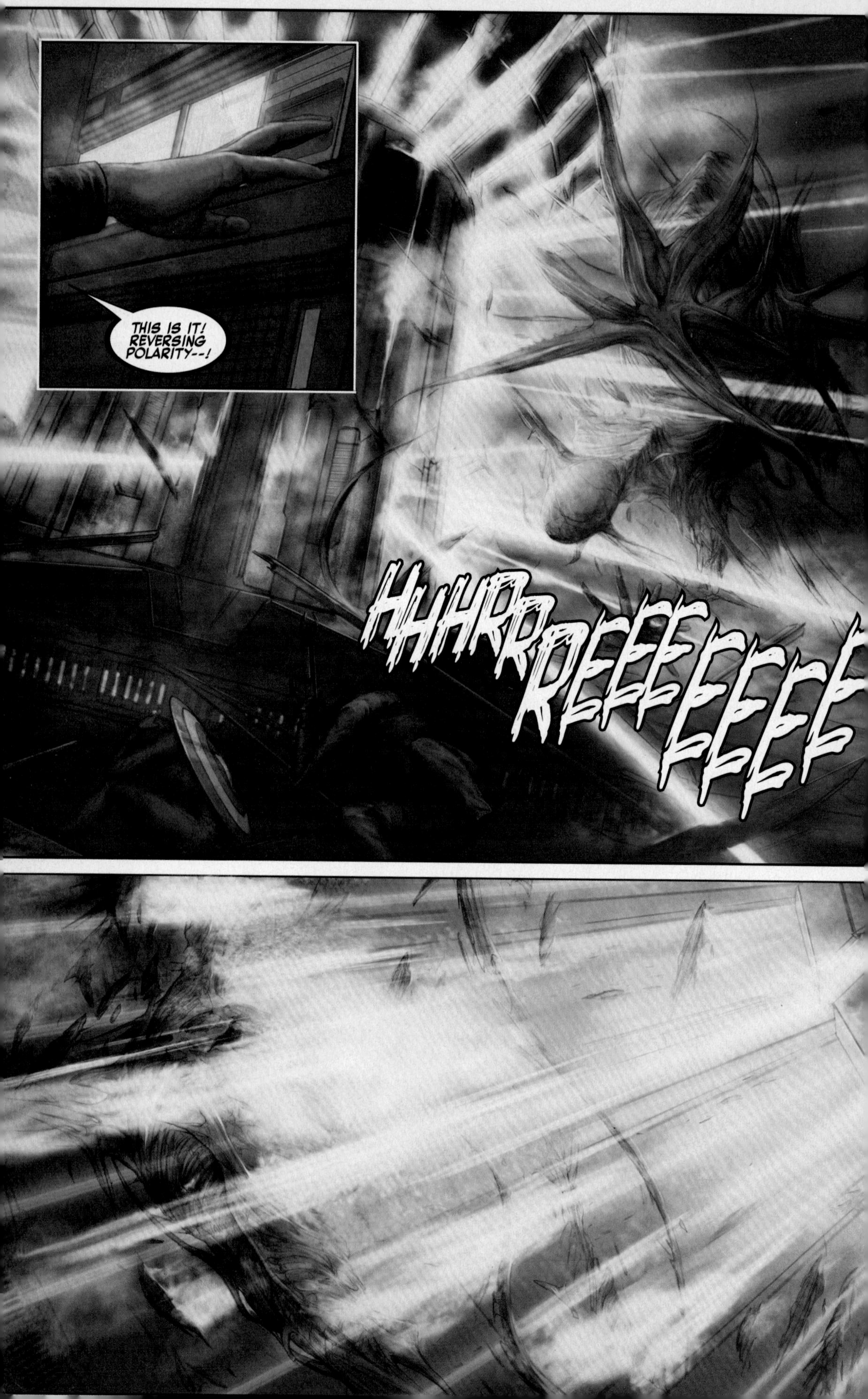
THIS IS IT! REVERSING POLARITY--!
HHHRRRREEEEEEEEEE

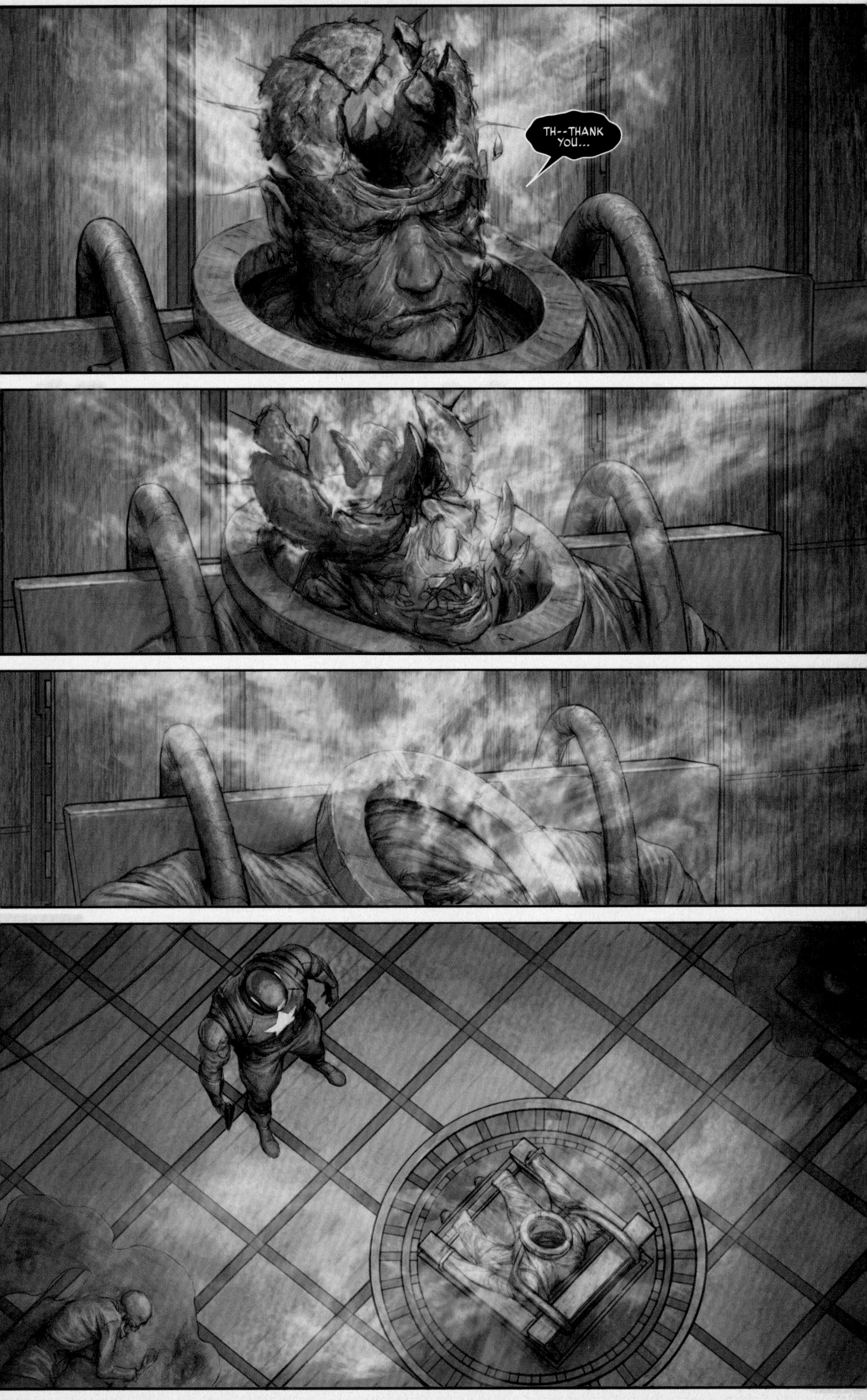
TH--THANK YOU...

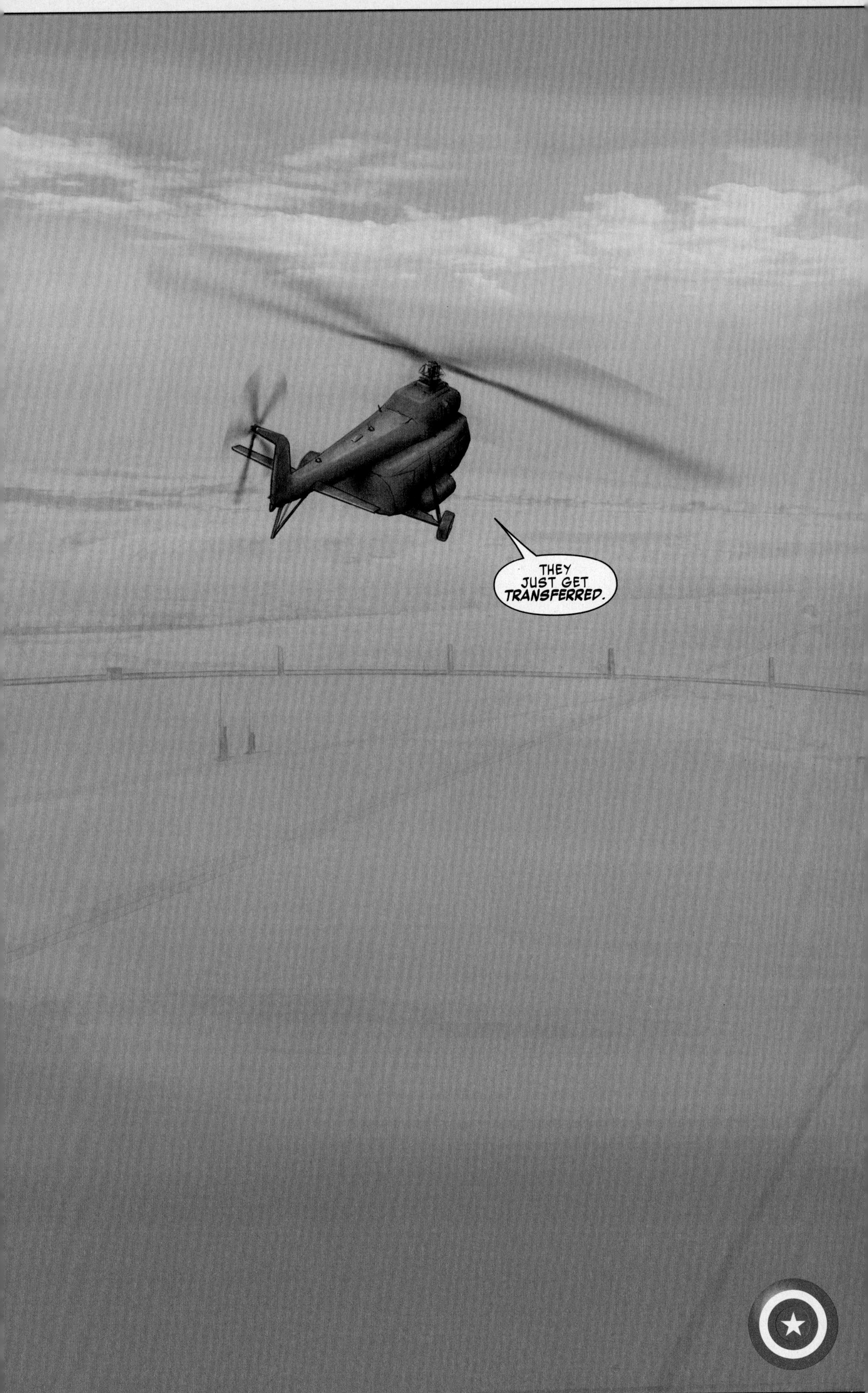
THEY JUST GET TRANSFERRED.

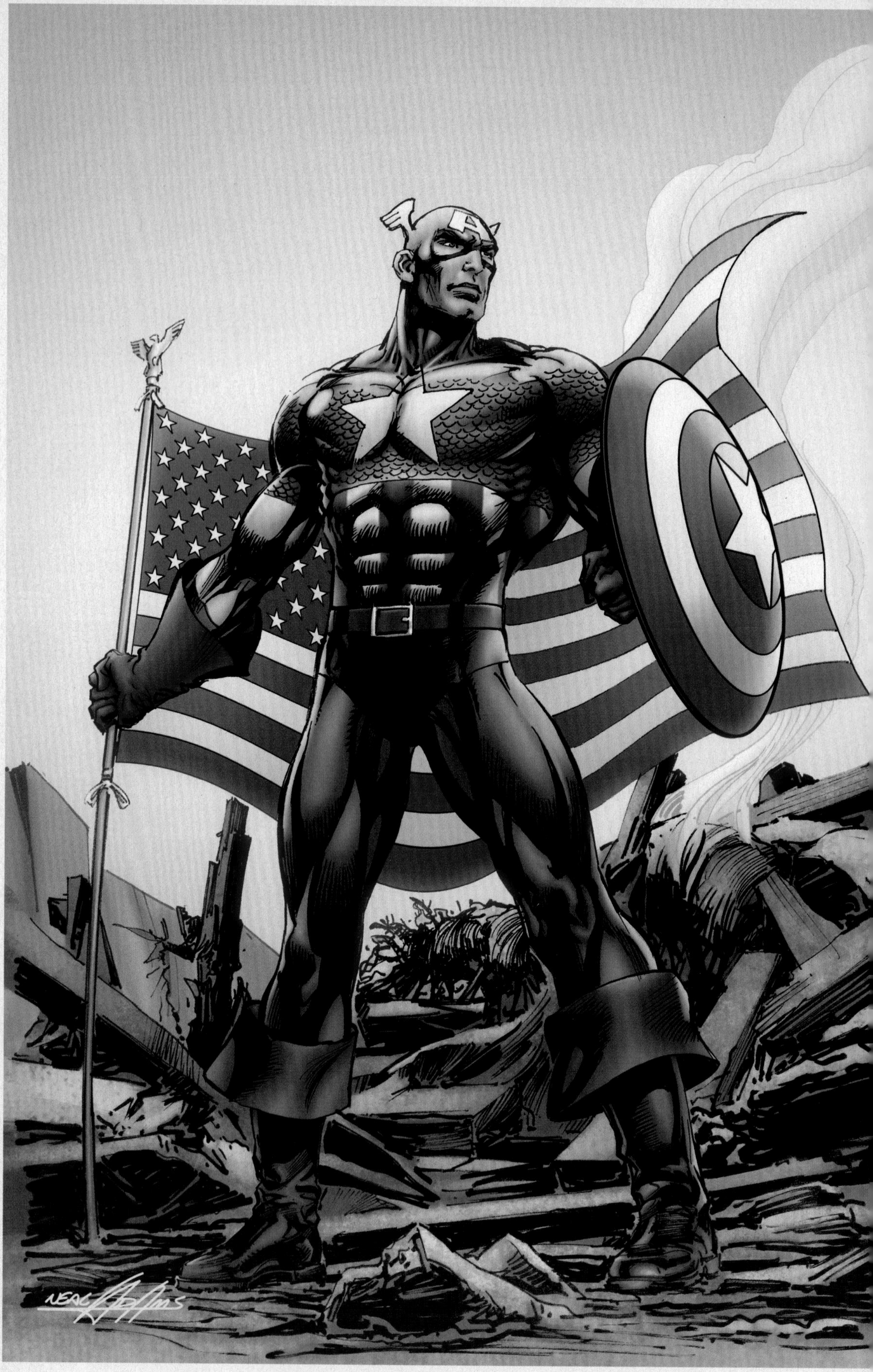

#1 LEGEND VARIANT COVER BY NEAL ADAMS & MORRY HOLLOWELL

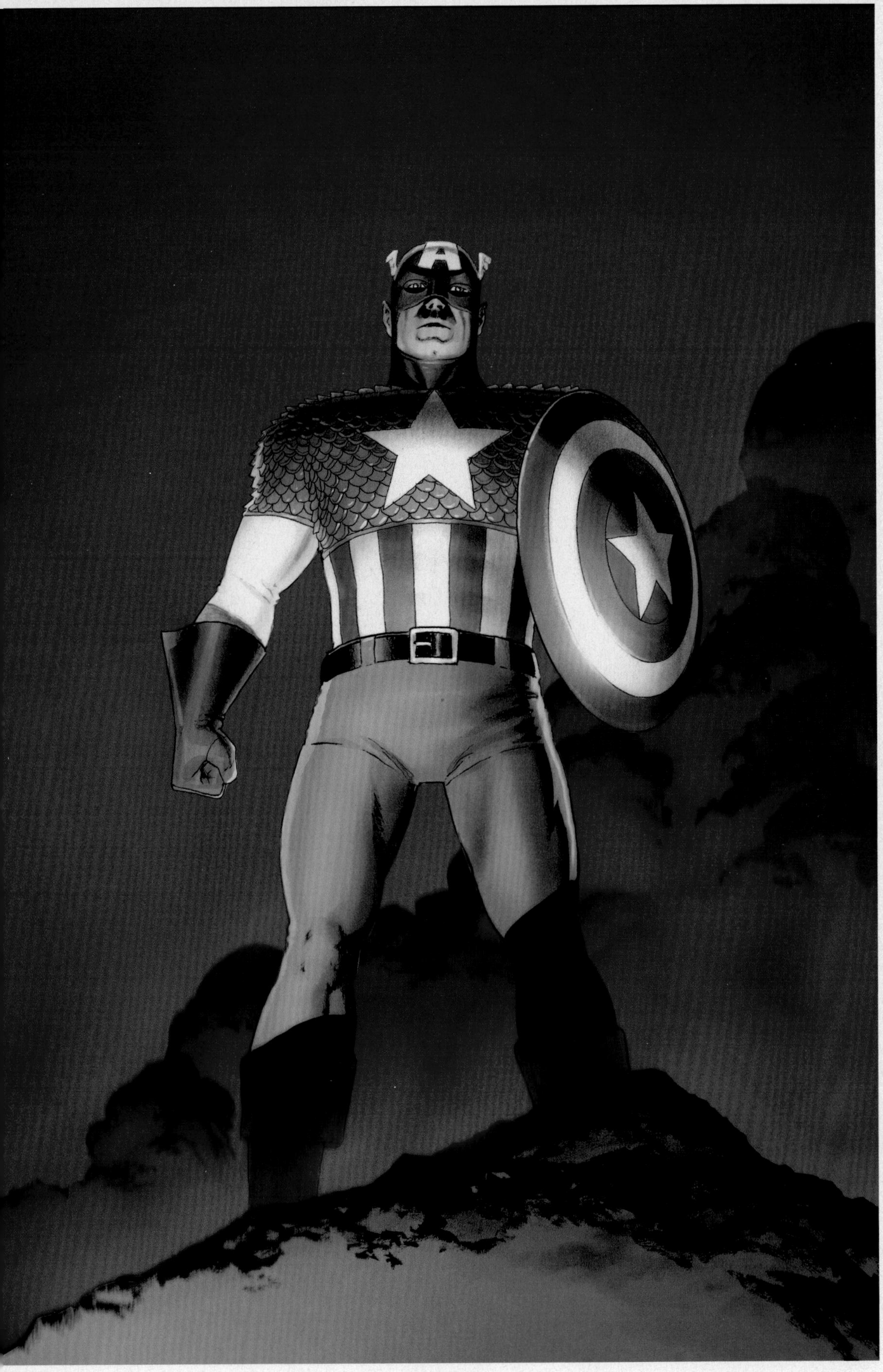

#1 MARVEL UNLIMITED VARIANT COVER BY JOHN CASSADAY & JASON KEITH

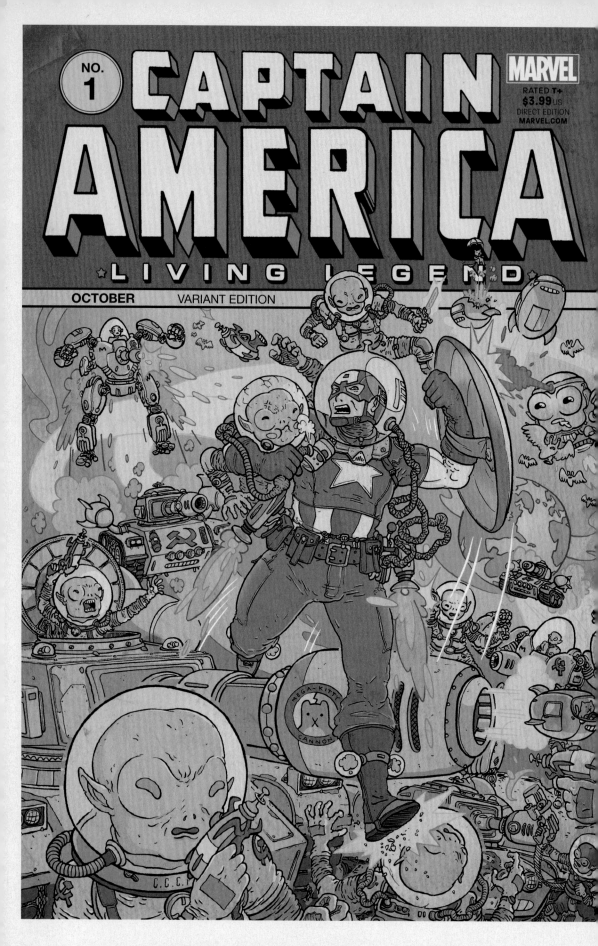

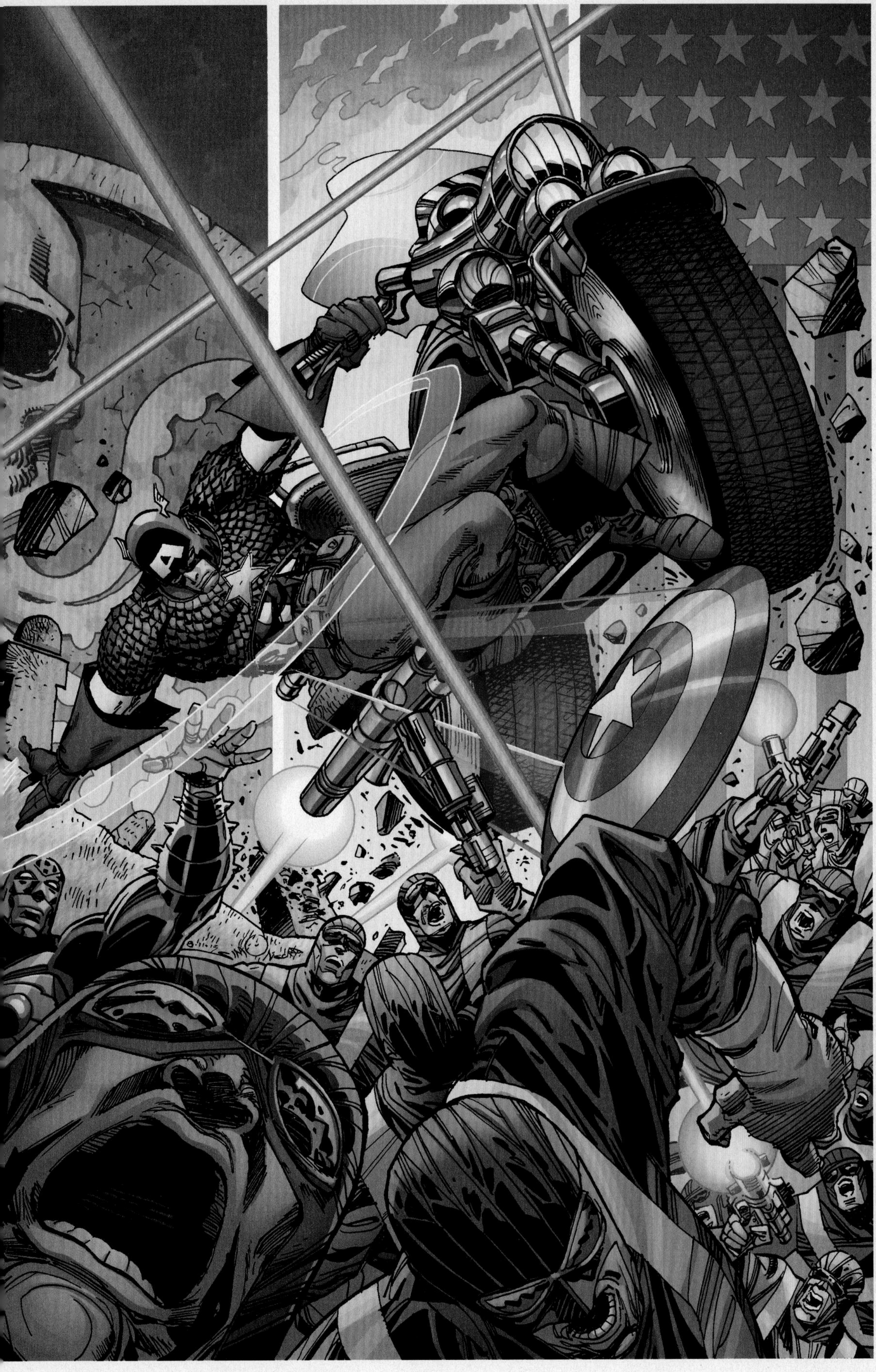

#2 LEGEND VARIANT COVER BY WALTER SIMONSON & LAURA MARTIN

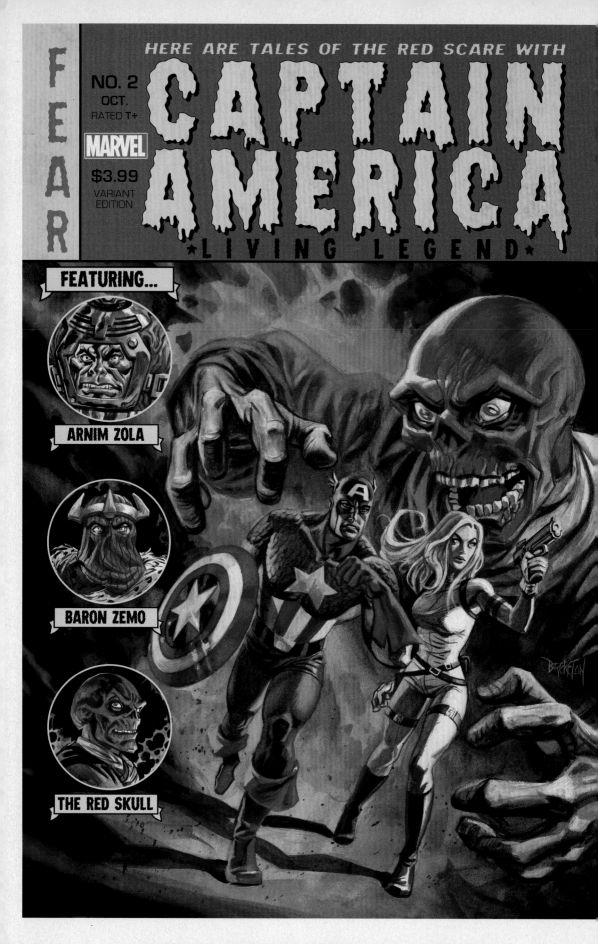

#2 VINTAGE VARIANT COVER BY DAN BRERETON

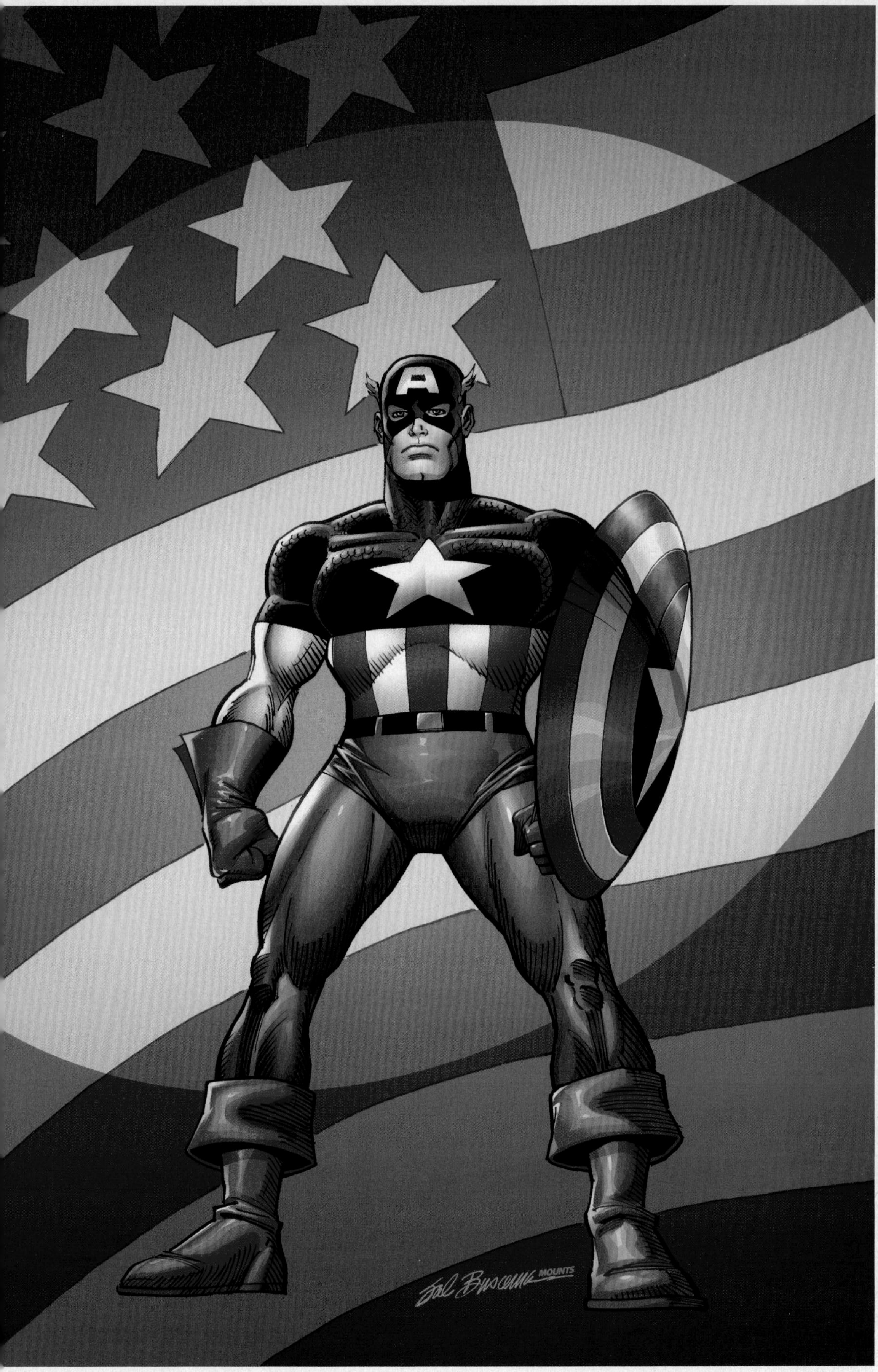

#3 LEGEND VARIANT COVER BY SAL BUSCEMA & PAUL MOUNTS

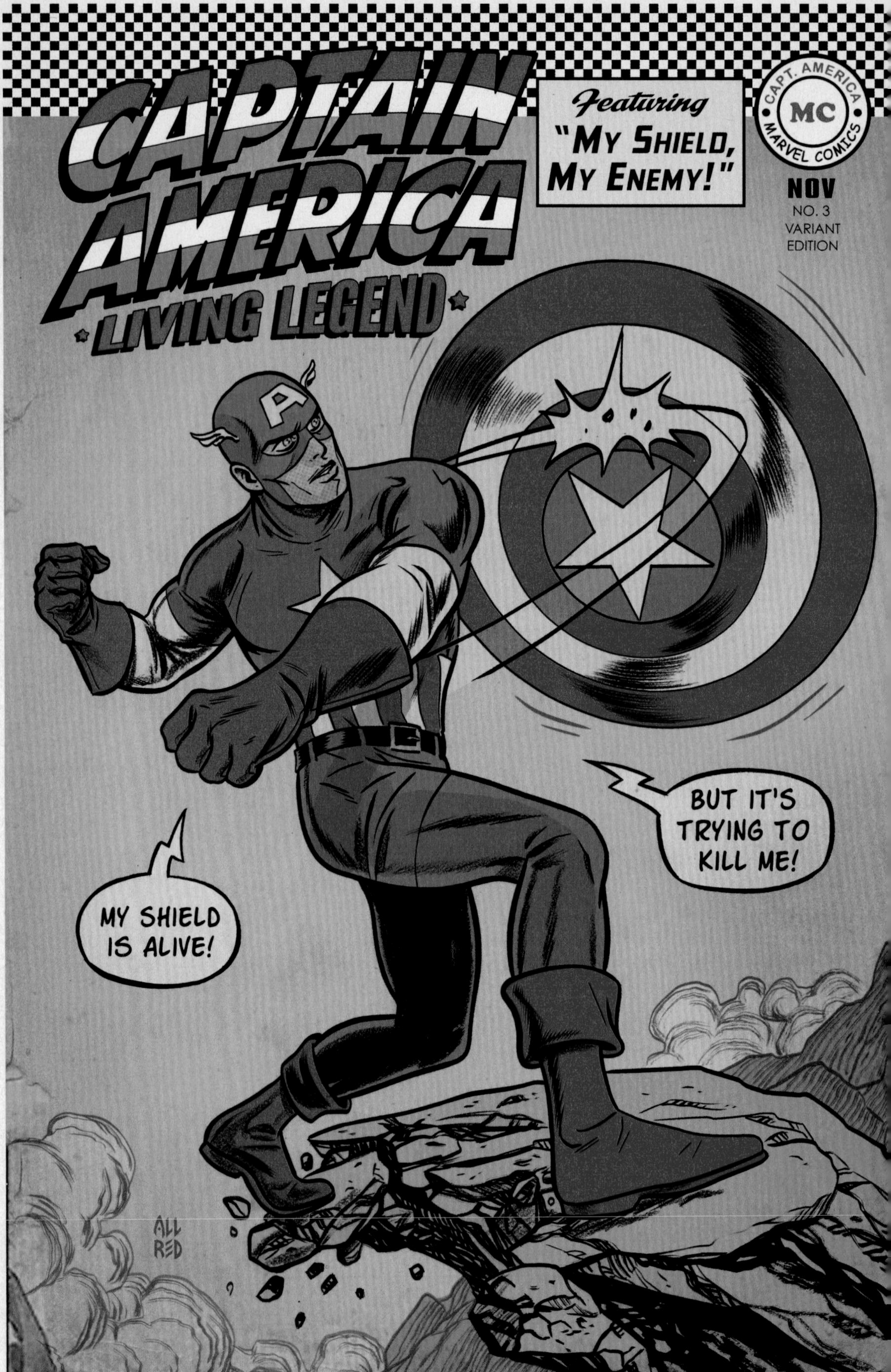
CAPTAIN AMERICA
LIVING LEGEND
Featuring
"MY SHIELD, MY ENEMY!"
CAPT. AMERICA
MC
MARVEL COMICS
NOV
NO. 3
VARIANT
EDITION
BUT IT'S TRYING TO KILL ME!
MY SHIELD IS ALIVE!
ALLRED

#3 VINTAGE VARIANT COVER BY MICHAEL & LAURA ALLRED

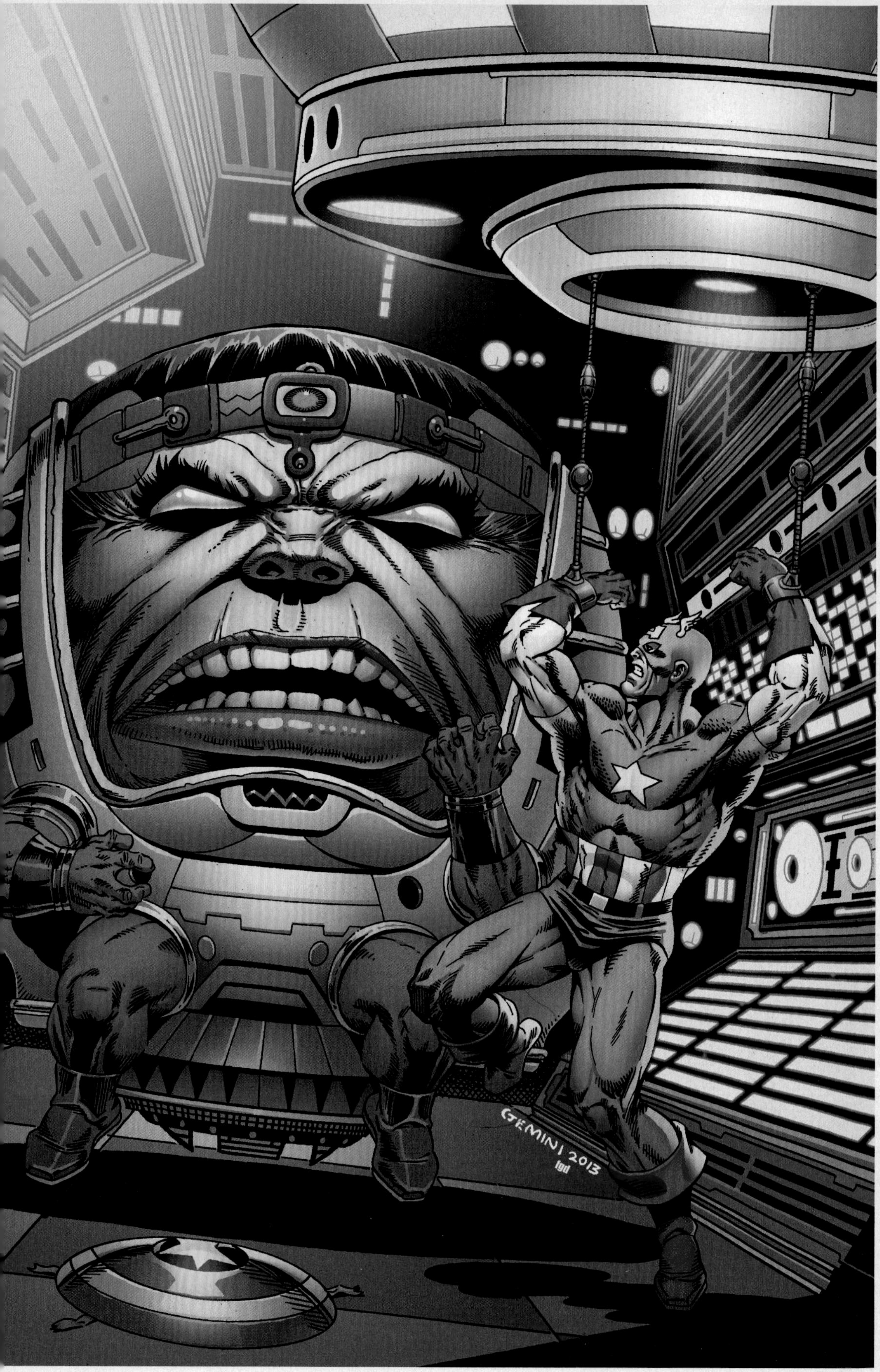
GEMINI 2013
fgd

#4 LEGEND VARIANT COVER BY JIM STARLIN, AL MILGROM & FRANK D'ARMATA

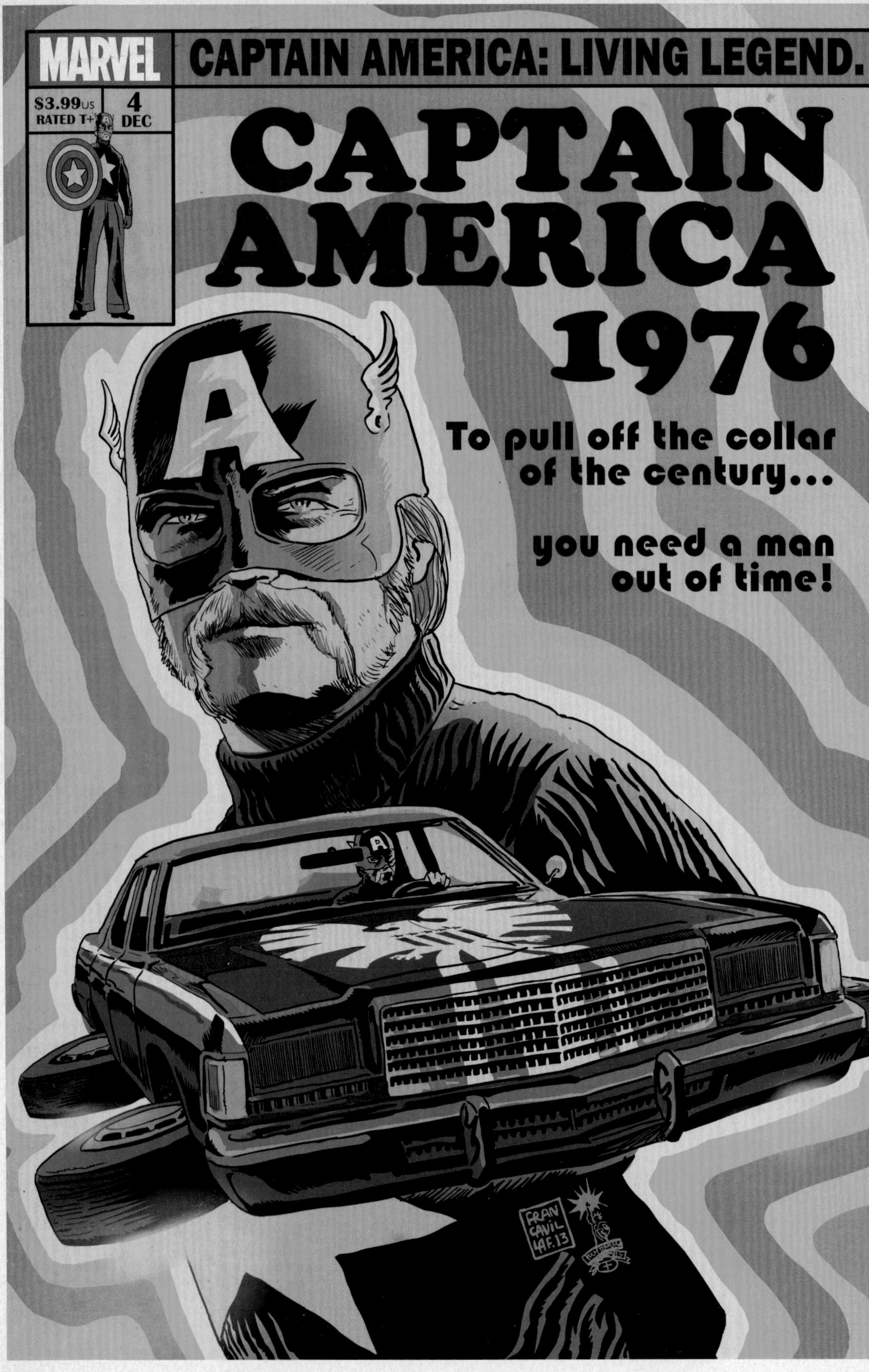
MARVEL
CAPTAIN AMERICA: LIVING LEGEND.
$3.99US
RATED T+
4
DEC
CAPTAIN
AMERICA
1976
To pull off the collar
of the century...
you need a man
out of time!
FRAN
CAVIL
LAF.13

#4 VINTAGE VARIANT COVER BY FRANCESCO FRANCAVILLA